The
Purpose
of
Life

by Alan & Jacqui James
A MEDITATION RETREAT
MODERN BUDDHISM

Jacqui James

1946 – 1989

The
Purpose
of
Life

*The Essential Teachings
of a Buddhist Master*

Jacqui James

AUKANA
BRADFORD ON AVON

First published 2008

Aukana Trust
9 Masons Lane
Bradford on Avon
Wiltshire
BA15 1QN
England

e-mail: info@aukana.org.uk
www.aukana.org.uk
Telephone: (01225) 866821, International: +44 1225 866821

The Aukana Trust is a registered charity (No 326938)

Acknowledgements
The publishers would like to thank **Jim Vuylsteke** for the preliminary editing of the text, for typesetting the book, and for his invaluable assistance and
guidance throughout the production process; **Garry Phillipson** for editing
suggestions, writing the foreword and back cover text, and much helpful input;
Trevor Day and **Felicity Cowie** for editing suggestions; **Sue Moyers, Mary
Valiakas** and **Ellen Foster** for proofreading; **Jason Rebello** for designing
the cover; **Peter** and **Susan Case** for technical advice; and **Tom Whyte** for
creative ideas and suggestions.

Typeset in Bembo 11/13.5 and Amerika Sans 18
Printed in Great Britain by Cromwell Press, Trowbridge

Cover printed by Opalprint, Midsomer Norton
Cover photograph copyright © Trinn ('Pong) Suwannapha 2007

A catalogue record for this book is available from the British Library

ISBN 978-0-9511769-9-3

Contents

foreword

Strange though it may seem, the book you are reading is about you. The pages that follow contain a diagnosis of your life in its most fundamental sense—the moments of joy, of frustration, the questions about how to live, and the nagging sense that there must be more to life than this. There is description, grounded in experience, of what to do in order to approach enlightenment—the fulfilment to which all genuine spiritual ways point.

This book is a collection of talks given by Jacqui James. Jacqui was a remarkable and inspiring teacher who walked the Buddhist path to its end and then taught within that tradition, though she reverenced and drew inspiration from many other spiritual ways. She died, aged only forty-two, in 1989.

The usual thing at this point would be to pay tribute to Jacqui, to try and convey a sense of her dynamic life, to say how many people she helped, and how much we lost with her passing. But there are two reasons to avoid such a eulogy here. First, any description of Jacqui could only be a pale, one-dimensional thing compared to the force of nature that she was. Second, she would not want this to be about her. Her concern was always to help her students by pointing to this present moment. Amazing tales about her—and there is no shortage—would miss the point. What she would want would be to help you, now. And to do this the message she conveys is that life has its problems. But if we learn to look at what is actually taking place—to really look, *now*—then we can see how those problems are our own creations, and how it is possible to go altogether beyond the self-imposed suffering of the neurotic mind.

Talking about the spiritual training, she once said:

> It's all aimed towards developing a soft, an open, a gentle mind—which is not out to get to the top of the tree, but is out to handle each moment as if it's the last moment; each object as if it's the one and only in the world. Then it's precious to you. You're not going towards 'a goal'—you're handling this moment, this thing, fully, totally, with your whole being.

So Jacqui would surely not want this book to start with an evocation of the past, no matter how inspiring and rewarding a time it was for some of us. Her message, always, was that the purpose of life is to experience what is happening right here, right now.

You may find that Jacqui's words speak to you, or you may not. If not, do not be disheartened. The search for life's meaning, for enlightenment, is certainly demanding, but it is a real quest with a real goal. If you have once felt the stirrings of the search then you would be well-advised to pursue it. Try to forget it, and the sense that something is missing from your life will just get stronger and stronger.

Jacqui spoke in a very direct, no-nonsense style. When teaching, and when delivering the lectures that appear in this book, she said exactly what needs to be done to approach and realise enlightenment. She was able to do this because she taught in an environment where students were in regular touch with their teachers, so that any problems or questions would quickly be talked through. In reading this book, of course, your situation is different. If and when you find things in the following pages which challenge your views, here is a suggestion about how to proceed: do not simply accept, or reject, the statements you find troublesome. Where possible, try out what Jacqui says, and evaluate for yourself whether or not it is helpful. And try to find someone you respect and who will discuss the issues at hand with you—ideally, someone who can justly call themselves a spiritual teacher.

Whilst one needs to be cautious in evaluating and choosing, genuine teachers can be found, in different traditions, throughout the world today. One very good source of practical instruction is the Aukana Trust—the organisation founded by Jacqui and her husband, Alan James—which runs a meditation centre, the House of Inner

Tranquillity, and associated monasteries. It is still directed by people who have completed the Buddhist training and are equipped to help the rest of us in our quest to resolve the mystery of this moment. The continuance of that work is the only epitaph Jacqui would want.

Real Buddhism

There are many forms of Buddhism to be found in the West today. There is Theravada Buddhism, Mahayana Buddhism, Zen Buddhism, the Pure Land School, and Nicheren Buddhism—to name but a few. They all have different practices, different ceremonies, different meditations, different style and colour of dress worn by their monks and nuns. The shrines in their temples are different. The Mahayana temples can be very ornate compared with the simple, classical lines of the Zen temples. The Buddha figures found in the different forms of Buddhism also vary enormously. Sometimes the Buddha looks very feminine, sometimes very human, but sometimes very odd because he is given huge ear lobes and an enormous spiked flame coming out of the top of his head, making it very difficult to relate to the image as representing a man seated in meditation or even representing, when the figure is standing, a man giving forth a spiritual teaching.

Theravada Buddhism has an order of monks who wear saffron-coloured robes and have their heads shaved. Mahayana monks' robes are maroon coloured and look quite different from the Theravadin robes, whilst the Zen religious wear black or brown. In Theravada the monks are celibate, but in Mahayana some are celibate and some are married. In certain Buddhist groups the emphasis is on study and chanting and ritual, whereas others decry these activities, saying they are peripheral to the main message and that if you really want to practise Buddhism, then you must devote all your time to meditation.

If you read the Pali Canon, the texts of the Theravada Buddhists, you come into contact with the teachings that the Buddha gave to his monks and to his lay followers that are contained in these lectures and discourses. But apart from this information, you also read about the people who were very close to the Buddha, what their personalities were like and what their level of understanding was of the *Dhamma*, the teaching. However, if you then turn to the Mahayana texts, you find that many of the stories about the Buddha's close disciples are quite different, and some of the Buddha's teachings and episodes in his life are also different from what you read in the Theravada texts.

All of these differences make one want to ask the question—'Well, which is the real Buddhism?'

Real Buddhism is not Buddha figures, it is not meditation centres, it is not monasteries, it is not Buddhist monks and nuns, nor is it Buddhist temples. Real Buddhism is not to be found in chanting or reading or listening to *Dhamma*. It is not to be found in stories of the Buddha or in chanting 'Buddho' a hundred times a day so as to increase one's wealth. Real Buddhism is not meditation that brings about bliss and religious visions.

So what *is* real Buddhism? Real Buddhism is looking deep into your own nature so as to come to the realisation that you create the world you live in. You create the heavens and the hells which you experience in your own mind. Once you understand *how* you create your own universe, you are no longer trapped by the heaven and hell states. You are free of them. Once free, suffering does not touch you.

But how do you look into your own nature? How do you do it? You do it by meditating. Real Buddhism could be said to be meditation— not just any meditation, but a particular type of meditation, that is, *vipassanā*. *Vipassanā*, insight meditation, is the close observation of mind and body so as to unravel its real nature, not to see how we *think* mind and body operate, but to see how they actually *do* operate.

We could say that real Buddhism is watching mind and body in an unbiased and impartial way so as to discover their true nature. Temples, pictures of the Buddha, chanting, *Dhamma* talks and such like are not the *act* of watching mind and body, which is why they cannot be considered real Buddhism. What these things do is assist us. Their presence is a reminder to us of what we should be doing if we are to be true followers of the real teachings of the Buddha. They remind us that we should be turning our attention inwards and watching the rising and passing away of mind and body.

* * *

When we take up the practice of meditation, our idea of what mind actually is, is very loose and woolly. We think we have never even given a thought to the size and location of mind, but most people visualise it as one object that is solid and compact. We are not sure whether mind is a large, single object like a football or a small, single, compact object like a walnut. But most non-meditators, as well as quite a few meditators, have the very definite idea that mind is located in the brain. That being the case, it cannot possibly be as large as a water tank, nor could it be as large as a football because it just would not fit into the skull.

But as for mind being the size of a walnut, well that is just too insulting a concept to even contemplate. Human beings are far too intelligent to have minds the size of a walnut—aren't they? And anyhow, all those thoughts and worries and creativity just would not fit into a mind the size of a walnut—would they?

Most people have a far more concrete notion than they realise of what mind is, what it does, and where it is located. Mind, to most people, is one object—it is compact and it is located in the head. And this one, single object does everything. It thinks, it plans, it worries, it hates, it schemes, it creates.

But is this a true picture of mind? Well, it is not the only picture. In the East, some believe that the mind is located in the heart, in ancient Greece, it was thought to be located in the stomach, and *vipassanā* meditators have yet another picture. If you want to plumb the depths of your own nature, if you want to come to practise real Buddhism, then concepts like these need to be examined. On closer scrutiny you soon discover that your ideas about mind are just that, ideas, and that they are not grounded in any personal experience whatsoever. You discover that all your views about mind have been picked up from other people and other sources of information, like television and books.

You come to realise that these concepts about mind do not have their foundations in unbiased and detailed observation of the workings of your own mind. The moment you do start to pay attention to *nāma-rūpa,* which are the Pali terms used for mind and body, you will come to a very different conclusion about mind—what it is, where it is located, and how it functions. And this time your views will be based on your own personal experience about the way in which mind actually does work.

★ ★ ★

As you do hour after hour of seated meditation, you come to notice that body and mind are different. Body is something which stays still and mind is something that reaches out towards body to identify it and classify it. Further, you come to notice after much repeated watching that mind is something which arises, lasts for a moment, then disappears. Sometimes it arises in the location of your ears, sometimes in your back, sometimes in your knees. Mind, in fact, arises in any and every location in the body as well as outside of it. And each time mind arises, it is quite different from the mind that arose a moment ago.

If you hear a group of people walking past you chattering, it is not the ear that hears. It is the mind that hears. People think that hearing and the ear are one and the same thing. They say, 'I hear people on the road outside chattering.' They assume that the ear, hearing, and 'I' are all one and the same thing, that they are the same event, a single, solid object welded together. But this is not so. This is not how it is in reality.

Sound is the physical object. It is body. It is *rūpa*. The physical object, sound, stands still, and the mind moves out towards that object to hear it. The actual experience of hearing is a function of mind. In Buddhism it is called hearing consciousness. Consciousness is only one aspect of mind.

What occurs in that moment of time is hearing, and that comes about dependent on the ear, which is also body, just like a sound is body, but it is a different body. So ear is one thing and hearing is another and 'I hear chattering' is thought, and it is another event yet again. There are three different happenings here. But because mind moves so fast, it seems as if all of these events are welded into one, giving us a wrong understanding of what is taking place. We are left with the distinct impression that what is happening is a single event which 'I' have brought about. We think it is the self which hears. Nothing could be further from the truth.

Having heard a sound, you will then identify it and say 'it is people chattering'. That label, 'people chattering', is mind. But it is a different mind from the mind that heard the sound. That mind has died and been replaced by the mind that says 'people chattering'.

★ ★ ★

Meditation is a training first in calming the mind and body. Much time must be spent in cultivating tranquillity. Once you get tranquil the mind naturally concentrates. Once it is tranquil and concentrated there are fewer objects in mind. There are not so many thoughts and sounds and physical sensations frantically chasing after one another to such an extent that they all appear to be happening at the same time.

Once you have become tranquil you will notice that a sound will come into existence, last for a moment, then disappear, and then a thought or a physical sensation or another sound will come into existence, last for a moment and disappear. The point is, there will be only one object at a time for you to notice. With this tranquillity of body and mind, objects slow down so much that they appear to be happening in slow motion. When the meditation gets to this point, there is so little going on that the attention is not distracted from noticing the mind reaching out to hear a sound. And you notice it as a distinct and separate event. Then you notice identification of the hearing take place, and you notice that it is quite a separate and different experience from the mind reaching out. After that comes the thought 'people chattering', and you notice that this is a different event yet again. You are aware of all of these events as they occur, and you are aware that they are separate from one another and different from one another. So your experience tells you that there are three events here, not one, and so never again are you deluded into believing that ear, hearing, and 'me hearing people chattering' are all one event.

Let me explain all of this in a slightly different way, in case you had difficulty in grasping what has just been said. When meditating, what you want to experience is the hearing as it happens. You are to train yourself to be clearly conscious that it is hearing you are aware of, not seeing or tasting or worrying. At the moment of hearing you need to be aware that it is hearing and that the act of hearing is mental, not physical. In other words it is *nāma*, not *rūpa*—it is mind, not body.

Once attention has moved on to the next stage, that of labelling the hearing as 'people chattering', you need to be aware as it is happening that the mind that took birth with hearing has died, and that that which is saying 'people chattering' is a new mind that has just been born. And as soon as the label 'people chattering' fades off, that mind has died.

The more you meditate, the more you start to build up a very different picture of what mind is and where it is located. You start to see mind as arising and disappearing thousands of times a day. You see each arising mind as separate and different from the minds that came before it and the minds that will come after it. You notice that the hearing mind is different from the wandering mind, and that the wandering mind is different from the mind that observes the body getting out of a chair.

You come to observe that 'you' at any given moment are only the arising of one of these minds, and that that mind is rapidly replaced by another mind. On other occasions 'you' are the arising of a body, and the body is then replaced by another body or by another mind.

The reason for meditating is to come to the experience for yourself that what you consist of is thousands and thousands of mental and physical bits which spring up and then fade away again, and that these bits just keep replacing one another rapidly and ceaselessly throughout the day and night, day in and day out.

However, you may well want to ask the question, 'But how can coming to see that "I" am made up of a collection of bits be of any advantage at all?' The answer is that we only crave to get rid of something or crave to hang on to something when we are convinced that it is solid and lasting. And we only suffer when we view life in this manner. Nothing is solid and lasting. But however much you understand this statement on an intellectual level and think you really *do* know that things change and are not solid and lasting, the fact is you do not know that from your own experience.

The way you can test whether your understanding is experiential or intellectual is to ask yourself the question, 'Is there any craving or hatred in my nature?' If the answer is yes, then your understanding is still only intellectual, and there is much meditative work for you still to do.

Trying to get rid of something or hanging on to it, hankering after sounds or sights or smells that are not present, wanting to become a different type of person from what you are now—all these are movements of mind, and any movement whatsoever brings on suffering and indicates that your understanding that everything changes is not yet deep enough.

The more you observe how rapidly mind and body are born and die, the more you calm down and stop trying to get rid of things or hang on to things. For you know from experience that the moment you start even to think of, say, shifting your position in the seated meditation so as to get rid of a back pain, that pain has already gone. The very thought of getting rid of pain is mind—is *nāma*. It is the birth of mind. The pain in the back was body—was *rūpa*. So the thought of shifting your position is the birth of mind. Once mind has come into existence, it means the pain has died, and so *rūpa* has died.

The more we experience for ourselves the rapid rising and passing away of mind and body, the more it hits us what a waste of time it is to make any movement to get rid of pain or to hang on to pleasure.

When we try to get rid of pain, that is hatred. When we dream about getting pleasure, that is craving. Each time you stop trying to get rid of pain but just let it exist, you have stopped hating for that moment. Hating and craving being reduced, the mind is less passionate. Being less passionate, it is calmer, cleaner, more balanced. Being all of these things, you have less suffering, which means, of course, that you are happier.

Perhaps you have remembered an argument you had with your partner, or you have remembered his long, gloomy face afterwards. Should your mind become filled and obsessed with anger but you find it difficult, if not impossible, to get sufficient distance from this mental suffering to approach the experience from a meditative point of view, this is because you have become so caught up and swept along by a stream of resentful and angry thoughts that you have forgotten all about watching what is happening in terms of mind and body. It never dawns on you that you could take the sting out of the situation, as well as increase your wisdom about the workings of mind, if only you would take one little mental step backwards and prise yourself loose from the gloomy thoughts for just a moment.

If you do manage to prise yourself free, then mind is cleared of anger for a moment, and if you have spent sufficient time at practising meditation, then you will remember to observe the rush of feeling in the solar plexus region and to note it as the birth of mind, and you will also remember to note that the thought 'how dare my partner behave like this', brings about the death of one mind and the birth of another. The feeling in the stomach is a completely different and separate event from the thought 'how dare they'. The thoughts that follow the initial 'how dare they', those thoughts that go over and over the argument, are yet another mind. This is the birth of the clinging mind, which is quite different from the mind that identified the mental picture of your partner arguing with you. The identifying mind was born and then died and, in this example, was replaced by the clinging mind. When the angry thoughts stop going round and round, then that is the death of the clinging mind.

★ ★ ★

On those occasions when you get totally obsessed with suffering and you just do not have sufficient presence of mind to remember that you can defuse the situation by practising real Buddhism, then remember the following story. It might help you to restore your balance, from which point you can return to practising real Buddhism.

I heard this story on the radio. This particular story was told by a Jewish Rabbi and my apologies to him for not remembering the story in greater detail.

He was at a social gathering and got talking to a woman who was very miserable because her relationship had recently gone wrong. It was the usual story of A loves B but B loves C and she was A. That day her young man had left her in no doubt that his affections lay elsewhere, and she was feeling very miserable about the whole affair. But she gathered herself together and asked the Rabbi to tell her a funny story so as to relieve her gloom. This he proceeded to do. When he had finished, she was laughing merrily and he felt good about having lifted her burden temporarily. Then she pulled herself up, went all serious, and said, 'Rabbi, tell me, what can I do to let go of this pain? I do not want you to joke and I do not want to listen to a sermon.'

He thought for a moment and said, 'When I was a young man, I invested quite a lot of money. I did not listen to the advice I was given and I lost the lot. I was very upset about losing that money. It is a custom within the Jewish tradition to give a gift to one another at New Year, but as I lost the money at New Year, every year after that when New Year rolled round my mind would become filled with gloomy thoughts about the lost money. One year at this festive time I wanted to give a gift to God, but what do you give to the person who has everything? I thought for a while and then decided that I would give away my thoughts about the lost money, because we are even more possessive with the things that go wrong in our lives than we are with the successes.

'Do you know what happened? Well, God must have taken that gift, because I never thought about that lost money again.'

The woman thought for a moment and said, 'I can relate to that. I see what you are getting at, but I have two problems: I am not Jewish and it is not New Year.'

'OK,' said the Rabbi, 'you are Christian. So why don't you start today? It is the seventeenth of February, which is Ash Wednesday and therefore the beginning of Lent, a very good time to give a gift.'

Adapting that story for your own purposes, when you, as meditators, get thoroughly caught up with negative thoughts—what can you do? When you get caught up with something, you invariably regard it as yours. It becomes 'my anger' or 'my resentment' or 'my hurt', and you find it very difficult to let go of your new possession. Why not give that anger or resentment or hurt away. Say the words mentally, 'I give this resentment, which is my possession, to you, my teacher,' or to whoever you have dedicated your meditation to.

Do you ever do that, dedicate your meditation to another human or non-human being? If you do not, this is how it is done. When you sit down to do an hour's seated practice, spend the first few seconds going over in mind what you wish to accomplish in the meditation. Say to yourself, 'I will turn the attention time and time again to watching body and mind coming into existence and fading away,' and also say, 'All the benefits that accrue from spending time attempting to develop wisdom I give away to my spiritual guide.' Or you can give away the fruits of your meditation to a parent or to a friend or to the devas, the heavenly beings, who occupy your house. If you were to dedicate your meditation to a thief, you would be reminded of inefficient qualities, and this would have a depressing, clouding effect on the mind. It is wisest to choose someone who is more spiritually developed than yourself, such as a *Dhamma* teacher, because the very thought of that person will remind you of concentration, mindfulness, generosity, and so on, qualities of mind which are noble. Thinking for even a brief moment about noble qualities will have an uplifting effect on you.

It really does not matter whether you do or do not believe that such gifts have an effect on the recipient or whether you do or do not believe there are such things as devas. What is important is the effect that these generous thoughts have on you. Practising giving away things you have acquired on a mental level makes you less possessive, more generous, and it heads you towards mental lightness and away from darkness. We think we can only give away physical possessions because we either forget or are ignorant of the fact that there is such a thing as a mental world which is just as concrete and real as the physical world.

When I was in my final year of school, everyone was concerned about what they were going to do once they left. Some were applying for university, some for college, some were planning a year off to travel, and the remainder hadn't a clue about what they were going to do. One girl in particular decided that her father's advice on the subject was absolutely right, and she was going to go in the direction that he suggested.

He wanted her to get the highest educational qualification she was capable of, and so he asked her to go to university and train as a doctor. He told her that people could take away her house, her goods, and her money, but they could never take away her education or the qualities of generosity, patience, energy, and love that she, by being a human being, was capable of developing if she chose to.

Clearly, he recognised that there is such a thing as a mental world and that goods can be acquired in that mental world which have more effect on you and are more long lasting than things of the physical world. He also told his daughter that when she died, she could not take her physical possessions with her, but that these mental possessions would accompany her after death.

Giving away the fruits of your meditative labours develops gener-osity just as much as the giving of a physical gift. A person can be generous or stingy with things of the mind in just the same manner as with physical objects. Take a look next time you are suffering and you will see that you are only suffering because you are being stingy in the mental world. When you are filled with anger or resentment or depression or worry, notice how you are hanging on to it, binding it to you, refusing to let go of this new possession, refusing to be cheerful, wanting to be angry and upset for just a little longer.

If you can remember the story the Rabbi told next time you find yourself caught in that stingy, possessive frame of mind, and you can bring yourself to give away your negativity, then the mind will brighten. Once this happens you can return to watching mind and body rising and falling. You can return to practising real Buddhism, which is the noticing of the three marks of *anicca*—impermanence, *dukkha*—suffering, and *anattā*—non-self, in your own body and mind.

I would like to end with the following advice from the Buddha (*Anguttara-Nikāya*, the Book of Nines, 'Velama Discourse'):

[T]hough with pious heart he took refuge in the Buddha, the Dhamma and the Sangha, greater would have been the fruit thereof, had he with pious heart undertaken to keep the precepts: abstention from taking life, abstention from taking that which is not given, abstention from unlawful sexual intercourse, abstention from lying, and abstention from intoxicating drugs and liquor, which are the cause of laziness . . . though with pious heart he undertook to keep these precepts, greater would have been the fruit thereof, had he made become a mere passing fragrance of loving-kindness . . . though he made become just the fragrance of loving-kindness, greater would have been the fruit thereof, had he made become, just for a finger-snap, the perception of impermanence.[1]

---

1. Adapted from Hare, E.M. (1978), *The Book of Gradual Sayings, Vol.IV*, p.265, Oxford: Pali Text Society.

Awareness

'Awareness' is a word you hear used time and time again when you come across meditation. You are told to be aware when you sit meditating. You are told to be aware of what is going on, from moment to moment, during the day.

But what exactly is awareness? Awareness is being conscious. There are many things of which you can be conscious. You can be conscious that it is a dull day. You can be conscious that you have a headache. You can be conscious that your friend is wearing a red dress. You can be conscious that your boss is in a bad mood. You can be conscious of sounds or smells or a stiff leg. You can be conscious of worrying about the health of an ailing relative. Which of these things is it important to be conscious of if you are a *vipassanā* meditator? Are all these things important? Or are only some of them important? Or are they perhaps all irrelevant, and there is something completely other that happens to you that you should be conscious of?

Before we go into depth as to just what it is a meditator should be aware of, let us take a look at the opposite of awareness—ignorance. For one of the best ways of finding out what awareness actually is, is to define what it is not. Therefore, we must take a close look at ignorance.

It is best to talk of ignore-ance rather than ignorance because 'ignorance' in the English language usually refers to someone who is intellectually stupid, and that certainly is not the meaning of the word 'ignore-ance'. Ignore-ance is the refusal to acknowledge the presence of something. It is to become conscious, for a very brief moment, of something which one finds so terrifying and so threatening that one turns away from it instantly, refusing even to acknowledge its very presence. That something may be a memory or anger or an idea someone is putting forth. Whatever that something is, it is always interpreted as painful, so painful that one just does not want to deal with it, and so one turns away from it.

A person who drinks heavily does so to ignore. He wishes to ignore the suffering he feels inside. I once knew a man with this problem. He drank more heavily when his troubles increased. When there was trouble at work, he would start drinking at midday and drink himself into a stupor by early evening. When there was trouble in his marriage, he would turn to drink to blot out the hurt he experienced from the continual rows with his wife. The bored housewife takes the odd tipple to smother the pain of boredom. The travelling salesman often drinks heavily to blot out his loneliness. Always, there is the attempt to smash out, to get rid of, to ignore a feeling which is unpleasant and looks threatening. One can ignore unpleasant feelings by blotting them out with drink or drugs or socialising or work. Or one can just pull the mind away from them and refuse to acknowledge their very existence. That way one thinks the problem of painful feelings is solved. Only a few have the wisdom to realise that the problem enlarges with the ignoring of it.

When individuals start to meditate, if they are employing drink as their way of ignoring what is happening to them internally, then they are encouraged to give up that extremely heavy-handed way of dealing with inner pain. Until they do give up drinking, they cannot really get started on the meditative path. *Vipassanā* meditation is all about facing up to and looking squarely at whatever is going on inside us. So right from the start of the meditative path, people need to give up all the coarser ways—such as drink and drugs—that they use, in order to blot out the inner pain, despair, and emptiness they frequently experience.

When we take a look at the less coarse way of ignoring, that of pulling the mind away from the unpleasant object and developing instant amnesia about it, even here we find ignoring can be divided into three types. For ease of explanation I am going to call an extreme case of ignoring 'coarse', a not so intense case of ignoring 'medium', and a very subtle case of ignoring 'fine', and give you an example of each.

This is an example of a coarse display of ignore-ance. From time to time I go up to a meditator and say, 'What is the matter with you?' 'Me?' he says, looking startled, 'Why, nothing.' He is not just saying that because he is being secretive and does not want to tell me what the problem is. He really believes that he is fine, that he is all right, that there is nothing wrong with his inner world. The whole of his face is covered with a greyish black haze, which is indicative of an extremely negative mental state. Always, there is hatred present in a person's mind when that greyish black haze hangs over his or her face. And apart from the hatred there will be a mixture of other hindrances running as well, like worry, and sloth and torpor.

Occasionally I like to check up to see if another meditator is capable yet of being aware of an external mental state. An external mental state is somebody else's mental state, whereas an internal mental state is your own mental state, and a *vipassanā* meditator is training himself or herself to become aware of both internal and external mental states. So wishing to find out whether a particular meditation student is able yet to detect another's mental state, I will ask her the question, 'How is so and so, the one you've been working with all afternoon?' If she can read the other meditator's mental state, she will say something along the lines of, 'Oh, she's running hatred, and it's shown in the way she's banging and crashing around.'

A great deal of ignoring is going on if a meditator is running strong hatred (shown by such things as the greyish black hue covering the face and the banging and crashing) and yet he himself is totally unaware of anything amiss and is surprised, if not shocked, that I should imply that he is somewhat off beam.

Ignore-ance of a medium or less severe nature is present when meditators know they are off beam, but when asked, 'Why are you in a bad mood?' they say, 'I don't know.' They are unaware of what mental action they performed that brought about the negative mental state, but they are conscious that they are in a bad mood. So there is less ignore-ance in this example than in the previous one. These meditators are conscious of the bad mood, therefore admitting there is suffering in the moment, but not conscious of what they did to bring about that bad mood.

The third kind of ignore-ance, fine ignore-ance, is even less blind than the two mentioned so far. It shows itself in the following manner.

I ask a meditator, 'What is the matter with you?' and he says, 'I am feeling off beam because I am worrying about my work load.' And he mentions how he is conscious of the negativity that is running in his mind. He is conscious that there are the hindrances of worry and hatred present, and he is conscious of the comparison between now, where he sees himself as continually overloaded with work, and the future, which he pictures as having lots of leisure time in it and very little work. He says he is conscious that this continual comparing, between what he has got in the present moment and what he wants, is craving for something other and hatred of the present situation. And he is conscious that because there is craving present, he is suffering. But somehow he has got locked into the hatred, and he does not know what it is he has missed—what vital factor in the chain of events he should have been conscious of, which he missed, which would have stopped him from getting locked into hatred.

What he was unconscious of, what he ignored, was the unpleasant feeling that had arisen due to the overwork. He did not like that feeling. He found it threatening, and so he quickly ignored it. The moment a meditator blots out from consciousness a feeling that he or she does not want to face, hatred for that feeling starts to build. And suffering is experienced.

All of this is fine ignore-ance. Fine ignore-ance is present when a meditator is conscious that he is in a bad mood, conscious of the hindrances of worry and hatred, conscious that he is comparing and that comparison is craving or hatred, and conscious that he has become attached to that hatred. Can you see that the meditator who had fine ignore-ance operating was conscious of so many more things existing in his mind than the meditator who was caught up with coarse ignore-ance, who was not even aware that he was in a bad mood?

★ ★ ★

From what has been said so far, it should be becoming clear that there is a definite link between ignore-ance and life appearing empty, meaningless, frightening, and painful. Therefore, if you get rid of the ignore-ance, you will also get rid of all that prevents life from being vital and totally satisfying. But how do you get rid of ignore-ance? The answer is simple: by developing awareness. You have to become aware, you have to become conscious of many things that up until now you have been oblivious of. However, you have to become conscious only of *certain* things. You do not have to become conscious of everything in the world. That would be an impossibility, and it would not be useful to you in your task of overcoming suffering. You do not have to become conscious that this morning it rained. You do not have to become conscious that the Bantu are an African tribe. You do not have to become conscious that oranges cost less in a supermarket than they do in the village greengrocers. You do not have to become conscious that your allergy to cats is due to having been attacked by one in a past life.

But you *do* have to become conscious of hearing as a separate and discrete event. You have to become conscious that when there is hearing present, nothing else exists in your world. At that moment in time there is no rain, no Bantus, no cheap oranges in supermarkets— all there is, is hearing. You have to become aware that that moment of hearing is consciousness. It is 'hearing consciousness'. You have to become aware that hearing is born, it lasts for a split second, and then it vanishes. This is called the birth and death of hearing. You have to become conscious of this birth and death of a moment. In the same way you must become aware of the other four senses, those of smell, taste, touch, and sight.

Apart from becoming aware of a sense consciousness for the split second that it exists, you need to become aware of what follows on from that. It will be a perception or a feeling or both. For example, you may hear a nightingale singing, which you find wonderful. Labelling the sound as 'nightingale singing' is the 'perception' and the pleasure that wells up in you at the sound of that bird singing its heart out is 'feeling'. You have to become conscious of the perception and the feeling and how they too only last for a split second, how they too, like hearing, are born, exist for a while, and then die.

Next, you need to become conscious of your response to that feeling. Do you want more and more pleasant feelings? If you do, you will make the mind move towards the sound. You will hold the attention on the bird song. You will not let it move away. You will keep bringing it back to the birdsong so that you can experience more and more pleasant feelings. You need to become conscious that this is craving for pleasant feelings. And that the more frequently you lock on to the sound, the greater the disappointment when the bird stops singing because the pleasant feelings also stop.

You need to become conscious of how craving produces suffering within you, for you will have no desire to give up craving and the attachment to it if you do not become conscious of how it leads to suffering.

Finally, you need to become conscious that there is nothing wrong with hearing, or the label you put on the sound to identify it. Nor is there anything wrong with the feeling that follows. Whether that feeling is pleasant or unpleasant, it is all right. What you need to be-come conscious of is that it is how you *react* to that feeling which determines whether you live in a world that is a hell or a world that is a heavenly place to be. If you react by trying to get rid of the feeling or trying to hang on to that feeling, then you condemn yourself to living in a hell state. You choose it. You do it to yourself. Nobody else does it to you. No god or demon out there does it to you. It is *you* who does it to you. You choose the type of world you live in.

Vipassanā meditation is an exploration into the world we create for ourselves. When we start to meditate, we set out to discover exactly how we have created that world and what we must do to change it into a heaven world. For it goes without saying that those who choose to meditate earnestly have already come to the realisation that theirs is not a heaven world, and that they are doing something, they know not what, which is turning their world into somewhere they would rather not live. You, in common with all other beings, wish to live in a world which is light and bright and happy. You know also, even if that realisation has not yet fully formed, that you *can* do something to bring about such a heaven world.

★ ★ ★

Having defined exactly what awareness is not, having also defined what it is a *vipassanā* meditator must be aware of, you then ask yourself: 'What do I do to bring about a higher level of awareness? How do I increase my consciousness of what is going on inside me?'

Besides attempting to increase your awareness by doing one or two periods of seated meditation each day, you can also increase your awareness during the day by trying to be more conscious of objects around you.

How many of you, when you enter a room, notice the colour of the walls? Do you notice any plants or flowers present? Consciously note everything when you come into a room—the colour of the furniture, the houseplants, the tables and chairs (are they in the same position as they were the last time you were there?). The lights—how many are there and are they all switched on, or are some of them off, and are the same ones off this time as last time? Is the floor clean or dirty? What is the dirt—spilt tea or dust? If the curtains are not drawn, is the sky as light this time as the last time you were in the room, or is the sky overcast, or is it blue, or is it night outside? And sounds—are there more or fewer sounds? Are the sounds of cars or human voices or radios?

This action of deliberately focusing the attention on the room makes you locate on the activity you are presently engaged in. It helps to cut off being caught up with the past, with thoughts of the family you have just left or the work problems of the day. Paying attention to objects around you brings you right into the present moment.

Having paid attention to the environment around you and got yourself into the present, the next step is to work your way inwards into yourself and focus on what is happening inside you. Is your body tense or relaxed? Is your mind quiet or are there many thoughts buzzing around? Are you still caught up with worries about things that happened during the day? If so, be clearly conscious that the hindrance of worry is present. Be conscious that when you are noting that your body is tense, at that moment all there is in your world is tension. There is no worry, no buzzing thoughts. Be conscious that when you are aware of the worry, the body tension has finished. It has died, and a new moment has been born which is called 'worry'. This is being conscious of the rise and fall of things. It is this continual awareness of the rise and fall of things which wears down craving and hatred.

If you look at a friend's floor and are aware that it is dirty, and then you are conscious of the mind spinning off and starting to worry about your dirty kitchen floor and how you have been meaning to clean it for days but just have not been able to get round to it—be aware that you are *doing* the act of worry as your way of trying to cover up the unpleasant feeling that arose when your eye came into contact with a certain external object, that object being the dirty floor.

Being fully conscious of the meeting point between data coming in through the senses and what you choose to do with that data is where *vipassanā* meditation really lives. You can respond to the data with hatred or you can respond with craving. In either case you choose to live in a hell world. Or you can remain equanimous, letting the data float in and then out, past your watching, alert attention—not grabbing it, not trying to push it away, not being disturbed by it whether it is pleasant or unpleasant. If you can manage this equanimous approach you will find you suddenly are living in a heaven world.

★ ★ ★

What are the benefits to you personally if you practise becoming conscious of things that you were previously unconscious of?

To start with, as your awareness of what is going on inside you deepens, you will find that you are rather disturbed by this heightened awareness. You will be disturbed because you will think that the meditation has made you worse, more angry, more restless, less concentrated. But it has not. It just makes you more conscious of what has always been present in you but which previously you had not the courage to look at. Then you settle down to the new you. And you realise that to become more conscious of the chaos that has always been present in your mind is a benefit because you cannot possibly do anything about sorting out the chaos if you are not conscious of its existence. That is the first benefit of increased awareness.

If you continue to practise steadily, you will raise your capacity. But you only raise your capacity to be more and more conscious if you work at it daily. This means meditating *every day*—not missing the practice for six days and then on the seventh having a binge of three hours seated meditation in the hopes that this will make up for those lapsed six days. If you continue to practise steadily and in the right manner, you will find that the world you inhabit becomes more alive, more dynamic, more interesting, richer. You will not be one to complain that most of the things you do each day, like travelling to work, are meaningless, grey areas in your life which you complete as hastily as possible and usually in a state of amnesia because you take refuge in a mental fog to escape a crushing sense of boredom and greyness.

I read a story once about a man who worked on Manhattan Island in New York. In order to get to work every day he had to catch a ferry, and he found that after he had been to work a few times, he knew the route very well, and so he started to block off from it, and he did not register any of that journey to work. It was one of those grey, foggy patches in his day. He then took up meditation, and he was amazed to find that his journey to work was extremely enjoyable because he started to notice the sparkling on the water. He started to notice the smell of the water. He started to notice the people in the boat. He started to become conscious of his journey to work, which previously he had just ignored. He was amazed to discover that every day was different. He had assumed that he knew the journey off pat and therefore it was boring and therefore he cut off from it. As soon as he started to meditate and started to be aware of changes in himself, changes in the elements, changes in people around him, as soon as he became aware of change, his journey was no longer boring but extremely interesting, even though he made that 'same journey' every day. For him, it was no longer the same after he took up meditation.

And you will find that once you have been practising this meditation for some time, if your walk to work is one of those grey, foggy patches in your day, you will notice that it changes beyond recognition. That foggy patch will start to have recognisable objects in it. There will be the occasional screech of brakes, the colourful dress of a child, the bark of a dog. And there will be feelings in response to those sense impressions. You will notice yourself feeling again. Previously, you would have sworn you were dead emotionally, all your feelings washed out. Now, all of a sudden, you are rich in feelings once again. They are not all pleasant, but at least you are coming to life—your world is enriching.

The benefits of becoming more conscious of what is going on inside you are all positive. You will learn, however, to redefine what you understand by the word 'positive'. It is a positive experience to be more conscious of what is going on inside you, even if what you see there is unpleasant. It is a positive experience to start letting go of that unpleasantness—the training teaches you that you must let go in order to lessen your suffering. It is a positive experience to have your inner world become more alive, richer, more three-dimensional.

These are all benefits from practising awareness of your inner world.

Vipassanā

If you are a housewife, then when you sit down to meditate the types of thoughts that will run through your mind will be concerned with household matters and the family. You will find yourself planning the evening meal, wondering if the drain is about to block up again, running through the items you must buy when you go shopping later in the day. You will find yourself making a mental note to pack young Geoffrey's swimming trunks in his satchel the moment you finish the meditation, because today is the day for his swimming lesson at school, and if you forgot those trunks, young Geoffrey would be so distressed, as he loves his swimming lessons.

If you spend your day in an office, then when you sit down to meditate the contents of your thoughts will be mainly concerned with office matters, concerned with the relationship with your boss and your fellow co-workers. Very little thought will be paid to the home and the running of it.

If the person who is a housewife starts to feel inferior because she thinks about nothing other than meals and shopping and washing—all of which she regards as extremely trivial and none vital to humanity— then she has fallen into a wrong view. She has fallen into an *attā* view, a view of self, a view that she is separate from the universe and not conditioned by it. When wrong view is present, she is bound to suffer because out of wrong view springs hatred or craving. Hatred and craving are *dukkha*.

It is inevitable that the housewife's thinking content will be mainly taken up with home and family because household chores and relating to husband and children are what she fills her day and night with, and therefore she is conditioned by them. She is not separate from these people and activities. Because she is part of them, they form the supporting condition for her thinking content. So her thinking content will flip from cabbage and white sauce for dinner, to the dog, to her son, to vacuuming, to the family budgie, and back to the pile of clothes waiting to be washed.

However, let her go on holiday and the supporting conditions change. Perhaps she and her husband go to Majorca for a week. They shut up home and leave the kids with the parents-in-law. When she meditates on holiday, she will notice a change in her thought content. Thoughts of the children will still creep in, but not as often as when she is at home. Thoughts of meal planning, vacuuming, Monday morning washing are all forgotten. They are replaced by, 'Wonder what's on the menu tonight? I did like that paella we had last night. That was a nice couple we met at the swimming pool this morning. Wonder what the Caves of the Dragon will be like? And let us hope the courier on this tour is better than the one we had yesterday afternoon. I must remember to put sun cream on my nose more often, otherwise it is going to get awfully red and sore.'

Notice, household matters have faded and holiday matters are looming large. We are all interconnected and therefore influenced by the environment and events that go on around us, and so if the supporting conditions change, so does the content of our thinking. With our housewife, the environment and mental atmosphere have changed, and so her feelings, mental states, and the contents of her mind have also changed.

The more clearly we notice how our thought content, our mental states, and our feelings change dependent upon supporting conditions, the more we realise how little control we have over our internal universe. This noticing starts to undermine the wrong view that we are separate from the world around us. When we think we are separate, we believe we can control the way we think and respond to the world.

Take a look the next time you attend a party. See how much control *you* have over your meditation the next day. Let us say you are there for four or five hours, at least until midnight. You are used to going to bed at 11pm for a starter. But on this occasion you only get to sleep at 2am.

You wake up at your normal time, 7am. Seeing that you are awake, you decide you might as well meditate at 8am, your usual meditation time, even though you feel rotten. You sit down to meditate for an hour and you say to yourself, 'Now, I am going to be very mindful. I am not going to fall into thinking. In fact, I am not going to think very often, and when I do, it will not be about today's activities or last night's party—it will be about the Buddha's teaching. I will not fall asleep or wrong concentrate by forcing and gluing the mind onto the breath. I will pay attention to the rise and fall of the feeling in the abdominal region associated with breathing in and out and the rise and fall of sounds, feelings, thoughts, and smells.'

So you start. You close your eyes. The mind settles gently on watching the rise and fall of the abdomen. It watches it once, twice, and then there is the thought of that woman at last night's party, the one wearing the red dress. 'Didn't she look awful? And that tall, dark fellow, he didn't seem to have much to say for himself, but he looked marvellous. Oh dear, I do feel slugged. Wish I hadn't stayed so long and had got to bed earlier. Wish I hadn't had that conversation with Marjorie. I must learn to guard my speech at parties . . .' Masses of thoughts about the party run on and on, and then all of a sudden oblivion—it is called sleep. Next thing you know, the alarm has gone off, and the hour's 'meditation' is over. Filled with thoughts of the party and sleep it was. Watching the rise and fall of phenomena never even occurred during the whole hour.

So you started off the meditation with all sorts of plans of what you were going to do during the next hour. And did any of them succeed? No, not one. Your resolution to control what your mind got up to failed miserably. It only failed because your approach to the hour was inefficient. There is no way anybody can control the activities of the mind, but you can come to understand how the activities come into existence and then pass away again. You can come to that understanding if you frequently notice how things change when the supporting conditions change. And that understanding brings calm and peace, but it is *not* attained via the route of control.

Control is to tell the mind it will do this or that in a given situation. It always fails because the mind goes its own sweet way and appears to do what it wishes regardless of your demands. When it does not do what you want, depression follows. Hours are spent indulging in rationalisations, recriminations, and endless speculations as to why the mind is so wayward.

Understanding is seeing clearly that the mind goes whichever way it wishes because it is conditioned by the past and present supporting conditions. If the supporting conditions are a party, then it will be filled with thoughts of a party. If the supporting conditions are the office, then it will be filled with thoughts of the office. And if the supporting conditions are house and family, then it will be filled with thoughts of husband, children, cooking, and shopping. To demand it to be filled with something other is fruitless and is a refusal to accept things as they are. Not accepting things as they are brings about suffering. What you have to do is to watch and notice how the contents of the mind change dependent upon the supporting conditions changing.

If you notice this, then gradually the mind will turn towards the right view of *anattā*. '*Anattā*' means that things do not exist separately but are interconnected. With right view becoming more established, the mind settles. It is not so concerned when, after a party, it does nothing but think about the party. Being more content to let what is present just be, the mind does not spin off so readily into hatred. The mind only spins off into hatred or craving when it is not content with what is present in the moment, even if the present is thoughts of a party. It only spins off into hatred when it thinks it ought not to be thinking of the party. When it spins off into hatred, ego is present and so suffering arises.

The advantage of coming regularly to a meditation centre such as ours, coming to lectures or group meditations or Pali Canon classes, or even coming to help around the house and garden, is that it becomes the supporting condition for your universe. The more often you are around, the more your mind will turn towards thoughts of *Dhamma*, the Buddha's teaching, and towards attempting to be mindful. As the House of Inner Tranquillity is a meditation centre and the place and the people in it focus all their waking hours on *Dhamma*, then when you are around such places and people your mind too will naturally turn in that direction.

★ ★ ★

Many meditators have come to realise that insight work is done at that level of mind known as 'access concentration', and, quite reasonably, they want to know how they can tell for themselves when access concentration is present and when it is absent.

Think back to a time when you were studying a book for a class, such as a Pali Canon discourse for a class here. You will remember that on some occasions you had no trouble at all reading the allotted number of pages, but on other occasions you had great difficulty. The mind just scattered everywhere. You found yourself reading the same line time and time again and still not understanding it even after the sixth time you had read it. The whole task of reading was an uphill struggle. In fact, it was a boring chore.

If, on those occasions when the reading is difficult, you look carefully at the mind and the objects present in the mind, you will notice that there is ill will present. Ill will is that sense of disinterest, sometimes tipping into outright dislike of the book you are trying to read. Also, there is probably flurry and worry present. Flurry and worry is present when the mind darts off in the middle of the reading, getting wound up about something incidental like 'Have I put the milk bottles out?' You cannot remember. The mind chews at it for some time and then decides that perhaps you had better go and have a look, and then— 'No, this is ridiculous!'—first you are going to finish the reading before getting involved with the milk bottles. So you bring the mind back to reading, and no sooner have you done that than it is off again, this time wondering whether you should pay the electricity bill or can it wait till next week. Then you start worrying about whether you are going to finish the reading in time for the class. Whilst all of this is going on, no reading is taking place. Along with the ill will and the flurry and worry, often comes doubt—doubt in your capacity to understand the material in front of you, or doubt in your capacity to come to grips with the meditative endeavour if you cannot understand the theoretical side of the teaching. When ill will, flurry and worry, and doubt are present with regard to reading, then they are nearly always accompanied by sloth and torpor. Sloth and torpor in this example will be a feeling of lack of energy, a lack of drive to do the reading—a general sluggishness about getting stuck into the task in hand.

So far I have listed four of the five hindrances. The fifth one is sensual desire. When ill will is present, sensual desire is usually absent but not invariably so. However, the most important thing to notice is that when any of the hindrances are present, their very presence destroys concentration. When concentration is absent, mindfulness is affected. It is weakened. Without concentration and with weakened mindfulness, keeping one's mind focused on a printed page and making sense of that print is an uphill struggle.

The presence of hindrances means the absence of access concentration. You will get to know more thoroughly when access concentration is present if you also examine the times when you are enjoying reading a book. If you look carefully, you will see that what is present in mind is joy with what you are reading. This is technically called *sukha*. There is also interest in the content of the text. This interest is *pīti*. Turning the mind to the lines in the book and keeping them on the unfolding story is, on these occasions, very easy. This is what is technically known as initial and sustained application of mind. When joy, interest, initial and sustained application of mind are present, then concentration comes naturally. Concentration has reached the level known as access. Mindfulness, too, is so much stronger under these positive conditions, and when all of these positive factors are present, then there is no room for the hindrances of ill will, sensual desire, flurry and worry, sloth and torpor, and doubt to enter.

However, you do not want the mind to get more concentrated than this, because if it does, it will then lock onto one unmoveable object and become fixed on that object. What you want for *vipassanā* is moving, varied objects—because when they are moving and varied, then you have the opportunity to observe one of the marks of change or unsatisfactoriness or non-self.

If you are aware of which hindrances are present when you are finding it impossible to concentrate on a book, then you will be developing mindfulness of mental objects. The hindrances are classified as objects in mind, and so if you do discriminate those hindrances which are present, even though you may find it impossible to get any reading done because of the lack of concentration, at least your time is not wasted, because you are aiding your insight to grow by being aware of mental objects, and so, even under these difficult conditions, you can still be practising *vipassanā*.

Access concentration needs to be present in order for the in-depth work of *vipassanā* to be done. By 'in-depth' work, I mean seeing one of the three marks. If concentration is not present, then there is too much falling into craving and hatred of objects. However, access concentration is more easily reached if you notice and can actually pick out the various hindrances for yourself. And you can only do this if you can distinguish them when they are present. If every time ill will or sloth and torpor or doubt or sensual desire or restlessness are present, all you want to do is get away from them as fast as possible, and you are desperately wanting to have happiness and joy and concentration present in mind, then you will never take a close look at those hindrances. If you do not look at them closely, you will not be able to discriminate them, and you will not know, for example, what flurry and worry is, even if it should accompany you all day. If you cannot discriminate, then intuitive wisdom does not grow.

If you sit down to meditate and you are aware, right at the beginning of the session, that some of the hindrances are present, then you will know immediately that today, for part and maybe all of your seated practice, concentration is going to be nonexistent. This is the really beneficial thing about seeing and knowing the hindrances and where this awareness aids you in reaching access concentration. Having observed so many times before the link between the presence of the hindrances and the absence of concentration, you relax. You accept that concentration is poor and that when concentration is poor, mindfulness too is spotty. You will also have observed through repeatedly watching the ups and downs of the mind that when concentration and mindfulness are in short supply, then the mind more readily falls into thinking or daydreaming or simply falling asleep.

If you truly accept the presence of hindrances, then they fade away when they are good and ready. But if you give them more fuel by hating them, then they hang around for ages, and if you are not even aware when they are present, then you can so often be adding to them with hatred without even knowing that you are doing so. However, you do become aware of the results of such blindness, and you become aware of the results by noticing that you just do not seem to be able to get it together meditatively. The meditation does not seem to be doing anything or going anywhere.

The meditation is not bearing any fruit because you are not seeing either the hatred of the hindrances or the hindrances themselves. So there is a great deal of dullness around, a great deal of ignore-ance of what is present.

If you notice the presence of certain hindrances, and therefore the absence of concentration, and you realise that you will probably more readily fall into thinking, especially if you are the type who spends a lot of your waking hours thinking—if once there is thinking present, you can accept its presence, instead of fighting it, then it will go away quicker. Also, you will be able to distinguish the hindrances because all your energy will not be taken up with fighting thinking. Fighting thinking is not wanting it to be present. *Fighting* is hatred of thinking. *Accepting* is keeping the mind still, not wishing for the thinking to go away nor wishing for it to continue.

Now it is at this point that the real skill of the meditator comes in: that of fully accepting the presence of thinking whilst making an attempt to stop thinking. Making an attempt to stop is applying right effort. If you do not make any effort, then the mind is likely to tip over into craving for the thinking process to continue.

This teaching is training one to walk the middle path between the extremes. With thinking it is walking between the extreme of indulgence in thinking on the one hand and hatred of it on the other. True acceptance of the presence of thinking is the middle path between indulgence and hatred. If you say to yourself, 'OK, just accept the thinking. This is the way I have been instructed to approach this whole question of thinking,' and so you sit there and think, that is not acceptance of thinking—that is indulgence in thinking. You have fallen off the middle path between extremes. You have fallen into the mire of indulgence. If you come to and realise that you have been thinking for the past ten minutes and get cross with yourself and regard the thinking as something which is preventing you from meditating properly, then you have once again fallen off that middle path. This time you have fallen into the mire of hatred.

You are practising the middle path if, when you come to after a long spell of thinking, you become aware that thinking has taken place, and then you turn your mind towards the primary object, the primary object being the feeling of the rise and fall of the abdomen. If the mind truly accepts thinking, then it does not hate it or wish it to go on. It just notes it and goes back to rise and fall.

★ ★ ★

Many people accuse those who work for their own enlightenment of selfishness. However, it is not selfish but the opposite, the most unselfish act a person can seek to accomplish.

There is a woman. She gets cross with her three-year-old son because he has just thrown his plate of porridge on the floor. If she then hates her crossness, she has brought about a selfish state of mind. At one level of meditation that crossness is all right, but the hatred of that crossness is inefficient. It is inefficient because when hatred arises, it is effectively saying, 'I should not be cross. I should be something other than what I am in the moment. I should be calm and controlled under all circumstances.' It is inefficient to hate crossness or calmness or sleepiness or clarity or irritability, because if we hate them, we are saying that the present moment should be something other.

As you do more and more meditation, and the noticing of what is going on in the mind and body gets more subtle, you come to realise that even the crossness is inefficient—that what actually takes place is that as the plate of porridge hits and spreads all over the floor, an unpleasant feeling arises in you. And it is that feeling you do not like. So the crossness, which is a shade of hatred, is towards the unpleasant feeling. But everything happens so fast that without sufficient training the mind does not notice that it is the unpleasant feeling it is reacting to, but thinks it is the child and blames the child. (This does not mean, however, that you must not discipline children when they throw their food around.)

So first meditators must learn how not to hate hatred, that is, they must learn how not to hate such states as crossness and irritability, and then they must learn to go deeper and subtler still and learn how not to get cross with, how not to hate, unpleasant feelings.

The Buddha, during his forty-five years of teaching, used to make frequent references to things he called 'cankers'. 'Cankers' are stains in the mind. Mind is pure, but an attachment present in the mind is like a stain that taints that purity. The Buddha categorised all attachments under four headings, four different stains that pollute the mind. Remove those stains and mind is pure once again. One of those stains is called the 'canker of becoming', which is wishing to be something other than what you are. So every time crossness arises and you hate it, or unpleasant feeling arises and you hate it, then the stain, the taint, the corruption, the canker of becoming has arisen because you do not wish to be cross, and you do not wish to experience that unpleasant feeling. You wish to become something other than what you are in the moment.

Perhaps you are sitting meditating and you are just watching sounds come and go, bodily feelings come and go, the odd thought come and go, an itch in the nose come and go, slight boredom come and go, and then all of a sudden you have the thought, 'There must be more to meditation than this. This is tedious and awfully trivial,' and so you step in and take charge. You pour more effort into seeing the beginning and end of things, or you pour more energy into staying for longer periods on the rise and fall. The moment you take charge, the stain, the canker of becoming, has arisen because there is a non-acceptance of the moment and a desire to become something other.

The instant we do not accept the present moment, conflict arises in the mind. Conflict is suffering. Suffering is craving or hatred accompanied by ignorance. When craving or hatred arises, a sense of 'I' is born, and when a sense of 'I' is present, selfishness is present. One is separated out from life and the people around one. One has lost contact with one's surroundings. A wall has been built between oneself and the universe. The smooth flow of phenomena has been temporarily stopped. One has become in-turned and highly self-centred.

Hatred and craving create suffering for you and those around you. Hatred and craving harm yourself and others. So can you see that to undertake a training to eliminate craving and hatred is *the* supreme act of unselfishness? When the training culminates, it brings about a permanent situation—in you—of non-harming of both yourself and others. And what can be more beautiful than a being incapable of harming the universe it dwells in?

Loneliness

Throughout a single lifetime, a human being passes through certain and distinct phases. Those phases will be concerned with such issues as career, having children, buying a house, moving home or creating a home, making money and gathering possessions, travelling, investigating spiritual matters, joining or managing a group, death, marriage, break-up of a relationship—what you as a personality want and need from life, work, and health. These are some of the phases that most of you will go through at one stage or another in your lifetime. Each phase can last for anything from a year to five years, but the most common length of time is two and a half years. During those two and a half years, an individual will focus his or her attention more strongly on one area of life than on any of the others.

For instance, you may focus your attention on marriage. For years you may have had very satisfactory short-term relationships with those of the opposite sex. You see your boyfriend or girlfriend several times a week. You have pleasant times together. You also have the occasional fight. The relationship satisfies a need in you. It never goes very deep. It is not too intimate. You do not see one another so often that you get on one another's nerves. You like it this way. The last thing you ever want to do is get too involved, for that may end in marriage, which is certainly not what you want. You like the casual relationship that does not pin you down too much, and when you get bored with it, you can abandon it without too many complicated repercussions, particularly as you are not married to that person. You are then free to move on to a fresh new encounter with another. You are proud of your single status. You even brag that you will never get tied down, and you pity those who, in your eyes, are burdened with the responsibilities of a marriage. Marriage is certainly not for you. Living free and being able to roam is what you ask of life.

One day you wake up to the fact that you are thinking more and more about your latest boyfriend or girlfriend. You cannot seem to get him or her out of your mind, and there is a growing yearning to spend more and more time with that person—to be more intimate, to be closer, to experience more fully this one-to-one relationship— and the only way you can see of getting that is by being married to that individual. Marriage follows and for several years there is a strong focusing in and on that relationship. You learn about one another and about one another's little idiosyncrasies—like how she always squeezes the tube of toothpaste just *anywhere*, thus successfully managing to mangle it, rendering parts of the tube useless, whilst he is very methodical in his approach, always squeezing the tube from the bottom and working upwards. You learn about little idiosyncrasies like this one. You learn how to adjust to these and how to overcome your annoyance if you should find the trait irritating.

You notice that certain freedoms are hampered, but also that new horizons are opened up. There is much to learn about oneself, about the other person, and about a relationship. Once you have fairly thoroughly explored this ground of a one-to-one relationship, which has allowed you to define yourself and become aware of how you deal with another, then the focus of attention moves away from it and into a totally different area. That area may be work or having children or a spiritual search or one of the other areas already mentioned. Of the various phases that a human being passes through in a lifetime, those that create the greatest sense of loneliness are the break-up of a marriage, the birth of the first child, children leaving home, and the death of someone very close.

The breaking down of a relationship, divorce, and the subsequent rebuilding of a life is, for most, a devastating experience and a period when loneliness is a frequent visitor. Loneliness is that sense of being isolated, cut off, unable to contact another. It is that sense that you are all alone, bearing the weight of the world on your back with no one offering any assistance and, worse still, no one understanding your problems or caring about them. So loneliness visits frequently when a relationship is breaking down, *even if* what you most desire in the whole world is the breakdown of that marriage.

Loneliness occurs at times when you least expect it, in a room full of people, for example, or at a dinner party or at a meeting. Loneliness, surprisingly, can occur when you are surrounded by people, people you know and care about and whose company you enjoy. Loneliness can also occur when you are with someone you love very much, whose presence you feel very relaxed in, and who you seek to be with as often as possible. And yet, mysteriously, when you are with that person, you can have periods when you feel distant, out of contact, cut off.

The arrival of a new baby in the home can also be a time of increased isolation and loneliness. The mother spends more and more time on her own, looking after and nurturing the child. She has far less adult company than during her working days, and she begins to miss that adult company. She feels isolated in her cosy nest, cut off from the world, out of touch with the flow of events. The increased loneliness brings in its wake a lack of self-confidence and a fear of taking the initiative to meet new people—even seeking out mothers in the same predicament can look like a daunting prospect. And along with this lack of self-confidence and fear, comes even more loneliness.

The husband in the family suffers too from loneliness at the arrival of this new baby, but his loneliness has its roots in different conditions. He is still mixing during the day with adult company, and, depending on his job, he may be meeting new people every day. Whatever the case, he is likely to have far more adult company per day than his wife. He is still very much in the swim of things. He does not feel cut off from the world, as does his wife. But where he feels cut off is from his wife—because, with the arrival of a new baby in the household, the wife's attention and very often her love as well get transferred from the husband to the child. The intimate relationship the husband once had with his wife is no longer there. He has ceased to be the centre of her attention. The child is the centre of her attention, and the husband must play second fiddle, and sometimes he is even ignored outright. When such an event occurs, he feels isolated, rejected, cut off, lonely, even though surrounded by wife and child.

A death of someone close is another life phase that brings in its wake that crippling sense of loneliness. This sense arises, even if the person who dies is someone one has been married to for anything from twenty to sixty years, and even if when he goes all one's friends make such disparaging remarks as, 'You are better off without him, dear. He was such a lazy slob who squandered all your joint resources, never did a day's honest work, got drunk frequently and picked a fight at the slightest provocation. You are far better off without him.' Even if the marriage was not successful and was frequently filled with heartache, for the one left behind there can still be times of loneliness. The longer the marriage has hung together, whether it was filled with bliss and harmony or arguments and violence, the more likelihood there is of loneliness.

One can understand how, when two people are very close and love one another deeply and then one of the two dies, how the partner left behind will suffer badly from loneliness. But how come, when two people live together, fight like crazy all the time and, by all accounts, hate one another on sight, how come when one dies the other feels lonely?

One can understand that when a woman has been out to work for several years, gives that up and stays at home to look after a baby, that the reduction in adult company and being pinned to the house most of the day is likely to bring about loneliness. But how come a husband, who not only has a wife but also has an addition to the family, a child, not any old child, but *his* child, how come he does not feel fulfilled but instead feels lonely?

One can understand a person feeling lonely when they are alone, but how come loneliness occurs when surrounded by people?

And then there are those really odd times when loneliness rears its head—those times when you would least expect it, those times when you are surrounded by close friends or in the company of someone you love. How come loneliness occurs then?

★ ★ ★

One has to ask the question, 'What is loneliness?' It is a sense of being isolated, cut off, not being able to contact another. I have heard it described like this: 'When talking with a friend, it was as if he was standing at the end of a long tube.' But these are only the symptoms of loneliness—it does not tell you anything about the origin of loneliness.

Loneliness occurs when there is a preoccupation with oneself. 'I'm all alone in this house. I don't see anyone from one day to the next and I don't like it. I want company.' 'I have nothing to do, especially now that I'm unemployed. I don't like having nothing to do, it makes me feel spare. I *want* something to do.' 'I need to be close to someone and yet, when I'm close, I feel smothered. I want a relationship and yet I want my independence.' 'I must leave this person. I must get away. She's terrible to live with. We must get a divorce. I want to be alone. I want to live alone.'

This continual focusing on what *I* want brings loneliness. How can we hope to have a relationship with another or with the world around us if we are continually focusing in on *my* ambitions, *my* health, *my* career, *my* worries, *my* happiness? If you are absorbed in yourself, you cannot possibly find space to relate, and if you are not relating, you will experience loneliness.

At the time of a marriage breakdown there is a tremendous preoccupation with what *I* want and what *I* expect from that relationship. After the divorce there can be a huge preoccupation with what I want my life to be filled with and what ought to be there that was missing from the marriage. This preoccupation with oneself brings about loneliness.

At the death of someone one loves there is a fear of all those empty days and nights, those long hours stretching into the future with nothing but the cat for company—again it is concern not about the one who has just died but about oneself and how one is going to cope alone.

At the death of someone close, someone one does not particularly get on with but has spent a fair proportion of time every day with and has done so for several years, even in this instance there can arise loneliness. One is preoccupied with how one's routine must change now that the other one has died, how there is no one to fight with, no one to insult, how I will now have to fetch in the wood and clean out the fire. 'He used to do that. I've got a bad back. I don't know that I can cope with all those heavy logs.' In short, there is a huge concern about oneself and the change in one's daily living pattern. And when there is a centring on oneself, there is loneliness.

At the arrival of a new baby, the husband is caught up with what he is not getting from his wife, and the wife is concerned about the lack of stimulation in her life. Both are concerned about themselves and what they are not getting.

In every instance there is a preoccupation with myself and what I am not getting. There is a wanting something from life or a rejection of something. One word for wanting something from life is 'craving'. One word for rejecting something is 'hatred'.

If there is craving or hatred in the mind, then there is loneliness. You may not call it that, but if you are mindful, you will notice the symptoms, and you will describe these as one of 'I feel utterly isolated,' or 'I feel out of contact,' or 'I'm not relating—I feel cut off from others and life.'

As craving and hatred are mental states grasped at by the unenlightened, then it follows that loneliness is something experienced frequently by everyone. It is not something confined to those 'certain phases in a human lifetime', those phases like divorce, death, or the birth of a child. Unless you come to experience *directly* that you create your own loneliness by choosing to hate or crave and then cling on to that state, unless you actually know this from your own meditative experience, you will not understand loneliness. And if you do not understand it—how it comes to be and how it ceases—then you will always be trapped by loneliness.

More sense is made of why you can be with someone you feel very attracted to, whose company you love, who you desire to spend a lot of time with physically, and yet still, when you are with him, there are times when you feel you are not contacting him. He feels separated out from you. He feels like a stranger.

When such states occur within you, you can be sure that what is happening is that you have become lost in what *you* want. You have become preoccupied with yourself. That preoccupation is unlikely to have anything to do with the other person. In other words, you will not be thinking about your relationship with that person, but instead you will have got caught up in concern about your job or about your health or about your holiday or about the neighbour you do not like or some other matter. You will have totally forgotten about the very existence of the loved one you normally spend hours thinking about, dreaming about, craving to be with. Now you are with them, what do you do? You shut them out by becoming preoccupied with yourself.

Preoccupation with yourself, in short, craving and hatred, is highly dangerous because it shuts out others and the world leaving you lonely, anxious, mentally aching, and dimly aware that something is wrong but not quite sure what, or how to cope with it. It can even leave you wondering about your own sanity.

★ ★ ★

It is not uncommon for meditation teachers to be asked by a meditator to confirm that he or she is sane and is not going out of his or her mind. Or the statement is made, 'If this continues, I'll go insane,' and the statement is made seriously, not in jest. Craving and hatred are indeed insanity, but the meditator is not going insane as clinically defined. What is happening is that he or she is becoming very conscious of how destructive the preoccupation with oneself is, and that such a state creates an imbalance, and that this imbalance is frightening. Provided the meditator stays aware and just watches the preoccupation with herself and watches the fear of it, then all is well. But if she becomes so frightened of the craving or hatred that she falls into the fear, then a very inefficient and nasty situation occurs where there is hatred of hatred, and the mind becomes locked in hatred and fear and totally absorbed in itself and its problems.

The only way to cope is to come to understand loneliness—just how it occurs, how it ceases. How does this mental state of loneliness operate? Freedom lies in understanding. Freedom does not lie in re-placing loneliness with fulfilment or company or loved ones. You cannot get freedom by replacing loneliness with anything. You can only get freedom by doing absolutely nothing but watching. By watch-ing you see how loneliness operates. When you see that, you have understanding. When you have understanding, you are free of lone-liness.

When you just watch, you come to know loneliness. And the first thing you observe when you watch is that as soon as there is a wanting to have something or a desire to get away from something, then there comes about this sense of not being in contact, this sense of utter isolation from everything around you. You will also observe that when the mind is totally absorbed in the moment, then there is just feeling or movement or thinking or smelling or tasting or touching taking place, and that this is accompanied by a sense of contentment and ease.

From all of this you will have come to realise that whenever there is a movement away from *now*, then craving or hatred arise and with that comes loneliness. When the mind sinks into the moment, there is no thought of 'me'. There is just an event that is born and dies, and on such occasions there is no loneliness—instead there is contentment and fullness.

★ ★ ★

Contentment and fullness is love. If we consider what love really is and what it is not, maybe we will learn just a little bit more about loneliness.

If you find yourself attracted to a person, someone you regard as beautiful or wise or witty or good company, there is a quality about the person that makes you want to get closer. Your attraction breeds a desire to be with that person, and so you manipulate life in such a way that you spend a lot of time physically close to him or her—talking, going to the theatre or for walks, or doing small tasks together. Small jobs around the house are not a drudge. In fact, they become a pleasure if shared with someone whose company you enjoy. Should this familiarity make the bond deeper, then there springs up that which we call love.

Now what is called love can too often drive a wedge between two people because it turns from true love into possessiveness: 'I want that person,' 'I want to be close to them,' 'I want them to behave in an appropriate manner,' 'I want them to change certain deficiencies of character,' 'I want them always to be with me and no one else,' 'I want them to do and behave as I say.' So what we call love quickly becomes an object out there which I in here see as my possession, which should do as I want. And the moment the mind views another person as mine, there is no longer love but the beginnings of growing loneliness.

If the mind is aware of its own movements, of the thoughts of 'I want to have,' 'I want to be close,' 'I want them to change,' if there is an awareness of these thoughts, then there is the possibility of non-action. If there is non-action, there is no loneliness. If there is no loneliness, there is a love—true love not possessiveness. Non-action is just watching the thoughts, seeing them as babblings of the mind, noting them as just thoughts, not taking them seriously—not believing in their content but just watching the wanting, the desire to possess, the desire to control.

You need to view all of these thoughts as if you were viewing bubbles on the surface of a river. There you are on a sunny summer's day, sitting on the bank of a fast flowing river, and on the surface of that river is a myriad of little bubbles. As you watch them drift by, some bursting as they hit a rock, some evaporating, new ones are born, and all are carried off into the distance as the river meanders its way towards the ocean. All the bubbles will die, and a myriad of others will be born and in their turn die long before the river reaches the ocean. None of those bubbles greatly affect or bring about a major change to that river because they have no substance.

If you can view those possessive thoughts, those wanting thoughts, those desire thoughts, like those bubbles on the surface of that river—if you can view them as just so many bubbles on the surface of the mind that have no substance—then you cannot harm yourself with them because you will not grab hold of them. Instead, the mind will just view those thoughts as so many substanceless bubbles drifting past to eventually burst and evaporate. With such an attitude of viewing, the quietness of the mind is not disturbed.

But should you not view thoughts in this manner but instead regard them as having substance, as somehow being real and solid, then you will take them seriously, and the mind will gear itself for responding mode, and action will follow. When the content of thought is taken seriously, the mind automatically rears up to act. And there is the view of 'me' in here that must act towards that delightful or painful thought out there. There is the view that somehow, someway I must *do* something towards these possessive, wanting thoughts. I must get rid of them, or if I am finding them particularly pleasurable, I must get them to hang around a bit longer. As soon as there is this acting, there is separation, and when there is separation, there is loneliness. If there is no movement of mind for or against loneliness but total attention, then, at that instant, there is both a total understanding of how you created loneliness as well as the ending of it. With the ending of loneliness, there is no sense of being cut off, isolated, out of contact.

When there is no loneliness, there is love. Love is not thinking about someone else. Love is not wishing to be with someone else. Love is not being with another. Love has no object. *Love is.* Love is being in the now, with no separation from the now. Love is contentment with *whatever* is present in the moment. Such a mind is sensitive, alert, conscious, and full of affection for whatever is. Affection wants nothing in return for its actions. It is fascinated by life unfolding before it and feels a deep affection for the mystery—a mystery it fully understands and yet still finds awe-inspiring. It does not demand that this mystery always present it with joyful events. If the mind demanded this, then there would be action.

The loving mind knows and accepts that some objects are pleasant and that some are painful, and because of that, it accepts *all.* There is no longer pleasantness that must be hung on to or painfulness that must be rejected, but rather there is just an event that comes into being and passes away. With this, there is contentment. Contentment is love, and when love is present, loneliness never again appears on the scene.

Of Wizards and Wise Men

Scattered throughout the Pali Canon, the texts of the Theravada school of Buddhism, are references to 'one who is released both ways'. Now what does this mean, 'released both ways'? It implies, does it not, that there are two paths, and that there is something to be gained at the end of each path? It implies that the two paths are different, and that they have different rewards at the end of each of them.

There are indeed two paths. One is the path of the wizard, and the other, the path of the wise man. The key to unlocking both paths is awareness, but the objects treaders of each path have to train themselves to be aware of are different, and that is why each path produces different results. Buddhism calls the path of the wizard 'mundane' (worldly), and the path of the wise man 'supermundane' (beyond the worlds).

I do not know what the dictionary definition of 'wizard' is. Nor do I know what those who call themselves psychics and magicians understand by the word 'wizard', but what I mean when I use the word 'wizard' is one who is accomplished in *samatha* (concentration) meditation and all its associated disciplines, and what I mean by the words 'wise man' is one who is accomplished at *vipassanā* (insight) meditation.

If one walks down the path of the wizard, one will develop understanding about human relationships and how they function. One will learn about the do's and the don'ts of any given life situation, like running a business, or being part of a group, or dating someone—one will learn what to do and what not to do if one wishes to get the best out of these situations. Some call such knowledgeable people 'street wise'. The trainee on this wizard's path develops a worldly wisdom by paying detailed attention to external objects, objects such as human beings and how they relate to one another, patterns that govern external events, and mental laws and how they operate.

Also included on the path of the wizard is learning about thought and how to control it. It is learning to control the mind to such a degree that, at will, one can cut out from everyday consciousness and exist for a while in a deeply tranquil state, an altered state of consciousness called *jhāna*. Once this is developed the person can become 'sensitive' to their environment. They can become what is often referred to as 'psychic', when they sense the feelings and the thoughts of others. Often they can sense other realms as well. This gives them more information about their external world, which allows them to handle it even more successfully. This success is wisdom. Being able to handle life wisely means that the wizard's day-to-day living runs smoothly.

Samatha training, which is part of the world of the wizard, if developed to its fullest potential, includes not only the capacity to hold one's mind on one object, like the word 'Buddho', but it also includes understanding the reason for such activities as giving and discipline. On this path one develops a deep understanding of actions and their results, and of rebirth and how it functions from life to life. One understands the world of animals, the world of gods, and the world of demons. One understands how they operate and how best to treat them if one wishes to live harmoniously with these other realms. *Samatha* training is much, much more than just learning to concentrate. One may ask, 'But for what purpose would one wish to become skilled at concentration and knowledgeable about such things as actions and results, rebirth, and other realms besides the human one?' A person undertakes this sort of training because he or she very much desires to become wise about the world in which they live.

As one journeys along the path of the wizard, one does become more and more wise about people, society, mental laws and how they operate, so that by the time one gets to the end of this particular path, one is released from ignorance. One is released from the ignorance about the way the world functions. This wisdom brings a freedom from the many problems that beset our day-to-day living.

As the trainee wizard gets more accomplished at his craft, his friends start to regard him as a 'wise old man' (or a 'wise old woman' if it is a female trainee), regardless of whether he is twenty or sixty years of age. His friends are drawn to him like pins to a magnet. They want the wizard to give them advice on how to handle career problems or money problems or sex problems or parent-child problems or old-age problems. They go to the wizard for advice on all manner of worldly problems. However, they do not go to him seeking the answers to such questions as 'Is there a God?', 'What is Reality?', 'How do I experience enlightenment, *nibbāna*?', or 'Can "I" even experience enlightenment or must I get rid of the concept of "I" first?'

Such questions one would not ask the wizard, for such questions and their answers are of no concern to him. He is not after discovering *nibbāna*. He is not after release from spiritual ignorance. He is after release from worldly ignorance. That is his realm. That is his domain.

If you want to be guided to the realm of *nibbāna,* then you must take your questions about *nibbāna* into the domain of the wise man (or woman). He has walked along the other path, the *vipassanā* path, the path of awareness, the spiritual path. It is the path to self-knowledge. It is an internal path. It is a path where one learns about internal relationships rather than external relationships. The trainee wise man is concerned with one of the sense consciousnesses, like eye consciousness, and how it relates to perception and feeling and then to craving and hatred. Learning all about such internal relationships is what occupies the interest of one who is training to become a wise man.

If you tread this particular path, then when you come to the end of it, you will find yourself released from all mental torment. You will find you have gained nothing but lost a lot and that that *losing* is the losing of a mental burden which you have carried around for lifetimes. Your friends will call you 'enlightened' or 'God-realised', and those who wish to have their own experience of being free, light, fresh, and open to all internal events without fear will come to you for your advice on how to journey into such a realm.

★ ★ ★

Because the worldly wisdom collected by the meditator who walks the path of the wizard is so visible, people throughout the ages have come to associate this type of wisdom with spirituality. The wizard's training produces in its practitioners some or all of the following qualities: peacefulness, tranquillity, gentleness, sympathy, compassion, and a powerful will. It produces people who can communicate with others, who understand human problems, and who have a workable solution for all such problems. These are external qualities—external only because they are so easily visible to others, especially to those who have not yet begun to train, and who therefore do not have the capacity to judge what true spirituality is. As these qualities are so easily observable to all, they are erroneously thought to be the qualities that one must develop in order to become enlightened. However, these qualities have nothing whatsoever to do with the path of the wise man. One who has got to the end of the spiritual path and is truly worthy of the title 'wise man' may exhibit none of the qualities just mentioned.

The path of the wizard and the path of the wise man are two very distinct and separate paths that end in different places. The phrase 'released both ways' refers to a person who has trodden both the path of the wizard and the path of the wise man. It is important that you know the difference between the two paths because if you do not, you may well be walking the path of the wise man (for that is what we teach at this meditation centre) but unknowingly steering your practice towards the path of the wizard. Should you secretly desire to develop worldly wisdom because you admire the qualities of the wizard more than those of the wise man, you will corrupt the path you are currently walking upon. When a trainee walks one path thinking they are developing the skills that belong to the other path—very little happens. Not much development of any sort takes place, either of a worldly or a spiritual nature.

It is like the person who wants to learn horse riding but goes to a swimming coach and splashes around in a swimming pool. He thinks that because horse riding is called a sport and swimming is also called a sport, the two are interchangeable and that by learning to swim, somehow he will develop riding skills at the same time. It would be clear to us that such a person will not develop riding skills, nor will he develop swimming skills to any great extent because his attention will not be fully on swimming due to his cofusion about the results he is likely to obtain from practising the art of swimming.

In a similar way, we get ourselves confused when it comes to the development of spiritual skills, for we easily get the world of the wizard and the world of the wise man muddled and think that somehow they both produce the same results. This is because society calls both paths 'spiritual' when in truth only one path is spiritual (the wise man's path), whilst the other is worldly. We also get the two paths muddled because the qualities developed by the wizard are so easy to observe, whilst those of the wise man are not. This is because no qualities at all are developed along the path of the wise man, and so we have nothing by which we can assess the path. The Buddha stated that he gained absolutely nothing from perfect, unexcelled enlightenment. How can this be? It is because the spiritual path is not one of adding things to oneself. That is the way of the world. The path of the wise man is a path where nothing is changed—where mentally you stand absolutely still, observe, and then make sense of what you have observed.

So if you cannot add anything, how can you journey anywhere? Strictly speaking, it is not accurate to talk about a wise man's path and its results—for in truth there is no path, and therefore there are no results. As you are already enlightened, you cannot go journeying around looking for something you already have. But as you do not know this yet, you have to make a journey. When you get to the end, you will realise that it is as though you need not have bothered with the journey at all—for the path was circular. It ended where it began. But you do not know this from your own experience, and therefore you must journey. And as you make this journey along the wise man's path, what exactly are you doing if there is nowhere to go and nothing to be achieved? You are 'doing' losing. You are losing your views—views like 'There is somewhere to go and there is something to be gained.' That is the burden I talked about earlier that you have been carrying around for lifetimes. That burden is the burden of views, and it is those views that hide *nibbāna* from you.

The more we know about the differences between the two worlds of the wizard and the wise man, the more likelihood we have of being successful on the path of our choice. Only those activities that lead towards *nibbāna* would I call 'spiritual'. All others I would call 'worldly'. Activities such as astrology, tarot, psychic development, healing, helping others—all these are worldly because they add something to us. They most certainly bring a happiness, but it is not a permanent happiness. It is temporary. If you want permanent happiness, then you must tread the spiritual path, the path of the wise man.

★ ★ ★

As the majority of what we teach at the House of Inner Tranquillity deals with the world of the wise man, I am going to devote the major part of this lecture to descriptions about the world of the wizard.

Let us imagine that there is a man who lives in Bradford on Avon and who runs out of sugar. He decides to walk into the town to buy himself some. His house lies north of the town, and in order to get into the centre he must pass through Market Street. Now, the end of Market Street that is furthest from the centre of the town is very narrow, and on one side of it there is a very high wall that drops straight down onto the street. There is no room for any pavement. And on the other side, the side opposite this high wall, are shops and a narrow pavement.

Our gentleman has to walk on this narrow section of pavement. And as he turns the corner into Market Street and steps onto the pavement, an enormous juggernaut comes hurtling towards him. As his eye catches sight of the lorry, his mind spins off, throwing up image after image that weave themselves into a fantastic story. He sees himself smashed into the shop window by this juggernaut. Some of his limbs are broken by the weight of the vehicle, and his face and arms are badly cut from pieces of flying glass, the worst cut of all being of a major artery in his left arm, the arm that he lifted to shelter his eyes from the oncoming vehicle. Next he sees himself lying on the pavement with a crowd of people gathering around him, whispering and looking shocked. There is blood everywhere. It is some minutes before the ambulance arrives, by which time he has lost considerable quantities of blood and is unconscious. Whispers are spreading amongst the crowd and several are asking, 'Is he dead?'

All of this is creative thinking. Nothing actually took place out there in the physical universe. It all took place in the man's mind and all because a juggernaut passed a little too close to him as he stepped onto the pavement in Market Street. Creative thinking is sometimes called imagination, and such imaginings have an effect on the body. The knees tremble and turn to jelly. The heart pounds. The mouth goes dry. The hands sweat. Blood drains from the face and one feels sick.

If the man walking down that street is a wizard, he will just laugh at his creation, for he is a man who is aware of the difference between creative thinking which has meaning and therefore can tell him more about the world in which he lives, and creative thinking which is an illusion, which is therefore useless, even harmful if he pays any attention to it. And he knows that this particular creation has no meaning, no matter how sensibly the story was strung together. That is why he will label it 'illusion'. Nonetheless, he will marvel at the fertility of the mind—how in a flash it can create a whole story that is so vivid, so emotionally intense, and so consuming of his attention that it is as if it actually took place.

As the man is a wizard, he is fully conscious of what has taken place in his mind and what effect that creation has had on his body, but because it is an 'illusion', he will not give it a second thought. He will just brush the creation aside. Nor will he pay any attention to his trembling knees, pounding heart, and nausea. He knows that all of these physical symptoms have been induced by his mental creation, and that because body is much slower to recover than mind, it will be some while, maybe twenty minutes, before the shakes and the sickness fade away. Furthermore, this wizard knows that these thoughts are not psychic phenomena trying to tell him about an event that is going to take place in the future. How does he know that this particular batch of creative thinking is not a psychic premonition? How is it that he is so certain? He knows, because from continuous observation over years of the thoughts and pictures that habitually run through his mind, the wizard has noticed a different tone between creative thoughts which have something worthwhile to tell him and creative thinking which is an illusion and which is mind just rambling on, churning out one bit of junk after another. He knows too that the majority of mind's creative ramblings fall under the heading of worthless junk. He knows the particular tone of thoughts and mental pictures that are worthless junk, and he knows under what conditions such illusions are most likely to spring forth.

This wizard is only too fully aware that suffering in the form of worry and fear would be his constant companion for hours if he believed this creation that mind has suddenly thrown into consciousness. He knows that the only skilful way to respond to all such illusive creative thinking is to turn away from the thoughts, to be unmindful of them, and to go back and concentrate on what he was doing just before the creation appeared, which was walking down the street. This way he knows that the body will settle down, and in a few minutes he will feel his normal healthy self once again. Such a person has learnt to control creative thinking. He does not allow it to control him. Control does not mean smashing the thoughts out the moment they arise. That is hatred and that is loss of control. Control means *awareness* and *knowing* exactly what category of thoughts one is being aware of. It means knowing the category, then withdrawing one's attention from the useless thoughts but investigating the useful ones. The person who knows all of this, knows the world of the wizard.

In the example just given, if the man walking down Market Street has little or no training as either a wizard or a wise man, he is likely to respond in one of the following ways.

He may be totally unaware of everything—unaware of the creative fantasy about being crushed against a shop window and unaware of the physical effects that that fantasy has on his body. His body will still go through the motions of being cold, sweaty, and nauseous, but he will not be aware of any of these physical things. He will automatically react with hatred towards the unacknowledged physical effects but will be unaware of the hatred. Years later, when he feels totally out of contact with himself and those around him, when he is existing in a shadowy, grey mental world where he hates himself and feels uncomfortable with himself most of the time, he will be mystified as to why he is in this state. 'Where has this unhappiness come from?' he will ask. It has come from his continuous ignoring of what was going on in his mind and body.

Or the untrained man may react to these thoughts of being crushed in yet another way. He may well be aware of the physical feelings of sickness and shakiness but be unaware of the creative thinking which brought this sickness about. As soon as he becomes aware of the physical sensations, there is a strong likelihood that he will worry about his health. He will wonder, 'Why is it I suddenly feel so ill for no rhyme or reason?' Because he starts to worry about his health, he is not remaining detached from the physical feelings that the mental creation produced. It is not possible for him to remain detached because he ignored the creative thinking that came before the sickness. Only awareness of the creation and the sickness can give him knowledge, knowledge of how the mental creation and the sickness are linked to one another. Only knowledge will keep him detached.

So should the gentleman not see the link between the mental creation and the illness but only be aware of the illness, he will fall into worry about his health. He will start wondering if perhaps he has contracted a dangerous illness. Maybe it is even terminal. He will hurry off to the nearest phone to make an appointment with his doctor. Much time and energy will be spent lost in a world of worry about his health and about how long he has got to live. It will take several hours, maybe even several days before he has seen his doctor, had the necessary tests, taken the necessary pills, and found out that nothing whatsoever was wrong with him in the first place. But during those days he will exist in a fog of worry. Such a man has no control over his imaginings. They control him. He does not even know he imagines, and he most definitely does not know the effect such imaginings have on his body. So he does not know that he has done this sickness to himself. Such a lack of awareness brings about suffering, suffering in the form of worry about his health. This suffering will come and go for days before it finally departs from his world. As he does not know about creative thinking and how to control it, his suffering may only cease when his doctor tells him that he has not contracted a rare disease, but that he is perfectly healthy and likely to last for many a year to come.

There is yet a third way that a man who is not a wizard may respond to a mental creation. Should he be one who *is* aware of the content of his thinking much of the time and on this particular occasion *is* aware of the creative thinking as it takes place, should he also be someone who is aware of the effect such thinking has on the body, then he will not be surprised when he notices feelings of nausea, weakness in the knees, and sweating of the palms of the hands. But should he not know the difference between creative thinking that is an illusion and creative thinking which should be used, he will not be able to remain detached. He will take his fantasy seriously and react with hatred or craving towards it.

* * *

Thinking which receives the label 'valuable' may be picked up and investigated to see what it can tell the wizard about the world that surrounds him. One type of mind-reading takes place this way. For example, a wizard may notice masses of thoughts drifting through his mind that are concerned with his career and the way in which it is going. He may notice that he is worrying about whether or not he is going to get that promotion that is coming up in the firm next month—or perhaps he should change jobs in order to ensure that he advances up the career ladder. Should the wizard notice these types of thoughts running through his mind and know that he never normally thinks about career advancement, he will immediately be alerted and investigate, for he knows that this thought is not his own. So he investigates to find out who, in his immediate environment, is worrying about his or her career. The wizard investigates all the thoughts that ran through his mind before the thoughts about career advancement sprang up. He also investigates all the thoughts that came after and during the thoughts about career. This way he discovers who it is that is concerned about their career development.

★ ★ ★

There are many things to be learnt besides just concentration medi-tation on the path of the wizard. One of those things is how to relate successfully to others. This type of learning comes from watching life and from wishing to learn from what one watches. This wishing to learn is very important, for it makes one open to all the cues that are constantly being fed to us by others.

For example, on several occasions I was witness to a woman who was rather poor at behaving in a manner that pleased others—which is another way of saying that she was bad at relating. She continued to deepen this characteristic by absolutely refusing to be mindful of what she did when in the company of others and of how they reacted to what she did.

A married couple who are friends of both of us invited Alan, my husband, and me to lunch. They have a very nice home. It is tastefully and expensively decorated, with a number of valuable antiques in each room. On this occasion the couple had prepared a simple but delicious Italian pasta meal which they had put in individual ramekin dishes and which we were to eat on our laps in the lounge. The dishes were a little too hot, and so that we would be comfortable whilst eating, the hostess fetched some small tables. One did not have to have a lot of knowledge about furniture to realise that these tables were very expensive. The hostess, not wishing to damage the tables, went off and fetched some mats to protect the wood from being marked by the hot dishes. She very carefully placed beside each person a table on which she put a mat, and then she placed a hot ramekin dish upon the mat. The host and hostess both left their dishes on the mats, bent over them and ate directly from them. However, once the dishes had cooled down sufficiently they picked them up, held them close to their mouths, and ate from them in that position. Every time they put their dishes back on the tables, they were very careful to place them squarely on the mats.

The woman, the one who constantly behaved in a manner which did not please others, picked up the ramekin dish, found it was too hot to handle, and dropped it straight back on the table, missing the mat entirely. In consequence, the hostess snapped, 'Don't put that hot dish directly on the table. Place it on the mat. That is what the mat is for.' The air went very tense, the host and hostess looked decidedly annoyed, the woman looked peeved, and the conversation remained strained for the remainder of the visit.

All that woman needed to have done was observe. The host and hostess were telling her exactly what to do by their very actions. They were indicating, by the way they were placing the hot dishes on the mats, that the tables were of value to them and that they liked to look after things that they valued. Observing other people's likes and dislikes and fitting in with them whilst under their roof, breeds harmony. Life runs more smoothly when there is harmony. If this woman had observed her hosts' behaviour and had followed their lead, suffering would not have arisen in her. But she chose to ignore the signals and suffering always is the result of ignorance. Ignoring external cues is the ignorance referred to on the *samatha* path. The training followed by one who is on the wizard's path demands that one is mindful of everyday events around one if one is to become skilled at handling worldly affairs.

* * *

All of this is a long, long way from the world of the wise man, who is not in the slightest bit interested in whether he relates well to others or not. He knows that no matter how skilled he is at living in the world, it is an endless subject—this learning to live successfully with parents, in-laws, children, partners, neighbours, and bosses—and that no matter how skilful he is, he is going to tread on somebody's toes almost every day, and that their reaction to his behaviour will give rise to an unpleasant feeling within him. So what interests the wise man is how to handle that feeling. He knows he cannot stop the arising of unpleasant feelings, and so he wants to know how to react to them in the most efficient manner so that he does not produce suffering on top of that feeling. Along his particular path he learns that the only way to handle feelings, both pleasant and unpleasant, is to see the link between feelings and how, when he tries to hang on to those feelings or to push them away, he suffers.

The trainee on the path of the wise man pays no attention whatsoever to the content of his thinking. He labels it all as worthless—even the mind-reading and psychic stuff is of no value to him. It does not help him on his quest, and so he dismisses it. He does not deny that thinking occurs. He is mindful that the process of thinking exists as a real event but that the content is unreal. He never gets caught up with that.

All the trainee does on this path is watch whatever comes in through one of the six sense doors, that is, the five physical sense doors of eye, ear, nose, tongue, and body, and the mind door. He watches things like the sound of a watch ticking, for example. He notes the sound rise and pass away. He notes the label 'watch ticking' rise and pass away. He notes the feeling that follows that label rise and pass away.

He observes the rising and passing away of things that are internal, and the more he observes how rapidly these things come and go, the more he realises the futility of trying to hang on to anything or push anything away. He realises this because it becomes so startlingly clear to him that things disintegrate rapidly. They have hardly arisen, and then they are disappearing, and so why bother trying to get rid of them. They are gone before one even thinks of trying. He also realises that the moment he becomes aware of something it has already passed away, because awareness only occurs once, say, the feeling has finished. So once again he realises the impossibility of actually being able to push an unpleasant feeling away.

When his noticing of this mark of change becomes strong enough, a transformation occurs within him. He becomes so disgusted with these fleeting objects, just because they are so fleeting, so ephemeral, so insubstantial, that he shrinks back from getting involved with them anymore. Because in the past he thought that these objects were solid and that they lasted, he felt they were worth loving or hating. But now he sees that they are not worth the fight. As he withdraws his desire to become involved with these fleeting objects, so his consciousness leans towards experiencing that which is permanent. He yearns to experience something that is not so unreliable as these changing, conditioned objects. As the trainee lets go of that which is impermanent, a curious thing happens—he finds that he is totally immersed in that which he has been seeking for years. He finds that he is immersed in the permanent.

Now he knows. He knows he always was immersed in *nibbāna* and that he always will be immersed in *nibbāna*. And he knows that all that had been hiding *nibbāna* from view was ignorance—the ignoring of the marks of impermanence, of suffering, and of non-self.

* * *

Finally, before I finish on this topic of the difference between the path of the wizard and the path of the wise man, I would like to point out that most spiritual disciplines combine the teaching of both paths and that we at the House of Inner Tranquillity are no exception to this rule. We do sprinkle mundane teaching in amongst instructions on how to become enlightened. The reason we do this is that many seekers of the wise man's path have their minds so filled with puzzlement and distress about day-to-day problems that they cannot possibly even begin to walk along the wise man's path until they have developed some evenmindedness towards these problems. And as they are worldly problems that bother these seekers, only worldly answers will bring about the dissolving of these problems. Once their minds are quiet enough and they are taking the ups and downs of day-to-day living more in their stride, only then are these seekers ready to begin the spiritual journey.

Women—
Their Bodies, Minds, and Meditation

I am going to talk about what must rank as one of the world's most fascinating topics. That topic is women. If it is not top of the list of people's most favourite subjects, it must surely come very close to the top. Women fascinate men. Women fascinate women. They fascinate because they are a puzzle. They are difficult to fathom. They seem so logical, reasonable, and happy one moment and then illogical, emotional, and tearful the next. These violent swings of mental states are infuriating, and it is hard to understand why they occur.

Men are an interesting topic too. But men are more consistent in their emotional and mental states, and therefore you know where you stand with a man. If he is grumpy in the morning, the chances are he has been like that ever since you have known him and is likely to be consistent in his morning grumps for some time into the foreseeable future. But she—she is happy, singing, on top of the world this morning. But tomorrow? Who knows? Not even she knows—maybe she will be happy and cheerful, but she is just as likely to be dark, irritable, and glowering. It is difficult to understand why there is the sudden switch, and the male partner can be forgiven if he wonders, 'What have I said or done wrong now?' Chances are he has said and done nothing wrong.

Although men are an interesting subject to talk about, and to contemplate the whys and wherefores of what makes them tick, because they are more stable emotionally, and therefore more predictable, they turn out not to be as fascinating as women. Nowhere near as many books are written about men and their psychology as are written about women. It is the unpredictability of the female personality that makes them such a mystery, and it is the mystery that makes them fascinating.

Men do not understand how women work psychologically. And women do not understand how women work psychologically. But if close attention is paid to the swings in the mental states, to the swings in emotions, and to the swings in the physical habits of a woman, then, over a period of time, a very definite pattern is seen to emerge. This pattern is directly linked to the hormonal shifts in the woman's body.

Now, to observe these patterns is essential for the female meditator. If she does not acknowledge them and float them up into the full light of consciousness, then these emotional swings dominate her, make her life miserable, and she is powerless to change the situation. She also hinders her meditative growth if she does not become aware of the vast psychological changes that occur at ovulation, before menstruation, and during her period.

It is also essential for the male meditator to come to awareness of and understanding of these patterns if he is not to fall into hatred of the females in his life. Nearly every man has an intimate relationship with anything from one to seven women. By 'intimate' I mean that he spends a portion of every day with that particular woman. She may be his mother, his wife, his daughter, or his work colleague. Think of the man who is married, has three daughters, has his mother living under the same roof as him, and owns his own business along with a female partner. He also has a female secretary. That man has intimate contact with seven women every day. He is totally surrounded by female minds, and when they swing downwards, he is affected. All of these women are not going to get moody and emotional at the same time, for the hormonal changes will occur on different days for each one of them, and so there is the likelihood of there being a strong tone of emotionality and irrationality in the atmosphere for a large proportion of every month.

Because the man is living surrounded by and absorbed in a very emotional and rapidly shifting mental atmosphere, unless he is very mindful, he will be unprotected and will fall into hatred and will not know how or why it happened. Thus, the incidences of rows and non-communication with the females in his life are likely to be far higher for the unmindful man than for the male *vipassanā* meditator who is conscious not only of his own shifting feelings and mental states but also those of the females in his environment. When he is conscious of this aspect of women, not only is it easier for him to guard his own mind from responding negatively to them, but also he can do practical things which help to lessen the tension in the atmosphere, thus making the environment more tolerable for both himself and them.

★ ★ ★

The female menstrual cycle is at the root of all the emotional swings and causes changes to take place mentally and physically, particularly at ovulation, before a period, and during a period. These changes have the most apparent impact on a woman's mental states and behaviour when she is premenstrual. Therefore, most of what follows relates to changes that occur in the few days prior to the start of a woman's period. Before I go on to discuss this aspect of the menstrual cycle, I would first like to consider the role that a woman plays in modern Western society, because this role strongly influences her attitude towards her bodily functions and the lunar side of her personality.

A human being's personality can be roughly divided into two parts—a lunar and a solar part. 'Lunar' is another term for femininity and 'solar', for masculinity. Both women and men have both these aspects within themselves. Awareness meditation brings these two parts, lunar and solar, into a more harmonious balance in each person, instead of one aspect being acknowledged and allowed to flourish to the detriment of the other. This is the more common state of affairs in existence before a person embarks upon raising their awareness.

A woman is mainly a lunar being, which is to say that the lunar side of her personality is very strongly developed. It is far more developed than it is in a man. The qualities of character associated with the lunar side are those of caring, nurturing, protecting, compassion, patience, and submission. Such things as homemaking and mothering are also lunar qualities. This lunar side rules food, breasts, feelings, intuition, menstruation, birth, motherhood, home, and family.

Before the industrial revolution, family life and the type of work one did were radically different from what they are today. The lifestyle was mainly agricultural, which meant that the whole family stayed in one place from birth to death, and each family member—mother, father, and each child—took part in the daily workload. Everyone was valued and needed for their work contribution if sufficient food was to appear on the table each day. So the old agricultural society in no way frustrated this lunar side. Instead, that society strongly supported it, for the traits of nurturing, caring, protecting are all qualities needed to successfully raise fruit, vegetables, grain, and farm animals. There is nothing more deeply satisfying for the lunar side of the personality than to be involved in raising the food it will later consume, bottling or preparing it, and finally devouring it.

This deep involvement with food keeps the lunar side of the personality alive. Also, the constant family contact of the old agricultural society was another activity that satisfied the lunar hemisphere. Families did not split up and members move off to other parts of the country like they do today. The norm was for the family to work the same land for generations, and the woman worked side by side with her husband and children—thus she was surrounded by an extended family of grandparents, aunts, uncles, husband, and children from the day she was born until the day she died. So working the land with her family gave full vent to all her lunar qualities. She could allow them to be expressed without them getting in the way of the role she had to fulfil in the society she lived in.

Today, however, it is a very different picture. Society's main thrust is towards industry, business, technology, science. We can no longer be called an agricultural society.

In order to survive and be successful in today's technological society, it is imperative that the solar side of the personality be emphasised. The solar side is the masculine side. The masculine side is analytical, mental, rational, aggressive, competitive, tough, active, and sexually conquering.

The solar side needs to express itself through its career and achievement. The lunar side needs to express itself through mothering. But today it is not enough just to be a mother. A woman needs to have a career if she is to feel a valued and worthwhile member of the society in which she lives. However, society's present evolution is at the stage where the woman is expected to be both a careerist and a mother. Should she confine herself only to a career, she is regarded as a failure, for society considers that she should have both a husband *and* children.

If she is only a careerist, she is regarded as some sort of hardened freak who has become too much like a man. If instead she decides to confine herself exclusively to the mothering role, she is still regarded as a failure because today's society places such a low value on feminine qualities to the extent that she will be regarded as someone who is 'just a mother' or 'just a housewife'. Whichever role the woman plays today, she cannot win. If she chooses to combine both the mother and career roles, which more and more women are choosing to do, then she is regarded as mediocre at both—not a very good mother and not a very good career woman.

There is a price to be paid for choosing to be born into today's solar society. That price is a dampening down, a suppression, sometimes even a repression, of the lunar hemisphere. And as it is such a huge part of a woman's psychological make-up, it is she who is more seriously affected and grows more neurotic by the repression.

In order to function successfully in a solar, masculine world, both he and she must dampen down the lunar part of the personality, and to assist this suppression of the feminine side, the woman starts to regard herself as the same as a man. She considers that if she is the same then she must be as good as him. She is conscious that she is different physically—she can hardly miss that—but she tends to brush this aside as being a superficial difference and not worth taking into account. The other thing she can hardly miss noticing, which is directly related to this physical difference, is that she gets periods. These she comes to regard as a nuisance, as getting in the way of her efficient functioning. So she pretends that she is not affected by them and ignores the physical and mental changes that take place at this time and tells herself that she is as good as a man any day.

Also, to function in the man's world, she knows that it is regarded as a weakness to be emotional and cry. She must be rational and logical, so she will further cut off from her lunar side. She will pretend it is not there, she will squash it down, and she will steadfastly refuse to look at what is actually there. And what is actually there is emotionality, all sorts of feelings, irrationality, and tears, and these are unacceptable in today's world if she is going to pull it together as a career woman and as a mother.

Many of the things that were intimately connected with the agri-cultural society, such as being surrounded by the family, growing and preparing food, just do not exist for modern woman. A family is not an extended one anymore, living in close contact all the time with members giving constant support to one another. Today's family is a nuclear one with mother, father, and 2.4 children, which splits apart when the children are in their twenties. More and more, there are thousands of miles separating children from parents. Divorce is on the increase, splitting the family up even further. So the lunar need to be centred in a home, surrounded by an extended family, and mothering everything in sight, is gradually being eroded.

The need to become a career woman, in order to be accepted by today's society or for financial reasons or both, means that she further denies her lunar side, for the solar, not the lunar side, must be allowed prominence if she is to survive in the technological business world.

No longer does she nurture and grow her own food—she buys it off a shelf in the supermarket. She does not spend time bottling fruit, making bread, or preparing lengthy dinners. She buys convenience, quickie foods from the local store and dishes those up instead. She has not got time to spend hours sweating over a hot stove, and thus the satisfaction the lunar side gets from being involved with food from the field to the table has been lost to most modern women.

* * *

If you think I am about to suggest that you go back to the land, get into self-sufficiency in a big way, and have lots of kids, you are mistaken, for I am not. This is the society that we have chosen to be born into, this modern, technological, Western society, and therefore not only is it exactly right for us but also we have the qualities of character to cope with it and to get the best out of whatever it has to offer. What we need to do is retrain in other ways of releasing our lunar side. We need to choose methods acceptable and available to our present lifestyle which allow the lunar hemisphere full expression without damaging our solar side.

Men today, just as much as women, need to allow their lunar half to surface and be incorporated into their whole personality if they are not to suffer psychological problems.

One of the most readily accessible ways to allow the lunar side expression is awareness meditation, because meditation is a lunar activity.

You are training yourself to be quiet, receptive, just watching, patient, surrendering to the objects viewed. What are these, other than lunar qualities? Feelings are also a part of the feminine side, and with the meditation, instead of denying feelings, you are turning right around, looking at feelings head on, and experiencing them fully. With meditation we learn to let these feelings exist. We learn to allow them their own space. We passively watch feelings rise and cease. We learn to refrain from controlling them. Controlling is masculine. When we repress our feelings, we are attempting to control them. It is a futile control, because not only does it not work, but it is self-damaging as well. All of this we learn from the meditation.

A meditative way will also encourage the development of giving, service, devotion—all of which are lunar qualities.

* * *

When I came to meditation I knew nothing about hormonal shifts in the body, let alone mental changes arising due to these shifts. It was my meditation teacher who introduced me to this aspect of womanhood. And I was not at all charmed when I heard about it, even less so when I began to observe the changes in myself.

I have since found that very few women are aware of what happens to them on a mental level during those five days before their period starts. So it is little wonder that men too are oblivious of this area. Given what has been said so far about the modern tendency to cut off from the lunar side, this chosen blindness is then not at all surprising.

Some women, those who keep up with the latest books on feminist issues, are more knowledgeable about the premenstrual syndrome, but it is on a very intellectual level—they have rarely observed the process to any great depths within themselves. They usually are the worst offenders at being blind to their lunar side because they deny their femininity, viewing it as something which somehow relegates them to second-class citizens.

An observation that has surprised me most since starting to teach meditation is noticing how strongly certain men are affected by the approach of the full moon. I mention it because a man who is affected shows identical mental changes around the full moon to those of the premenstrual woman. If you want to know whether you are affected by the moon, then you need to keep an eye on the calendar, noting when the full moon is due to occur and looking out for any significant shifts of mental states before and during the full moon. If you are affected, then everything that I am about to say on the woman's mental states just prior to her period is relevant to you too.

About five days before a woman's period starts, there is a rapid drop in the level of the hormone oestrogen in her system. This heralds certain mental changes. Body and mind are closely linked. When there is a change in one, there is a change in the other. So, dependent upon a hormonal change in a woman's body, there come about certain mental changes.

Typical states that arise at this time are anger, irritability, and confusion. A woman is more accident-prone before her period. She is more likely to be untidy in the home—finding it too much trouble to wash the dishes, make the bed, tidy up the rooms—yet at the same time, she gets irritable if the house is untidy. An understanding partner will assist in tidying the home at this time of the month because he will realise that, just before her period, life is something of an uphill struggle for the woman, and tidying up can be viewed by her as an insurmountable problem. As confusion is one of the mental states rampant during the few days before a period, and untidiness is a sign of confusion, then being untidy at this time comes somewhat naturally.

Because the place is disorderly, she will then get irritated and bad tempered but will seem powerless to do much about it. She is powerless because there is so much hatred around, and hatred saps the energy. The powerlessness is actually a lack of energy. So the understanding partner who helps her tidy up is taking away those tell-tale signs of confusion. As her environment becomes more orderly, this has the effect of calming her down. As she calms down, her hatred lessens.

Some women respond quite differently when premenstrual and become overcharged with energy, rushing around the house cleaning everything in sight and woe betide the person who gets in her way when she is in this type of mood.

In the few days before her period, a woman has awful trouble making sense of heavy intellectual books. If she tries to study the Pali Canon at such a time, she will find she understands very little of it. If she looks again at those selfsame passages after the period has begun, she will discover that she can comprehend them easily. Before her period she really should not be reading anything heavier than a typical, chatty women's magazine. If she does wish to pursue her reading along spiritual lines, then she should confine herself to the lighter, non-study books.

The trouble is that during this brief phase before the period starts there is so much self-hatred running around that the woman drives and drives herself at the difficult books even though she cannot understand them. She gets more and more irritable because she cannot understand, thereby adding further hatred to the pile of self-hatred that is already around.

The sensible approach would be to lay off the book until the period has come and gone. But being sensible is at a very low ebb at this time. One of the reasons the mind cannot understand what it is reading is that it has a tendency to distort the words. It either misses out words here and there as it is reading or it adds words, thus giving a completely different meaning to the sentence than the one the author had intended. Moreover, the mind is unaware that it is doing it.

The other ways self-hatred manifests is in clothes and food. She nearly always wears her most ugly clothes at this time. She justifies her actions by saying that the old clothes are her most comfortable as they are looser and baggier than anything else in her wardrobe. She adds that as the body has put on weight due to water retention, which is normal just before her period, most of her outfits are too tight, her old clothes being the only ones she can comfortably fit into. She already feels ugly because of the body suddenly growing larger due to water retention, and the old clothes add to her feelings of a lack of attractiveness and femininity. Feeling less attractive, she hates herself more, thus adding once again to the hatred that is already running.

With food, she lacks sense. She will eat all the wrong foods. She will eat lots of fatty food, chips, fried bread, and the like. She will eat rich foods, fattening foods like cream buns. These are all comfort foods. She feels like an unlovable creature at this time—a monster, with lots of violent and angry thoughts flying around. To placate these, she stuffs herself in a desperate attempt to keep at bay all those unpleasant feelings. Unfortunately, her body cannot cope so well with fatty, rich foods when premenstrual, and so she very often ends up feeling sick. Then she is disgusted with herself and so adds yet more self-hatred.

I knew a woman who used to make a very rich meat dish which

contained pork, sour cream, wine, and lots of butter. She made it only once every twenty-eight days, and every time after eating that dish she was sick. She grew to loathe it but felt driven to make it. Four months passed before she realised what was going on, which was that she only made that particular recipe during the five days before her periods, when her system could not possibly cope with the rich ingredients. She then realised that she had been making that dish as a gesture of hate towards herself. If she made it at a time when her system could not cope, she was bound to get sick and end up hating the dish and herself. So as soon as she realised all of this, she stopped making that recipe in the days immediately before her period started.

Another aspect that runs at this time is argumentativeness, which is just another facet of hatred. The way it manifests, though, is that everyone is wrong, especially the man in the woman's life. Anything the boyfriend or husband has to say is wrong. If he says it is a fine day, she will say that it is not. If he says the sky is blue, she will say it is not—that it is turquoise. If he says things change, she will say they do not. Anything that he says is wrong.

This is one area in which the male can really help to keep things cooled down. If he knows nothing about the premenstrual syndrome, his anger will rise at this point and he will retort with a snap, saying something along the lines of, 'You're wrong.' Before long there will be a rip-roaring argument underway.

Apart from the argumentativeness, the woman is also supersensitive. She imagines that she has been slighted by the most innocent and casual of remarks. This brings on either a flood of tears or a flood of anger.

The mindful male who has come to recognise all the signs of the premenstrual phase does not fall into hatred himself when he notices his female companion getting argumentative. He keeps very mindful of the unpleasant feelings rising up in him. He does not respond with anger towards them, and he *does not* answer her back. He is much more likely to agree with what she is saying, recognising that she is only expressing an opinion, and all opinions, after all, are only 50 per cent right, so she is entitled to her 50 per cent. Even if he secretly thinks that she is wrong on this occasion, he would not be foolish enough to say so, not if he wants to assist in keeping things as smooth and as harmonious as is possible during this difficult time.

So the two states that flare up frequently during this premenstrual phase are hatred and confusion. Where the problem actually lies is not in the hormonal change, nor in the mental changes, but in the *resistance* to these changes. And because she resists, she hates. Because she hates, she is confused.

★ ★ ★

For the female who is the perfect meditator there is no resistance to the rapid changes that take place mentally and physically before her period. She does not resist the lunar side. She accepts it. There is no resentment of changes in weight, size, or health of the body. She does not wish them to be other than they are. She accepts them.

She does not fight the change in the tone of the mind either. She is not disturbed in the least by being supersensitive. She does not resist the dulling of the mental faculties. She just watches. When there is no resistance, there is no anger or confusion, and so there is no premenstrual syndrome. Those around her are unaware of the period coming and going, so peaceful is the atmosphere compared to the old days when those five days before the period were marked by tears and tantrums. Even she only knows of the approaching period by checking her period calendar and by the occasional dulling of faculties, the proneness to tiredness, and the slight change in mental tone.

It is the anger, the self-hatred, and the confusion that make those five days in a woman's twenty-eight day cycle so stressful for herself and those around her. Banish confusion and hatred, and there is no longer a vast noticeable difference between the time around periods and the rest of the month. The character becomes more stable, no longer experiencing violent emotional swings.

Until the female meditator has fully trained herself in awareness of the moment, there are certain practical things she can do to lessen the stress of the premenstrual syndrome.

First, eat sensibly. Stay away, as much as possible, from oil, butter, cream, rich foods, and excessive amounts of sugar. Eat plain, simple food, grilled or boiled, with plenty of fresh fruit and vegetables.

Do not read study books. Read light books, preferably with a spiritual or meditative theme.

The five days before the start of the period is a time to withdraw from society, not a time to get more involved with it. This is because the mind is naturally going inwards to focus on internal changes. It is a struggle to keep the mind pinned on externals, and socialising requires the mind to be focused on externals. The mind's natural flow is to go inwards, and hence concentration comes more easily at this time, and the spin-offs from balanced concentration, such as intuition, arise more readily.

It is best not to have dinner parties every night during those five days leading up to periods, nor is it wise to dash around during the day visiting friends. That would only increase your tension level.

Keep chores to a minimum. Allowing more time to yourself also helps at this time. If you drive yourself to keep you and your home tidy, even though these are the last things in the world which you wish to do, this will lessen the confusion. After you have fulfilled whatever tasks you have to perform, if you are able, give the rest of the day over to yourself to be quiet and withdrawn from society. Give it over to knitting, sewing, or meditating—generally potter around—all of which is very healing. If you have children, see if you can find someone to look after them for an afternoon, so that you can have some quiet time alone. Quietness, solitude, meditation, all soothe the turmoil. Your children are likely to reap the benefits of a more mentally balanced mother, and so there is no need to feel guilty for having abandoned them for a few hours.

★ ★ ★

How do ovulation, her period, and particularly the time before the period affect a woman's meditation? Drastically and badly is the short answer. In the early days of her meditative training, she is pretty useless during these times. She is useless only because there is so much hatred and confusion around. Because there is hatred, this knocks out her drive, energy, and self-discipline. So the first thing she does is miss several days meditation, mainly during those five days leading up to her period. If the meditation routine is broken, it is extremely difficult to get it going again. And if she does not actually *do* the meditation, she cannot get any benefits from it.

After she has overcome this hurdle and is managing to do the practice regularly, the next problem that she faces, which renders the meditations unproductive, is the vast quantities of hatred and confusion that overwhelm the mind when she is premenstrual.

Well, if there is one benefit from living in a society that values solar rather than lunar qualities, it is that it admires perseverance, drive, courage in the face of adversity—all of which are masculine qualities. Because these traits of character are admired and a woman does not want to be left out, she wishes to display these traits with the same ease as most men, so she draws heavily on her solar side to overcome the problems of the lunar half of herself. By courageously keeping going with the meditation during the 'stormy' times and applying perseverance and drive during her 'sane' times, she gradually begins to develop the capacity to see and to watch objects, no matter whether they are pleasant or painful.

She then applies this capacity to be mindful to the premenstrual time, and by now she does not get so caught up in hatred. From time to time, she can actually notice what is going on without wanting it to be other than it is. *Now* she has the perfect opportunity to turn her premenstrual syndrome into something very valuable from a meditative point of view. She can turn what was a useless time into a very fertile time, a time when she can learn much about one of the most important aspects of Buddhism, and that is *anattā* or non-self.

She comes to be aware that no matter what she wants, no matter how much she would rather not have impaired judgement, irritability, confusion, tears, or anger around in the five days before her period starts, they are there every month. Regularly as clockwork, the mental states turn up on her mental doorstep every twenty-third day of the twenty-eight day cycle. No matter what she does, they are there, as large as life and twice as ugly. So she learns from careful and systematic watching that it is pointless fighting them—they are there to stay for a certain length of time, and as long as she has a female body and has not reached menopause, she is going to experience those strange feelings and emotional swings in a regular cycle.

The moment she comes to that realisation, the hatred and confusion lessen, and her clarity of mind increases in leaps and bounds. The next thing she notices is that, although she gets more or less the same mental states every month, they differ in intensity each month. Sometimes they are very bad, other times, not so bad. She notices that dependent upon the supporting conditions, these mental states last for a long time or a very short time, and that the supporting conditions also affect the intensity of the irritability, the anger, the impaired judgement, and so on.

Next she notices how rapidly they come and go. And by this time she is beginning to view these mental states not as 'my anger', 'my confusion', 'my dullness' but simply as 'anger' or 'confusion' or 'dullness', and she notes that these states arise dependent upon conditions and cease when those conditions cease. Now she is really beginning to experience *anattā*.

The woman, therefore, if she trains herself in the right way, has the rare privilege of being presented every lunar month (and that comes round ever so quickly) with fuel in the way of her premenstrual syndrome, upon which the fire of wisdom can blaze up and take her far along that path leading towards *nibbāna*.

Thinking

Most meditators regard thinking as one of the greatest obstacles to successful practice. If they spend the major portion of an hour's seated meditation going over and over different thoughts, then, when the hour is finished, they usually feel somewhat depressed and regard that day's meditation as having been a complete waste of time. As most people hate to spend a whole hour not accomplishing what they set out to do, there is the tendency for the meditator, next time he or she sits down to meditate, to put massive amounts of energy into keeping thinking under control so that it does not occupy so much of the hour.

Certainly the meditator's heart is in the right place. He does need to do something constructive if attachment to thinking is a problem for him. However, although his assessment of the situation is accurate, that is, the meditation is getting corrupted by too much thinking and he must do something about it, the way he goes about solving that problem is not always in his best interests. He usually resorts to the way of effort, trying to squash out thinking by force of will. Although this is one of the recommended methods of controlling thinking, it is rather a crude option and one which should only be used when all else has failed.

When he tries to hold thinking at bay by force, what the meditator discovers is that one of three things happens. Thinking may increase— it just seems to be everywhere, shooting off at all angles, getting speedier and speedier, and accompanied by a sense of excitement and tension. Or his mind goes dull and certain pains occur either in his body or head—and when the meditator gets up from his chair, after the hour's meditation is over, he is quite likely to find that his eyes are out of focus, his vision distorted, and he feels sick in the stomach. Or he will find that his attempts at controlling thinking have certainly brought about the desired results—he no longer thinks, but neither is he conscious of anything else! Most of the hour is now spent in sleep rather than in thinking.

What I want to do is introduce you to some other ways of handling thinking rather than always resorting to effort to cope with the problem. The use of effort as a way of controlling thinking is described in the Pali Canon in a very colourful way. It says that the meditator 'with teeth clenched, tongue pressed up against his palate, subdues, restrains and dominates his mind with his mind.'[1] It is a crude method, a last resort method, to be used when all else has failed.

There are four other ways of quietening thinking so that you can get the mind into a calm and concentrated state and hold it there.

★ ★ ★

Before I go any further, I want to make quite sure you understand what is meant by 'thinking'. Thinking is a set of words that pop into mind and which link together to form a concept which makes sense to you, a concept like 'My sister and I get on very well together,' or 'My brother and I fight a great deal.' Each concept is accompanied by a feeling. The first thought, 'My sister and I get on very well together,' will be accompanied by a pleasant feeling. Whereas the second thought, 'My brother and I fight a great deal,' is likely to be accompanied by an unpleasant feeling. The thought is not the feeling. They are two separate things. But the thought and the feeling rise up so close together that it is hard to separate the one from the other.

Some thoughts appear not to be accompanied by any feelings at all, like the thought, 'I must switch off the light.' Such a thought does not give us a pleasant feeling but neither does it pain us. Thoughts about switching lights on or off are actually accompanied by a feeling

---

1. Technical language that appears in quotes throughout this chapter is drawn and adapted from the 'Discourse on the Forms of Thought', Horner, I.B. (1976), *The Middle Length Sayings, Vol.I*, pp.152–156, London: Pali Text Society.

but it is a neutral feeling. Hence we tend to regard such thoughts as being without feelings, which strictly speaking is not totally accurate. All thoughts are accompanied by a feeling which is pleasant, painful, or neutral. We might decide that a particular thought has no feeling, but it is actually accompanied by a neutral feeling. And thoughts accompanied by neutral feelings do not usually trouble us. It is the thoughts that are accompanied by a pleasant or a painful feeling that cause us a problem.

When you look closely at the whole process of thinking, you will see that it is not the thought which is the problem, nor is it the feeling accompanying that thought which is the problem—it is the getting *attached* to the thinking which is the problem.

A jealous thought, for example, produces a very intense and unpleasant feeling, but if you can just watch the thought and the feeling and in no way grab hold of either of them, then there is no problem. It is when the jealous thought is quickly followed by another jealous thought and another and another that you have a problem. At this point life becomes closed in, grey, and miserable. You have become attached to thinking. When this state of affairs occurs, the meditator definitely has a problem with thinking which needs solving.

Note that I am only regarding thinking as an obstacle to the meditation practice if you get attached to it. A thought which comes up and then fades off is no problem. No matter how intense the feeling is that accompanies it, the thought still fades off. It is only when you reach out and grab hold of that thought and go over and over it that the mind becomes polluted and a state of suffering arises.

If a meditator wishes to develop intuitive seeing, he or she must keep the mind steady, calm, and concentrated for much of the day, and in order to do this you need to get rid of those inefficient thoughts which threaten to destroy the calm.

Words are such dangerous things because I am sure that when I used the word 'calm' you instantly built a mental picture of those times when there have been very few thoughts in your mind and 'no feelings' accompanying those thoughts. And you have decided that that is what is meant by 'calm' and is what you are supposed to be aiming at. You are going to be very disappointed because that state is very rarely achieved. The state of calm is a much more dynamic state than that. It is possible to have many thoughts coming and going and yet be very calm. Calm is what comes about when you do not get *attached* to thinking.

There are such things as efficient thoughts and inefficient thoughts. 'Efficient thinking' does not refer to the content of your thoughts. Whether you are thinking about painting the ceiling, financial difficulties, or a point of *Dhamma*, all are equal. The content of your thinking can be about something very ordinary and mundane, like painting the ceiling, or something lofty and uplifting, like the wonderful qualities of the Buddha. It matters little whether you are thinking about the ceiling or the Buddha—what matters is whether you become attached to those thoughts.

It is the attachment, or lack of it, which determines whether the thought is efficient or inefficient. 'Efficient' means thinking which you are not attached to. You neither want it to be there nor do you want it to disappear. You are quite at ease with the thoughts. You are not trying to hold on to them nor get rid of them. This means you have not taken the content of your thinking seriously. You do not believe in it and view it as a real entity that you must manipulate.

Efficient thinking is thinking where there is no reaction of either a craving or a hating nature towards the content of your thoughts. Because your reaction is pure, no suffering follows.

Your thinking may produce plenty of unpleasant feelings, but unpleasant feelings and suffering are two different things. Successfully following the noble eightfold path, the Buddha's way to enlightenment, eliminates suffering, but it *does not* eliminate unpleasant feelings. No spiritual way does that. Unpleasant feelings are part and parcel of the human condition. Suffering, on the other hand, is something *we* create. Therefore we have control over whether we do or do not suffer. If we do not want to suffer, we do not have to. But it does take a certain amount of intuitive seeing to discover why we so often choose to suffer. And the possibility of intuitive seeing flashing forth is definitely blocked when we get attached to thinking.

'Inefficient thinking' is thinking which produces suffering. And it only ends up in suffering because we become attached to the content and either hate the content or are entranced by it, wanting more and more of the pleasurable feelings the thinking is bringing up. For example, we can experience a sexual feeling at the thought of someone. We just keep on thinking about that person in order to continually reproduce those feelings which we find so thrilling.

* * *

A person gets attached to thinking from time to time during the day and from time to time during an hour's seated meditation. Sometimes a day or two will go by with no attachment at all. One is not constantly attached to thinking, but counteracting remedies, such as those I am about to suggest, should be used when you get attached. For the rest of the time leave thinking alone and just observe it.

One way of getting rid of inefficient thoughts is to 'attend to a characteristic which is associated with skilled states of mind'. For example, a person may pay attention to the faults in his or her job and marriage. If a person is turning his thoughts over and over on how much he hates his job and hates his marriage and hates life generally, he is attending to how awful things are. He is 'attending to an unskilled, inefficient characteristic'.

If one constantly thinks about the faults in a situation or in a person, then very quickly hatred rises up. And once hateful thinking has been created, it is very easy to get trapped in it. Thoughts then just go round and round, finding fault first with this thing, then that thing, then the next thing. Once hateful thinking gets a grip, it is pointless trying to mindfully watch the hatred you have stirred up. All that happens then is that you get even more caught up in the hatred.

It is at this point that one has to bring in the solution of 'attending to another characteristic, one which is associated with what is skilled', in order to put a stop to the attachment to hateful thinking. So the person who hates his job and his marriage and is fed up with life generally— rather than paying attention to the faults in his life, he should pay attention to the good points in his life. He should turn over in mind his blessings—how he is alive and healthy, is well fed, and has a roof over his head when thousands of the world's population are homeless, starving, and sick. Such a person should turn over in mind how he has all of these benefits of health, food, and home because of having acted efficiently in the past. Whatever present benefits you have in the way of home, food, education, money, or coming across an effective spiritual way, you deserve. These blessings are the results of your wise and efficient thinking and physical behaviour towards these things in the past. Spending time dwelling on the good in your life is one way of getting rid of attachment to fault finding. When criticising arises, attention to the opposite 'characteristic' of noticing the good points in a situation or a person balances the mind off, and the inefficient thinking that has arisen falls away.

If you do the same when craving thoughts arise, that is, pay attention to the opposite 'characteristic', craving thoughts will disappear. Hatred sees only the faults in things but craving is just the opposite. When craving is present, you see only the good points and the benefits to you personally if you can obtain that item or that person. To bring the mind back to balance, you have to focus in on the faults. For example, say you want a new car desperately, and you are getting obsessed with thoughts of possessing a particular make of car that you saw recently as you walked past your local car show room. You have gone into quite a few fantasies: visualising yourself driving around in this car, showing it to your neighbours, picturing your work colleagues going green with envy when they see the car in the firm's car park.

To counteract the craving fantasies, reflect on what a nuisance it is to own a car, especially a new one. You have to clean it more frequently than an old car, otherwise it very quickly does not look new anymore. Reflect on how you will get very upset if somebody bumps it or scratches it. And, if you happen to give a lift to a friend in this brand new car of yours which you are so very proud of, and the studs in his jeans happen to rip the upholstery, you will be mightily upset. Whereas with your old battered car, what is another rip? It has so many anyway. In other words, paying attention to the *faults* of owning a new car sobers the mind, and so you are far more willing to give up the attachment to those thoughts about a new car.

When you use this technique of paying attention to a 'characteristic which is associated with what is skilled', either concentrate on the opposites of hatred and craving, which I have just explained, or attend to the mark of change or body mindfulness.

An example of attending to the mark of change would be, instead of focusing on 'What an awful world we live in—it is full of violence and corruption,' which will quickly bring on hatred, focusing rather on how that thought popped into mind and now it is gone. Two seconds ago you were listening to the news on the radio, and now you are planning the evening meal. And the thought of 'what an awful world we live in' was sandwiched in between listening to the radio and planning the evening meal. Isn't it amazing how quickly thoughts come and go?

If you focus on thoughts arising and passing, it takes the attention right off the content of the thought. As soon as you pay attention to the content, there is a great likelihood of arousing a passion. But if you pay attention to how thinking comes and goes, rather than the content of that thinking, then you are paying attention to *anicca*, a 'characteristic which is skilful', and which will arouse a mental state free of passion, and which is calm and steady.

Another 'skilful characteristic', which I mentioned you could pay attention to, is body mindfulness. Say you are out in the open air, in the garden, doing a spot of weeding, and into mind comes the memory of a telephone conversation you had earlier in the day with your mother. Yet again she was telling you how to organise your life. At the very memory of her interference, up wells annoyance. You grab hold of the memory and start chatting to your mother in your mind, telling her where to get off. Your thoughts go over and over the subject. There is much hatred and therefore much suffering.

Try pulling the attention away from the thinking and placing it on your body. Attend to your arm stretching out to pull out a weed. Be inside the body and feel it stretching upwards as you stand up. Pay attention to the body as it walks, and again pay attention as it bends over another section of the flower bed to start weeding there. Take the attention away from thinking, and place it on attending to the movement of the body and its postures of bending, stretching, walking, standing. Note these different postures. This is paying attention to the 'skilful characteristic' of mindfulness of body, instead of paying attention to the 'unskilful characteristic' of finding fault with something someone has said.

I have mentioned four different 'characteristics' which are likely to arouse a skilled state of mind if you pay attention to them—counting your blessings, noting the faults in the object craved for, attending to the mark of change, and mindfulness of body. The idea is not to use all four techniques one after the other, but rather to use the one that is relevant to the type of thinking you are currently obsessed with, or to use the one that appeals to you most and which works for you. This applies not only to the technique of 'attending to a characteristic which is associated with what is skilled' but also to the next three techniques, which I am about to elaborate on.

In short, use the first technique you can remember when you find yourself trapped in thinking. If it does not work, try another one then another one, until you find the technique which works for you. And remember that it might work for you today, but tomorrow it may not work, and so tomorrow you will have to try one of the other ways of getting rid of troublesome thoughts.

So far I have explained that 'attention to unskilful characteristics' found in the content of your thinking is likely to end up in hatred or craving, and that the way to extricate yourself from that painful position is to focus on the 'characteristics within thinking which are associated with what is skilled'. This is technique number one for putting a stop to attachment to thinking.

Technique number two is to 'scrutinise the peril' in your thinking. Take a look and note what the outcome is of a bout of hateful thinking. Once the thoughts have died down, what do you observe about yourself and the other person? The first thing you will notice is that you feel worn out. You want to go and hide in the cupboard or go to bed to get away from the world. You feel mentally bruised.

And what has telling the other person off in your mind done to them? Does it change them? No—they are just the same as they have always been. Your bout of fighting with them in your thoughts has not changed their personality one little bit, and furthermore, it puts a strain on the relationship between the two of you, because next time you meet there will be a barrier, a sort of remoteness between the two of you. This tension will have to be broken down very quickly, or you will find yourself easily catapulting into another argument which will further damage your relationship.

To 'scrutinise the peril' in your thinking means to reflect on the fact that what you have observed are the results of hateful or craving thinking. The results are always detrimental to you personally. Hatred leaves you feeling worn out, exhausted, lonely, your enthusiasm for life temporarily sapped. Craving leaves you feeling thwarted, frustrated, restless. It saps your energy but not as badly as does hatred. Furthermore, if you indulge in such thoughts, they produce painful feelings in the moment and painful feelings in the future. Don't you always feel awful when you first set eyes on someone you have been having a go at in your mind? Also, you have created a groove in mind, so it will be much easier for you to go down that hate groove in the future. When you go over and over hateful thoughts, you find that it is much easier to do the same again the next time someone upsets you or when life does not go the way you think it ought to. Such hateful thinking guarantees further unpleasant feelings and more suffering.

Reflecting on the painful results of hating or craving thoughts helps you to let go of your attachment to these thoughts.

Method number three is 'forgetting unskilled thoughts'. Have you ever had the experience of a very small pain appearing in your shoulders whilst you are sitting meditating? I don't think there is a meditator who has not had this experience! And have you noticed that if you pay attention to it, in no time at all it has magnified a hundredfold. Suddenly the whole of your upper back is throbbing with tension and pain, and you do not know how long you are going to be able to bear it.

What did you do wrong? Why did that pin prick of a pain suddenly grow into a giant monster? It is because you paid attention to it. As soon as your attention was caught by the pain, quick as a flash, you thought, 'I hope this pain isn't going to increase.' With that thought you visualised the pain growing, and what you visualise *happens*. Mind works very, very fast. Do not think you have to be going over and over something before it becomes a reality in the world. One moment you fantasise about a pain which you hope you will not have to experience, and in the very next moment there it is, as large as life, for you to experience! Very obliging is mind—it frequently delivers the goods before your thoughts have even had time to finish drying off!

What can you do about this situation? What you do, as soon as you notice the pin prick of pain in the shoulders, is to bring about 'forgetfulness and lack of attention' to that pain. Just forget about the pain. The same goes for all sorts of troublesome thoughts. Perhaps you are concerned about a particular relationship. As soon as you notice that you are thinking about that relationship—drop it. Forget about it. Do not pay any attention to thinking about the relationship. This is method number three—cultivating 'forgetfulness of, and a lack of attention to, unskilful thoughts'.

If none of the suggestions mentioned so far for tackling troublesome thoughts works for you, then perhaps the final method, method number four, will.

The final method is to analyse the 'function and form' of your thinking and to find out why you do it. For example, why does a person worry? Why do you worry about an exam or a social engagement or a plane trip? You go over and over the forthcoming event in your thoughts because you believe that by doing so it will make that particular event turn out successfully. You also constantly think about the event to calm yourself down. There are lots of agitating and unpleasant feelings running around at the prospect of sitting an exam or entertaining the boss or getting into an aircraft. And you believe that if you think about the event often enough, it will quieten the agitation and get rid of all of those unpleasant feelings. You think about the forthcoming event because you truly believe it is to your profit to do so. As far as you are concerned, it is going to calm you down, get rid of the unpleasant feelings, and ensure that the event goes smoothly.

If you invest much time thinking about the forthcoming event but still you do not feel settled, you come to the conclusion that you have not thought about it enough yet. You decide you could not possibly have covered all the angles properly, and that is why you still feel so disturbed. So you continue to think about the forthcoming event.

How mistaken you are. You have come to the wrong conclusion because you have not looked closely enough at what actually happens to you and to that event when you eventually get to it.

What happens when you constantly worry about something is that whilst you are thinking about it, you feel agitated, uncertain of your own judgements, and you experience much suffering. When you eventually get to the event you have been worrying about—let us say it is a social engagement—what you will discover is that because you have been spending so much time thinking about it, you are crippled with self-consciousness, and your conversation and responses are very stilted and sometimes inappropriate as well. So, horror of horrors, the social engagement is a nightmare and does not turn out as successfully as you had hoped it would.

When you look at the reasons why you indulge in worry or hatred or craving, you will note that you do so because you assume that it is profitable to you to think in this way. If you then take a look at the 'form' those thoughts do take—that is, they produce agitation, self-consciousness, and suffering, rather than the calmness and successful outcome that you had hoped for—then it is easy to abandon attachment to worrisome thinking.

I have covered four ways of overcoming inefficient thinking: 'attending to a characteristic associated with a skilled state of mind', 'scrutinising the peril' in inefficient thinking, 'bringing about forgetfulness of unskilled thoughts', and analysing the 'form and function' of your thinking to find out why you do it. If you can implement these four ways of handling thoughts when you get attached to them, then you will find that inefficient thinking will die right down, and that you are much calmer and concentrated for longer periods each day. Once this happens, the right conditions have been brought about for intuitive seeing to readily arise.

The Power of Patience

All people know that patience is a good quality, and that if you have a great deal of it as part of your character, you are most fortunate. From a very early age we are told about patience. If a child is whiny and irritable because he cannot understand how his new toy works, a parent will come along and say, 'Be patient.' If a student gets close to tears because she cannot master a new maths problem, the teacher will say, 'Be patient.' We do not advance very far in life before someone says to us, 'Be patient,' so we get the message very early on that patience is a good quality to have, and that if we do not have it, we would be wise to develop it, the implication being that patience will help us enormously to get on in life.

And that is very true. Patience is not only helpful in day-to-day living, but it is also very helpful to the spiritual endeavour.

I read recently that there were certain qualities of mind that a spiritual devotee had to develop in order to get their meditative life off the ground, one of which was patience. But the author felt that a meditator did not really get impatient until he or she had been meditating for some little while and had begun to realise the enormity of the task they had undertaken—only then did the meditator get impatient.

I am not so sure about that. I have known several people who have started meditating and, when they hear that the goal of the meditative life is enlightenment, they think, 'Right, I'll allow two months for this task. If it proves to be a bit more complex than it appears on the surface, I'll give it two years—maybe. Once I've got that out of the

way, then I can really get down to living life.' Such thinking is a sign
of impatience.

Others do not think along those lines, but within the very first week
of meditating on their own at home, what happens? They open their
eyes and take a peek at the clock, convinced that the alarm mechanism
has malfunctioned, only to discover that a mere ten minutes has gone
by since they sat down. Such action on the part of the new meditator
is a sign of impatience.

Others sit down, close their eyes, and it is not long before they feel a
heaviness in the head. There is a sense of pressure above the eyebrows
and the body feels tense and uncomfortable. These meditators are concentrating wrongly due to impatience.

There are many other signs of impatience—one is bursting out of
the meditation, eyes open and staring, long before the half-hour has
ended. When this happens, the meditator usually decides to abandon
the seated practice, reasoning that it all seems such a waste of time just
to sit there doing nothing but thinking. 'I might just as well go and do
something useful, like have breakfast,' grumbles the meditator.

Sometimes falling asleep is a sign of impatience. Another sign is
when a meditator is constantly plagued with thoughts of wishing that
the seated practice was over, whilst others show their impatience by
frequently asking their meditation teacher where they have got to on
the meditative path. Some will frequently moan about the fact that
they have been meditating for a long time and they do not seem to be
getting anywhere. They are also displaying impatience.

The only reason why anyone would wish to get rid of impatience
when meditating is that the meditation gets so very uncomfortable
every time impatience rises up in the mind.

Impatience is present when the meditation is physically painful,
when you are bored, and when progress is too slow for your liking. And
what is the most prominent mental state present at such times? Is it not
despondency? Aren't you somewhat depressed with your meditative
endeavours? Aren't there thoughts running through the mind like,
'What is the point of this? It all seems a lot of effort for nothing?'

At such times you think of abandoning the practice—and many do.
You may not abandon it forever. The next day will find you back on
your chair having another crack at meditating. But if you allow such
thoughts to run frequently and you do not do anything to check them,

then it will not be long before you will not be coming on as many residential courses as you used to, and then one day you will wake up to the fact that you have not sat down to meditate for a whole week. Giving up the spiritual endeavour is the end result of impatience. A meditator needs to recognise impatience when it is present and do something active to put a stop to it.

★ ★ ★

From the list I have just given of the signs which indicate when impatience is present, you have probably decided that you do have a fair amount of impatience in your temperament after all. You would be most unusual if you did not. However, I have yet to meet someone whose impatience comes out in quite such a dramatic manner as did Swami Rama's.

Swami Rama is a Hindu monk and spiritual teacher who tells many a fascinating tale about his training in a book called *Living with the Himalayan Masters.*[1]

When he was a young man and under training, he wanted desperately to experience *samādhi. Samādhi* is a very deep, concentrated meditative state. His teacher had told him that unless he sat completely still for four hours, he would never attain *samādhi.* So he practised sitting from childhood onwards, but he failed to attain this concentrated state.

After much study he became a teacher, but he was dissatisfied with his role. He felt it was dishonest to teach meditation when he had not reached the required levels himself and was not enlightened. He felt that it would have been more appropriate if he had taught philosophy in some university or other, rather than instructing monks in a monastery as he was doing.

So one day he went to his teacher and said, 'Master, today I am going to give you an ultimatum. Either you give me *samādhi* or I will commit suicide.'

'Are you sure?' asked his teacher.

'Yes,' he said emphatically.

'Go right ahead, my dear boy,' was the calm reply.

---

1. This story has been adapted from Rama, Swami (1986), *Living with the Himalayan Masters,* pp.411–14, Honesdale, Pennsylvania: Himalayan International Institute of Yoga Science & Philosophy of the U.S.A.

Swami Rama was a bit taken aback. He did not expect his teacher to reply in such a fashion. He had expected him to tell him to wait for ten or fifteen days. His teacher had never been rude to him before, but on that day he was exceedingly rude. He told Rama that going to sleep at night did not solve any of his problems—he still had to face them the next day when he woke up—so committing suicide would not solve any of his real problems either: he would still have to face them in his next life. He ticked Rama off roundly, pointing out that he had studied all the scriptures and so knew from what he had studied that suicide was regarded as a silly and negative thing to do. 'But,' said the teacher, 'if you want to do it—go ahead!'

Swami Rama had heard much about *shaktipata*, which means 'bestowing the energy', and he told his teacher that he had not yet bestowed the energy on him. He went on to moan about how he had been meditating for seventeen years and had ended up with nothing but a headache when he closed his eyes to meditate. His teacher did not say anything, so Rama continued moaning about how he did not find much joy in life, and how he had been wasting his time all these years. His teacher had told him it would take fourteen years to achieve *samādhi*, and yet here he was seventeen years later and still he had not reached *samādhi*. And to cap it all, he had followed faithfully everything his teacher had told him to do, and yet it was not working.

'Are you certain that you have followed faithfully everything you have been taught?' his teacher asked, and then added, 'Is this the fruit of all my years of teaching you, that you are going to commit suicide? And anyhow, when do you want to commit suicide?'

'Right now,' said Swami Rama, 'I am of no use to the world and no use to you.' And he got up and walked towards the nearby River Ganges so as to drown himself.

'Wait a minute,' said his teacher, 'You can swim, so the moment you jump into the Ganges you will start swimming. You had better find some other way of drowning if you are going to do the job properly.' And he suggested that Rama tie a heavy weight round himself to ensure that he stayed below the surface of the water.

Rama was a bit upset at his teacher saying such things, especially as his teacher had loved him so much in the past, but he went and got some rocks and tied them to himself. When his teacher saw that he was indeed serious, he said, 'Wait, sit down there and in one minute I will give you *samādhi*.'

Swami Rama did not know whether his teacher was serious or not, but he figured he could wait one more minute before committing suicide. So he sat down on the ground in his meditation posture. His teacher went over to him and touched his forehead. He instantly entered *samādhi* and remained there for nine hours. When he emerged he said the experience was indescribable.

* * *

Although this story had a happy ending, it only had such an ending because at the last minute Swami Rama abandoned impatience. This allowed him to break through into that area of deep concentration which he had striven towards for so many years.

It looks as if the teacher transferred something to him, but the teacher did not transfer anything. Impatience arises when there is goal orientation in the mind. Goal orientation is when you are holding in mind an idea of what you want to achieve by meditating. If you find yourself constantly comparing your meditation in the moment with what you think you ought to be achieving, then you are goal oriented. If you are tense and you want to be calm, then you are goal oriented. If you are tense, and you are aware there is tension present, but you return the attention to the rise and fall with no thought as to how you want the meditation to develop once you get on to the rise and fall, then you are not goal oriented.

Swami Rama had to be goal oriented, otherwise he could not have worked himself up into such a state about not getting anywhere. He must have been constantly comparing his meditation, where he got nothing but headaches, with what he wanted to be happening, which was to find himself in a deep, calm, tranquil state. As soon as there is even the slightest trace of wanting the moment to be different than it is, the mind is stained, and it instantly becomes tense and untranquil. And deep concentration cannot occur unless the mind is tranquil.

Swami Rama's experiences of lack of joy and a headache when meditating are very normal. There are far too many meditators who overwork whilst they are meditating and so find it most uncomfortable. What they are doing wrong is that they are pushing themselves towards what they think they should be getting in the meditation—in short, they are goal oriented, and being goal oriented, they work too hard.

It is not uncommon for meditators to push and push, and in this way work themselves up into quite an emotional state, where their bodies and minds are racked with pain, and they are so desperate that they force themselves into a mental corner where there seems to be no escape. At this point they mentally give up and decide they cannot do the meditation any more, just like Swami Rama did. He drove himself into a mental corner where he really had no choice but to carry out his threat to commit suicide.

It is when meditators are cornered that they give up, and to their utter amazement they start to meditate in the right way, and the peace, tranquillity, and joy they experience then is marvellous. And what have they given up? They have given up trying to do the meditation. In other words, they have abandoned craving. They have abandoned their selfish desires to get somewhere. As soon as meditators do that, they find themselves meditating properly for once. And that is just what Swami Rama did—he gave up. What he gave up was his ego, which had been standing in his way. Once he did that the meditation worked. But look what he had to drive himself to before he was prepared to abandon his ego.

Impatience is one aspect of ego. Many people find it quite difficult to understand what ego is: impatience is ego, jealousy is ego, revenge is ego, hatred is ego. In short, all craving and hatred are ego.

* * *

In order to overcome impatience, you need a change of attitude. If impatience arises at all, it is because you are approaching the activity in front of you—whether it is meditating, compiling a computer pro-gramme, or cleaning the bathroom—with a wrong view. You are wanting to get it over and done with. You are wanting to get it out of the way, so that you can proceed on to something else which you consider more pleasurable than what you are doing in the moment.

As soon as you have got this goal of something which is bigger and better but beyond your experience in the moment, you are in trouble. So the change of attitude you need is to convince yourself that the moment *now* is what you are really after in life, and if you can do that, then you will find the present moment is very enjoyable.

Can you see that if you could accomplish this, it would be a complete reversal of attitude to the way you had viewed life previously? Previously you had thought that enjoyment lies off in the future, but now you think that enjoyment is only to be experienced when the mind stays in the moment.

Usually the first objection is, 'How can I do anything unless I have a goal in mind?' Yes, you do have to have a goal in mind, but it only takes a split second to imagine what it is you want to achieve in the future. It takes next to no time to conceive of the goal of making an untidy cupboard tidy, for example. Right now the cupboard is untidy, but you can picture in your mind that sometime off in the future, in several hours from now, that cupboard will be in order. It only takes a split second to do this picturing of what you want to accomplish. Once this picturing is done, it is important to forget all about the goal.

Say that one day you decide to travel from Bradford on Avon to London by car. Having established the goal—which is to arrive in London—it is now important to forget about London. You definitely need to decide where you will finally end up, otherwise you would just drive round in circles, which would be futile. But having decided you want to end up in London, you should now forget about that and concentrate on the first bit of the journey—getting from Bradford on Avon to Holt.

If, as you drive along, you look at the fields and the trees, you notice when you change gears, and you notice the cars in front of you, in no time at all you will find you are in Holt, having thoroughly enjoyed the journey so far. If you now direct the car towards the next bit of the journey—getting from Holt to Melksham—and again turn your attention to what is going on inside and immediately outside the car, in no time at all you will be in Melksham, having been aware of many things as well as having enjoyed the drive and the countryside along the way. If you keep your attention in the present, you will continue in this same enjoyable manner until you arrive at your destination—London.

If you were constantly to hold the goal of arriving in London in mind, all you would be interested in would be getting there. With this attitude, you will be frequently looking at your watch and then looking at the map and then looking at the signposts and sighing and thinking, 'Oh dear, I've only travelled ten miles. I've only just arrived in Melksham. I've hardly gone any distance at all and it's taken me half an hour. At this rate it's going to take hours and hours to get to London. It's still another hundred miles! I'm hot and I'm tired. I wish I hadn't decided to go on this journey. It seems to be taking forever. I think I'll abandon the endeavour and go home instead.'

Excessive concentration on the goal—the goal in this case being London—can only result in getting impatient with everything that lies between Bradford on Avon and London, because it seems to be standing in the way of your arriving in London. There would be little interest in the roads you have to travel along and the villages and towns you have to pass through, and these, along with the time that lies between the start and finish of the journey, would be viewed as things which have to be endured, and the quicker you got through it the better. Something that has to be endured is never enjoyed. To come to enjoyment one must forget about London and pay attention to the journey on a moment-to-moment basis.

So to enjoy meditation the same principle applies as enjoying a long journey—you need to relax into each moment, moment by moment, and forget about how it is going and when you should arrive at some profitable meditative state. You want to be constantly telling yourself to cultivate the attitude of travelling and forget about arriving. That way craving to achieve is cut down.

★ ★ ★

Swami Rama exhibited strong signs of impatience. Now I want to tell you about Sister Tenzin Palmo who shows the opposite approach towards the meditative endeavour—she shows an attitude of patience.[2]

Sister Palmo is an Englishwoman who lives in Northern India. Shortly after her twenty-first birthday, she became a Tibetan Buddhist nun. Today, twenty-four years later, she is still a nun. She was recently interviewed by a Buddhist newspaper reporter who wanted to know

---

2. The following story has been adapted from an interview with Sister Tenzin Palmo that appeared in a Mahayana newspaper from Khatmandu, Nepal which was received by the Aukana Trust in May or June 1988. The original newspaper was lost, and we were unable to locate the source material elsewhere. The publishers approached Sister Tenzin Palmo directly for permission to quote from the interview, and she kindly allowed us to reproduce extracts from the interview here.

all sorts of things about her life—such as what first attracted her to Buddhism, why she went to India, how she met her teacher, and what life was like after she became a nun.

For the first six years as a nun she was the secretary to her teacher, Khamtrul Rinpoche. One day he told her that she had been working for many years, and it was now time she went away and practised meditation. He sent her to the mountainous region of Lahul, which is near Ladakh in Northern India. There she lived for eighteen years.

For the first six of those eighteen years she lived in a *gompa* (a Tibetan monastery), but she was not very happy with it because it had quite a social atmosphere due to all the monks and nuns sharing the same monastery, even though they lived in separate little houses. She felt it was not suitable for doing retreats and decided to build a house some distance from the monastery.

A fellow nun pointed out that her plan was impossible because it took money to build a house and she had no money. 'Why don't you go and live in a cave?' asked the nun.

'We've discussed this for many years,' replied Sister Palmo. 'There are no caves, and if there were caves, then there is no water. And where there is water, then there are people, which makes it unsuitable for retreats.'

But the nun she was talking to persisted. She said that only the night before she had remembered how, some time back, she had heard about a cave which had water and wood and was very beautiful. Most people did not know where the cave was, but there was one eighty-year-old nun still living in the monastery who could remember where it was, and she took them to see it.

As soon as Sister Palmo set eyes on the cave, she was determined to stay, despite everyone protesting and saying it was not suitable because it was too far from any other habitation. There were no houses in the locality. The nearest building was the monastery, which was one and a half hour's walk away, and that at a brisk pace, and, as one would expect in a mountain region, it was all uphill. In the winter the cave would be completely cut off by snow, and in the summer nobody would go anywhere near it, because there was nothing around other than pasture land. All these things made it quite unsuitable.

But Sister Palmo was determined. She got some masons and some helpers to build a wall on to the front of the cave with windows and doors in it. Then she moved in, and there she stayed for almost twelve years.

The interviewer was most curious to know how she liked living in a cave and how she acquired food and water. She said she loved living in a cave because it was quiet, there was nobody around, and the temperature was naturally thermostatically controlled, as it is in all caves, so it was warm in winter and cool in summer. As to food and water—for the first eight years she collected water from a spring about a quarter of a mile away. After that she had water piped in. She ate rice, sourdough bread, *tsampa* (roasted barley meal), and dhal (a simple pulse dish), and she had a small garden in which she grew potatoes and turnips. She said that she stayed very healthy on this diet.

She had different routines depending on whether she was on retreat or not. When she was not on retreat, she would do some meditation, read a bit, garden, do some sewing, paint pictures of Buddhas and *bodhisattvas* (beings dedicated to helping others free themselves from suffering) which she could give away as presents, and sometimes she would write out religious texts as she was the scribe for the monastery. She commented on how she never felt lonely.

When she was on retreat she did nothing other than meditation, a bit of reading, and the things she just had to do. One retreat she did lasted for three years.

One of the questions that the interviewer asked was, 'Do you feel that you've made any progress from doing these retreats?' And as you listen to her reply, do bear in mind that she lived in that cave for twelve years, devoting all day and every day to the meditative quest.

Sister Palmo's answer was, 'I hope I've made some progress after training my mind all these years. However, the more you realise, the more you realise how much there is to realise; and at the same time, you realise there is nothing to realise. So, it's an enormous job, not something that is going to be finished in this lifetime.'

* * *

Now tell me, did your heart sink at that reply? There she is, someone who has been a nun for twenty-four years, twelve of which she has spent living in a cave, often doing retreats three years at a stretch—all of which makes your one hour's seated meditation a day and one or two weeks' of retreats a year look a bit on the mean side. And yet after all those years dedicated to meditation, she is still not enlightened and talks about enlightenment taking many lifetimes to accomplish.

If your heart did sink as you realised how much time she has devoted to the spiritual search, and still she is not enlightened, then it means you are impatient. It means that lurking in mind, either consciously or unconsciously, you have the goal that you must become enlightened soon—and the quicker the better—so that you can get the burden of meditation over and done with. The meditative way is correctly named when it is called 'a burden', because it is a lot of work which frequently you will not feel in the mood to strive at.

If there is any impatience in the mind, it actually undercuts the task you are trying to do, which is to calm and still and purify the mind. Therefore, patience is one of the attitudes you need to cultivate if you are to travel along the meditative path quickly. And the way to do that is to encourage yourself to view life in the following way: 'Enlightenment may take a thousand lifetimes to accomplish and that is OK by me—I am quite willing to work at it for one thousand lifetimes, two thousand lifetimes, even three thousand lifetimes if need be. I will work at the spiritual path for as long as it takes.' And running side by side with that view should be the opposite attitude: 'Enlightenment is possible in this very lifetime. Therefore, I shall turn my attention and efforts constantly towards the spiritual so that I do become enlightened this lifetime, not in the next one or the one after that, but in this very lifetime now.'

Cultivating the view that enlightenment may take a thousand life-times allows you to relax and take your time, because, after all, what is the rush? You have so much time at your disposal. Such a relaxed attitude is needed for tranquillity and concentration to come into existence. However, the inherent weakness in the 'it takes a thousand lifetimes' view is that you might think that as it is going to take so long, why bother to work at all? You might just as well leave the meditative endeavour to another lifetime.

So you counteract that weakness by encouraging the growth of the opposite view—that enlightenment will be achieved in this very lifetime. This gives a sense of urgency. It makes one sort out one's priorities as to what is and what is not profitable to the spiritual life. It prevents laziness and prevents one from giving up the meditative endeavour entirely. With these two views existing side by side in your mind, you will find that you have the correct balance between too much and too little effort. That keeps at bay all the troubles that beset meditators when their efforts are unbalanced.

When one day you wake up to the realisation that you have not mentally bounced at hearing stories like that of Swami Rama and how long it took him to experience *samādhi*, or that of Sister Palmo who had, likewise, been meditating for years and yet still was not enlightened, then you know that you are well on your way to developing the power of patience.

Why 'power' of patience? Well, a mental factor, such as patience, is a power once you can turn it on whenever you need it. Patience is a power once you can recognise that a certain thought or a certain life event is likely to make the old habit pattern of impatience arise and you can switch on the patience. This can only be done when you know exactly what patience is and have so cultivated it that you can turn it on whenever you need it.

When you have the power of patience directed towards enlightenment, then progress along the path is sure and steady. As long as you keep working, nothing can stop you from eventually coming to full enlightenment.

One Key to Wisdom

There are many keys and many doors to wisdom. Each key has to be found and each door unlocked before a complete revolution of your mental universe can take place. One of those keys has a little brown label attached to it, and written on that label is one word, 'impeccability'.

Impeccability is all about rules. Impeccability is all about doing things correctly and, in order to accomplish that objective, rules are laid down by the teacher. If those rules are followed, then a meditator achieves impeccability. Impeccability is about following rules and it is about learning why they exist in the first place. If you do not comprehend the purpose for the existence of rules, resentment and war with authority figures will be the outcome.

When a man or woman becomes a Buddhist monk or nun, they undertake to follow a set of rules which are called *Vinaya*. But here I am not in the slightest bit interested in these traditional sets of rules because usually only monks and nuns know what each *Vinaya* rule is, and it is only these people who follow the rules and give any thought as to why discipline exists at all, when in actual fact understanding rules and the purpose for their existence is a must for every spiritual traveller whether lay person or monk. So I am not going to deal with the traditional *Vinaya* for monks and nuns but with the non-traditional rules, the ones that are not written down in a formal system but which nonetheless exist and which need to be followed by every spiritual traveller who wishes to make sense of the dissatisfaction that exists within himself or herself.

First, I want to draw your attention to the five hindrances that block successful meditation. They are sensual desire, ill will, sloth and torpor, restlessness and worry, and doubt.

Now one of the ways of eradicating the last two hindrances, those of restlessness and worry, and doubt, is by understanding the nature of the *Vinaya* discipline. If you, a lay meditator, define '*Vinaya* discipline' in too narrow a sense, then when you come across a reference in a book to the fact that one of the ways of overcoming worry, restlessness, and doubt is by understanding the *Vinaya* rules, you will automatically dismiss that particular method of eliminating the hindrances thinking, 'Oh, that can't possibly apply to me because I am not a monk.' And with that attitude you will be throwing away one of the keys that opens one of the doors to wisdom.

Wisdom about yourself is to be found in simple little things like the right way to wash a window, the right way to walk amongst wild flowers, the right way to plaster a wall. If you think wisdom is to be found only in sitting on your backside meditating, you are in for a huge disappointment, and you will be looking for many, many lifetimes before you find the Buddha within.

To train to find that Buddha within, that wisdom within, involves more than just sitting in silence. It involves training your whole attitude of mind. If your attitude is right, then mindfulness and concentration unfold naturally. They are what is produced as a result of right attitude. You can bash away all you like at trying to develop mindfulness and the capacity to stay in the moment, but nothing will happen if your attitude is wrong.

For example, a person who earns their living by thieving may decide to take up meditation and may find they can manage to do four hours of meditation per day, but they would not get any results because their attitude to life is faulty.

Correct attitude means being reverential towards things that you should be reverential towards. Sometimes those things will be inanimate objects like cars, doors, or rooms, and at other times they are animate objects like flowers and human beings. Correct attitude and impeccability, which is correct doing, are linked. You can only manage to be impeccable if you are reverential in attitude.

Let us start with what would be the correct behaviour towards something like wild flowers. If you are being impeccable, you will walk amongst a field of wild flowers, enjoying their beauty, but not picking them. Picking wild flowers shows a lack of reverence for something that should be revered. It shows a coarseness and dullness of mind. It indicates a person breaking a precept, the precept of taking that which is not given, and yet the individual picking the flowers is not sufficiently sensitive to even realise that they are breaking a precept. If you ever pick wild flowers, look at your motives for doing so, and then maybe you will get some idea of what I mean by a lack of reverence in the mind. A person picks wild flowers because they find them beautiful, and they wish to hang on to that beauty and to preserve it for a few more days in a jar of water on a mantelpiece. Also, such a person likes the idea of acquiring something for nothing.

So the motives behind picking the flowers are craving, craving for sensual pleasure and craving for saving money—that is why the mind is coarse and dull at that instant. Anything negative in mind makes it dull at that moment.

If you grow flowers yourself for the purpose of picking and displaying round the house, well that is completely different. You have put toil and sweat into growing them and money into buying and caring for them. Those flowers belong to you, to do what you wish with, and so of course you can pick them. And if you apologise to the plant as you pick one of its flowers, that is a nice gesture. It breeds a consideration towards a living thing, and it expands the mind's definition of 'living thing' to incorporate objects other than human beings.

Impeccability is behaving in a sensitive and right manner towards one's environment without being gushy and sentimental on the one hand or coarse and insensitive on the other.

If it so happens that a meditator does not know instinctively how to behave towards such things as picking wild flowers, then the teacher will make a set of rules for that person, a set of do's and don'ts with relationship to flowers, and those rules, if faithfully followed, would protect that person against their own cravings. When craving, even just for wild flowers, is prevented from expressing itself, then that person's mind grows more sensitive as the years roll by. The more sensitive the mind is, then the more easily can it see what is going on in the moment.

Now let us look at the correct way to behave in a meditation room: the correct way is to take off your shoes or slippers before entering.

Why, you may ask? After all, it is only a room, and all one is going to do in there is sit with one's eyes shut watching thoughts and feelings and such things rush past.

Well, there is no rational reason why you should take your shoes off. There is no reason why you should not dance and shout and scream in the meditation room if you so wish. However, to wear shoes or to behave inappropriately shows a lack of reverence towards the meditative endeavour. Lack of reverence ends up in completely outrageous behaviour like that described in Roshi Jiyu Kennett's autobiography, *The Wild, White Goose*, which is about her years of training in Japanese monasteries.[1]

She tells the story of one Western couple who made passionate love on the floor in front of the altar of the temple she was running. She was not very impressed by their inappropriate behaviour and threw them out. Later she discovered that this couple made a habit of copulating in temples, which had resulted in their being thrown out of temple after temple across Japan and arousing the disgust of the local people wherever they went.

Reverence towards buildings dedicated to the spiritual ideal is common to most religions. Roman Catholics insist that women cover their heads when entering their churches, this being a way of paying respect to what one is trying to do when entering that building. Admittedly, covering one's head or taking one's shoes off can degenerate into a ritual which seems meaningless. But even action which has turned into ritual can still breed reverence and sensitivity of mind.

Not cultivating the right attitude results in the mind getting coarse. To help people cultivate the right attitude, rules come into being, rules like: 'Take your shoes or slippers off before entering the shrine room.' Again, why do people leave their slippers on, especially when they see others taking theirs off? They leave them on for a variety of reasons. They are too lazy to remove their slippers. Or they do not wish their feet to get cold—thus being over concerned with their own creature comforts. Or they do not wish to conform—thus being over concerned with their own individuality. Or else there is just a complete oblivion

1. Rev. P.T.N.H. Jiyu-Kennett, Roshi (1978), *The Wild, White Goose, Vol. II*, p.159, Mount Shasta, California: Shasta Abbey Headquarters of the Reformed Soto Zen Church.

of what is going on around them so that they do not even notice people taking their slippers off. Every one of these reasons is an aspect of craving or hatred or just lack of mindfulness.

★ ★ ★

Meditation training is teaching one's mind how to view life so that it reveals to us happiness and wisdom rather than sorrow and frustration. And that training involves more than just sitting meditation. Take as an example a runner. If he wishes to compete internationally and win medals, he needs to do more than just practise running. He has to watch his diet. He may have to eat certain body-building foods. He has to watch his sleeping habits. Going to discos every night and staying up until two in the morning just would not do. He will have to have a coach to train him. He will have to organise the entering of races plus the arrangements for getting there and the accommodation once he is there. He will have to watch his smoking and drinking habits, maybe even give them up. He will have to do all this, as well as running several miles a day.

So training to become a top class runner involves more than just running. Doing physical exercise, regulating sleep, watching diet, alcohol, and cigarette use—all these aspects are necessary to become a top class runner. One cannot say that one aspect is more important than another—one can only say all are necessary parts of the whole. All make up the training to become an international runner.

So it is with spiritual training. Doing just sitting meditation is not good enough. It is the largest and most important part of the training, but it remains sterile if other aspects of the training are not fulfilled, specifically the aspect of impeccability. As already mentioned, impeccability is doing things correctly. It is plastering a wall correctly. It is carrying shopping loads in and out of the house correctly. It is cleaning a room correctly. There is a right way and a shoddy way. It is not that the shoddy way is wrong and evil, but from the spiritual training point of view, it is unhelpful because it does not do anything to curb inefficient mental habits.

If a meditator regularly puts on soiled clothes, socks with holes in, and dirty shoes—it is shoddy. It is not impeccable because untidy dress indicates a confused state of mind. A well-trained meditator will take great pains to dress tidily, ensuring that clothes are clean and pressed wherever possible, that stocking seams are straight rather than zigzagging round the legs, that nail polish when chipped is removed and reapplied rather than left in a chipped state for weeks, and so on. All this attention to tidiness of body makes inroads into lessening mental confusion as well as laziness. Crumpled clothes, chipped nail polish, holes in socks—all are only tolerated because the person is too lazy to attend to them. There is nearly always some 'rational' explanation to hide their laziness, like: 'I am above unimportant concerns such as washing and ironing and how I appear to others.' And the person believes that they are more evolved because they are not concerned about petty details like cleanliness and neatness.

Some meditators are naturally tidy. Others are not. Those who are not are told that they must not appear in this meditation centre with holes in their socks. They must wash their clothes more often. They must take care of their appearance. The rule comes into existence, not for the purpose of criticising the meditator's dress-style or for getting him or her to look smarter, but to curb the meditator's mental confusion and laziness, which expresses itself through untidy dress.

It is interesting to note that amongst the *Vinaya* for monks, there is a whole set of rules governing how monks must wear their robes and what attitude they should have towards their clothing.

A meditation teacher telling a lay meditator how to dress and how to behave with respect to clothes is laying down a rule which in spirit is no different from that governing monks' behaviour. It is just that it is expressed in terms relevant to the layman and what he wears for his lifestyle.

When meditators are told 'do this, not that', then that is the definition of a rule. If the meditators understand that the rule is there to curb their inefficient mental states then they will be delighted to follow the rule, because they now view rules as something they choose to follow so that they can bring wisdom into their life. So the rules will not be seen so much as things which restrict 'my freedom', which I resent and therefore must fight against, but rather rules are seen as a way of behaving which I choose to follow because it profits me to do so.

When a meditator comes under full-time training at this meditation centre (and by 'full-time training' I mean that the trainee lives in the Centre for several years or becomes a monk or nun) such a meditator will find him or herself subjected to a whole host of rules. And some of those rules will have been created specifically for that individual, to decrease his or her particular weaknesses and to encourage the growth of impeccability.

Every full-time meditator is expected to achieve impeccability with respect to menial tasks performed in the house and garden. Some full-time meditators have large doses of impeccability naturally, so are given very few rules to follow and are rarely corrected. Others have many rules to follow and frequently get corrected until their body fulfils the task perfectly, even when their mind falls apart—for most people can do a reasonable job of something like cleaning a room, especially when they are in a good mood, but as soon as they are mentally off colour, their work standard falls dramatically.

A fall in work standard is not impeccable. I would regard such a person as untrained. Meditators are fully trained only when they can perform a task perfectly, regardless of whether they are in a good or a bad mood. Once this standard is achieved, they are fully trained with respect to impeccability and the correcting ceases and the rules fall away. But by this time impeccability is so automatic and natural for them that they cannot break the rules even if they try. Behaving impeccably is so ingrained that it just takes over.

★ ★ ★

So far, I have been talking about impeccability training for those who are under our roof constantly, but all meditators can train themselves along this line whether or not they are in contact with us daily.

Let me give you a few more examples of what I mean by fulfilling a task perfectly and which mental inefficiencies are curbed by the right approach to that task.

First, any job you have to do, whether it is cleaning a door, vacuuming a carpet, building a cupboard, or mucking out the pigs, should be done at a medium pace. If you do a task too fast, you encourage the growth of impatience. If you do it too slowly, your mind will wander and you will fall into daydreams and you will lose heart about completing the task. And one of the things all meditators are trained to do is to fulfil what they start.

One of the first instructions given to students at the House of Inner

Tranquillity is that when you sit down to do half an hour's meditation, do half an hour, not more and not less. Do not be tempted to sit longer if it is going well and do not give up if it is going badly. Do exactly the length of time you originally decided upon when you sat down. That way, you train the power of volition, which is a vital factor for successful concentration. Also, by completing the length of meditation you originally decided upon, you train yourself in truthfulness. One aspect of truthfulness is keeping promises, and fulfilling a task you have set yourself is keeping a promise to yourself.

As another example, say one has to redecorate a room. Apart from pulling all the old wallpaper off, one will also have to fill in the cracks, sand down the wall, and size it before one can begin to hang the new wallpaper.

If you have got the task of filling in the cracks and you want to accomplish this job impeccably, what are the do's and don'ts of approaching it? First, you must set a goal in mind so you know in which direction you are heading. The goal is to fill all the holes and cracks on each of the four walls with polyfiller. Then forget that goal. You know where you are going and what you want to accomplish by setting the goal. Now forget the goal and concentrate on each moment and on each bit of the wall, working at a medium pace and doing the task to the best of your ability. When you have completed about a quarter of the wall, recheck it to make sure you have not missed any bits or filled in a section poorly. With rechecking you can redo the bits you have done badly, making the end product that much better.

The job would not be impeccably done if someone has to redo the polyfillering because your workmanship is so below par. The job would also not be impeccably done if by doing one job you created three others for someone else. Do you know what I mean by that? If somebody slaps polyfiller around with abandon so that as much poly-filler goes on the floor as on the wall and then does not immediately clean it up, someone at a later date will have to scrape it off the floor before a carpet can be laid. The polyfiller by this time would have set solid, so it will take much longer to clean up than it would have done if it had been attended to the moment it was spilt.

Poor workmanship or creating work for others by being careless shows that inefficiencies are present in mind. The do's and don'ts about approaching polyfillering, or cooking for that matter, or dusting, or mowing the lawn, include not being goal oriented about it. When a person is goal oriented they have their sights set on finishing the job and moving on to the next job, so they pay very little attention to the doing of the job. Such a person sees only the goal, which is constantly held before the mind's eye until the job is completed. The end is all important to them. The means are just there to accomplish the end. This makes the person very tunnel visioned. They do not notice what is right under their nose. In short, the hindrance present is ill will or impatience—impatience to get the job done.

In the spiritual sphere the means is vital. If one pays attention to the means, that implies one is paying detailed attention to the moment, and therefore, if there is anything different about the moment from previous moments, one will notice it, or if there is anything one has missed noticing, one will, with time, spot it.

Perhaps after completing the task of polyfillering you go into one of the decorated rooms. You are tired and you want a cup of tea, and so you get yourself a drink and then throw yourself into a chair. Now that would be sloppy action. It would not be impeccable, because your clothes are likely to be covered with plaster dust and bits of polyfiller.

If you do wish to sit down in a decorated room after doing some dirty building work, fine, but once you get up to leave, you should return the room to the state it was in before you entered it. Bits of polyfiller stuck to a chair and dusty footprints across the carpet would not have been there before you entered the room. Someone going into that room, if you have left it sprinkled with polyfiller and dust, would be able to say, 'Oh, so and so has just been in here.' The action is only impeccable if, after having had your drink, you leave the room the way you found it, so that others would not even realise that you had been there.

★ ★ ★

Each human being, once an adult, should walk through the world lightly. Using it lightly means taking only that which one needs from the environment, then leaving it as best one can the way one found it. It means using the environment in such a way that others coming by afterwards would not know that one had passed that way. Walking through the world lightly and impeccability go hand in hand. When one of these qualities is being developed, the other is getting developed automatically.

If you leave a tidy room untidy, it is not impeccable behaviour because someone will have to come and clean it up after you. It shows that there is no consideration present for others because there is no thought about leaving the environment attractive for others. Leaving a room the way you found it will foster in you consideration for others plus mindfulness of body plus mindfulness of the environment. In traditional Buddhism this is what is known as being 'mindful of an external object', because you will have to be mindful of what the room looks like on entering if you are going to put it back the way you found it.

Once you get a hold of how to put into practice the concept of walking through the world lightly, then you will be able to tighten up on activities where at present you may well be leaving your mark. For example, how many of you on entering a bathroom, either at home or in a friend's house, find the toilet seat and toilet cover down but then leave one or both of them up when you depart? That is very much leaving your 'mark' in the toilet. It shows that you have passed that way. And do you even notice whether the lid and seat are up or down?

Or how many of you find a door closed, but after you have passed through it, you leave it wide open? Are you even mindful as to whether the door is open or closed? Doors are usually closed for a reason—to cut down noise or heat loss or dust. If you consistently leave doors open, it will not be long before someone explodes, yelling, 'Close that door. Anyone would think you were born in a stable.'

These are two very small examples, but spiritual wisdom grows out of attending to small, simple, everyday things. It does not grow out of getting lost in large issues like *anattā*. *Anattā* is much more likely to be understood if you pay attention to simple, daily tasks.

I think you can see that if you go out of your way to be impeccable and to walk lightly through the world in respect to toilet seats and doors, you have to be mindful, otherwise you will not even notice whether the seat is up or down or whether the door is open or closed. So, by attempting to behave impeccably towards such simple ordinary everyday events, there comes increased mindfulness as well as thoughts of others' welfare, because you will be thinking, 'If I put this toilet seat and lid down, it looks more attractive. It cuts down smells. It is ready for use by the next person.' Living harmoniously in a group is only possible provided your day is made up with lots of little considerations, like the one just mentioned. And almost every one of you lives in a group. If there is more than just you living in your house or flat or bedsitter, then you are part of a group.

Rules, whether for layman or monk, are designed to breed mindfulness in the person practising them. They are also designed to decrease inefficient qualities of mind and increase efficient qualities.

A third benefit of rules is that they bring about an increase of thoughtfulness for one's fellow beings, which allows a huge number of people to live together under one roof and not be at one another's throats the whole time. Amongst the monkhood, wide differences in people's education, their class position, and their personalities can be the breeding ground for considerable tension. But if everybody is following the same rules, then harmony between individuals is more easily established.

* * *

Much research has been done by psychologists and the like into non-verbal communication between individuals who are attracted to one another. A man and a woman, for instance, who meet for the first time and like one another, will want to chat to one another and get to know each other better. It is observable that within minutes of meeting they start to imitate one another's actions. When she picks up her glass to take a drink, he picks up his glass at the same time. When he turns his head away, she turns her head away. When she picks up her cigarette, he picks up his cigarette. The degree to which they imitate one another indicates the depth of their liking for each other. A salesman (if he is wise or is it if he is cunning) will copy the gestures and speech patterns of his customer if he wishes to make certain of clinching a deal.

As people imitate one another if they like one another, that fact can be put to good use by making people who are unlikely to instantly get on follow a set of rules that makes them behave in the same manner towards dress, eating, tasks, and so on. In this way, a liking for one another gradually begins to develop.

Written and unwritten rules governing any meditative group,

whether that group is lay or monk, are designed to provide the supporting conditions to bring individuals within that group to enlightenment as quickly as possible.

Digressing slightly, Thai women regard men who have been in the monkhood as desirable catches. This is because by keeping the *Vinaya* discipline they become house-trained. Many of the minor rules for monks deal with such issues as how he should dress, how he should behave when appearing in public, what small duties he should perform towards others, especially his teacher, and how he should eat (in other words, the rule deals with table manners). All this makes a person house-trained and considerate of others and thus a desirable person for a woman to wish to live with for the rest of her life.

It really is very important to understand what part rules play in one's spiritual development. One needs to realise that they are present for one reason only and that is to bring about impeccability. Impeccability is doing things correctly. This is only possible with the correct attitude. If the correct doing and the correct attitude exists, then concentration and mindfulness grow easily and, when they are present, wisdom develops.

Evenmindedness

There are two types of evenmindedness—basic and advanced. Basic evenmindedness comes about by encouraging the growth of three separate knowledges: (1) the knowledge that actions have results, (2) the knowledge that internal events are short-lived—they come and go very quickly—and (3) the knowledge that the development of the capacity to be unmoved by praise or blame is essential if one is to have any stability of mind.

Let us take the first knowledge, the knowledge that actions have results. If you have a thorough working understanding of this principle, then you will know that the living conditions you were born into, the type of parents you have, the standard of education you received, and all the things that filled your life when you were young and that fill your life now have only come into existence because of actions you made. If you truly *know* that from the moment you are born until the moment you die you create the world you live in, then it is much easier to take full responsibility for all the delights and horrors of the past, the present, and the future. Once accepting one's lot has become an ingrained mental habit, then evenmindedness starts to grow. And one of the ways of encouraging the growth of this understanding that actions have results is by reading at least six or seven books on the subject of rebirth.

Once *kamma* and *vipāka*, action and result, are thoroughly understood, one comes to accept the conditions one grew up in: one's mother, father, brothers, sisters, one's standard of education. One learns that it is no use feeling outraged if one's father had a nervous breakdown when one was sixteen, and so the family had to uproot and move to a different town where there was a less demanding job available for him. One learns it is no use feeling resentful because the disruption affected one's schooling, and one failed the 'O' levels that one sat just after moving. And failing one's exams means a lower standard of education and thus a lack of job opportunities. It would be fruitless holding a grudge against one's father and blaming him for one's low standard of education because one has acted so as to get that man for a father in the first place.

But people do hang on to the bitterness aroused by such events and rarely make the connection between the action of hanging on to the past and their failure to be happy in the present. The event has come and gone. One cannot alter it by being resentful of it. If one allows resentment of the past to run, one only works oneself up into a froth, which leaves one feeling worn out, but, worse still, the past event remains unchanged. Recognising this, one realises that not accepting the past is a waste of energy—it achieves nothing.

The second knowledge that assists in the development of evenmindedness is the observation that all internal things are short-lived—they come and go very quickly.

We observe that our feelings and thoughts are just like bubbles on the surface of water. They last for a second and then they are gone. How can we possibly take seriously something that lasts for a second and then vanishes? You would think a person was crazy if you saw him or her bending over a river trying to catch the bubbles off the surface of the water. You would think him crazier still if he told you that he intended to take those bubbles home, pour plastic into their centres, and place them on a shelf, so as to gaze upon those bubbles for the remainder of his life.

You would naturally think such a person crazy because you know it cannot be done. The bubble will burst. It is only a matter of time. This bubble may last longer than that bubble, but, as time is measured, the life of a bubble on the surface of water is very, very short. And yet, when we experience a pain in our backs, or when someone says something cutting to us, or when we remember something we said which we are ashamed of, we fail to recognise that these events have the same life span as a bubble. It is very short. But what do we do? We try to capture it and fill the experience with plastic, so that we can preserve it and keep looking at it. Unfortunately, we do not just attempt to capture the pretty pleasant bubbles that rise up when someone smiles at us or gives us a compliment or an unexpected gift—we try to capture the unpleasant bubbles and preserve those too. It is crazy. Who wants to look at a black, twisted bubble that has a sense of failure or jealousy or resentment captured inside it? And yet that is what we do—we clutch to ourselves our negativity and try to preserve that.

If only we could recognise that all conditioned things, all feelings, all mental states, all mental content, all thoughts are like bubbles: they spring to life, reach a peak, and then burst—gone forever, never to return. And the time that it lasts is oh so short. So why take them so seriously? You do not take bubbles on the surface of water seriously. Why? Because you *know* they can only last for a fraction of a second. You know that a bubble has no centre, and so it has no substance. But you think that what happens to you in life is different in nature to the bubble. But it is not—it is the same. When you understand that your thoughts, feelings, mental content have the same short life span and insubstantial nature as a bubble on the surface of water, then you will be able to stop taking them so seriously, and thus the overall tenor of your mind will become much more even.

The third knowledge to be developed to really ensure that basic evenmindedness runs for most of the day, every day, is to be unmoved by praise and blame.

The majority of folk would claim they cannot cope with blame very well but that they are fine with praise. They can cope with praise. But can you? If your loved one is not paying any attention to you at a party but is laughing and joking and speaking with others and totally ignoring you, can you cope? If your partner is lost in a world of his or her own for a few days, can you cope, or do you start demanding attention? If you are not complimented on a meal you have cooked or a new outfit you have just bought, can you cope with the lack of acknowledgement? If the answer to any of these questions is no, then you cannot cope with praise. You cannot cope because you actively seek and expect praise.

Praise comes in many forms besides the spoken compliment. It can come in the form of a loved one paying attention to you either by listening to what you have to say or by being constantly at your side at a party, or praise can come in the form of being given a gift.

If you actively seek praise, then you are attached to it, and your spirits will sink if you do not get what you consider is your fair share of praise. If you need something from outside of yourself, like praise, in order to feel complete, then you are at the mercy of the environment, and it is guaranteed that any evenmindedness you do have will be short-lived.

Now when it comes to blame, that is a difficult area and needs much work to get stability towards it. Blame can come in the form of being told that you have not done a job correctly, or it can come in the form of being told that certain aspects of your personality are unacceptable. Blame can also come in the form of relatives criticising the way you choose to run your life. Blame comes in many forms and always arouses unpleasant feelings within us.

If you are at odds with a parent or a spouse or a boss, where you are not so much fighting with them but they are fighting with you and trying to control and dominate you, you can reflect that in one way at least you are fortunate. To have to deal with someone you find difficult can be a great gift. It can strengthen and deepen one's wisdom, *provided* you approach the interpersonal conflict with the right attitude. Most soul searching, that is, trying to understand what life is all about and what part you play in the scheme of things, is done in times of pain and such difficult relationships are painful.

Even if you had such a relationship in the past and did not make the best use of the gift of an enemy and emerged from the experience somewhat twisted and lacking in self-confidence, then now is the time to rethink your attitude to past or present obsessive behaviour from others. Such relationships, if we approach them properly, are wonderful gifts because they give us the opportunity to become evenminded towards blame and have the added benefit of flattening one's sense of self-importance.

If you did not have someone to knock the stuffing of self-importance out of you when you were young, let us hope you come across it in your daily life now. It will come in the form of an unpleasant marriage, unpleasant boss, unpleasant children, or unpleasant neighbours. And if, when you come across this teaching, there is no person in your life knocking the edges off your self-importance, then you may find that your spiritual teacher needs to take up this role by getting fierce with you in order to lessen your self-importance.

If you are really intent on self-discovery, you will find you cannot withdraw from the teacher-pupil relationship. Perhaps all your life you have withdrawn from unpleasant situations, but now you find you cannot withdraw because you crave so much to discover the mysteries of the universe. But you are trapped. What to do? Your once supporting, encouraging spiritual friend, your teacher, your *kalyāna mitta*, has turned into a fierce and terrifying figure. What can you do? You want to know the secrets of the universe, and yet you cannot handle the guide who will show you the way. You feel trapped. You want to know the mysteries and yet not *this* way. This way is too painful. You wanted a nice, sweet, kind, understanding guide, not this tyrant. With sinking heart you realise that if you give up, perhaps you will never find a guide, because you know that there are not many who are qualified to guide travellers right to the centre of the mysteries. Great depression engulfs you. 'What shall I do?' you keep silently asking. 'What shall I do?' I will tell you what you do. You stay and fight. How do you fight? By being evenminded towards praise and blame. Let the teacher scold you, let him praise you, but do not let your mind become shaken by the blame, nor let your mind wander into hatred for the teacher. If you do, you are still very weak and have much to develop before you can hope to make headway with advanced evenmindedness.

How do you develop evenmindedness towards blame? You develop it by not taking yourself so seriously. Your boss says to you that you are a slow worker, and you have got to speed up. How do you react? Perhaps you get upset. Perhaps you get indignant. You think, 'Who does he think he's talking to?' Or you say to yourself, 'He's judging me unfairly. I'm a much better worker and much more thorough because of my slowness than my fellow work colleagues.' All of this would be taking yourself seriously.

If the boss's comments hurt, the hurt is no big deal. It is only a feeling—unpleasant, maybe, but only a feeling. And feelings come and go very quickly. But when you add to that feeling by getting indignant, by arguing in your mind with your boss, then you have a problem. And who has created it? You have. It is you who do not like the unpleasant feeling and so have made a movement in mind to get rid of the feeling. It is you who have taken yourself and your feelings so seriously and are demanding justice because you think you have been unfairly judged.

Taking yourself seriously is being puffed up with self-importance, and when you have that, you have *dukkha* (suffering).

Let what the boss says roll off you, like water off a duck's back. The hurt you cannot get rid of. Experience it, but then let it go. Do not clutch it to you by getting indignant with what your boss says. I can assure you that there will be many more comments of a similar nature made to you before this month is out. It may not be your boss who says nasty things to you—it may be your wife or husband or child or friend or the lady in the shopping queue who accuses you of queue jumping. Are you going to get indignant with all of them? If so, I can predict that it is going to be a very unpleasant time for you.

And where is your evenmindedness in all of this? It does not exist. You are swinging all over the place emotionally, dependent on what people say and do towards you, all because you take so seriously the feelings and thoughts that rise up in response to what others say. You believe it all.

One way of helping yourself to avoid taking your feelings and thoughts so seriously is to cast your mind back to the past, to a time when you were wound up about something. Do you recall how upset you were on May the 9th 1984? Oh, you cannot remember that day, let alone whether or not you were upset. Can you remember what an emotional stew you got into during the week commencing Monday, 7th of May 1984? Ah, you cannot remember anything from that week either. So how important was the upset if you cannot remember it now?

And there is bound to have been something you wound yourself up about during that week, Monday, 7th of May to Sunday, 13th of May 1984. It is a certainty that you experienced resentment or anger or fear or anxiety or excitement about something someone said to you which you interpreted as criticism or as praise. If no praise or blame came your way to upset you, then it is highly likely that you had a memory flash of past blame during that week in May 1984.

I am sure you have noticed from your meditation experience to date that the mind is all over the place in a day—up one minute, down the next, bored the next. It is hard to stay on an even keel for twenty-four hours, let alone seven days. So it is fairly reasonable to assume that during the week 7th–13th May 1984, you lost evenmindedness and got steamed up about some real or imagined blame or praise situation, even though you cannot remember the event now.

What seems an all-important unpleasant feeling now, which 'I must get rid of', is forgotten about by the next week, sometimes by the next day, because it has been replaced by another unpleasant feeling which becomes all-important. Because we take the momentary unpleasant feelings so seriously, we cannot tolerate them. Thus we make negative moves to get rid of them. As every action produces a result, this lands us with all sorts of problems in the future.

When you are feeling anxious about your job or your marriage or your children or when you are mad with someone because they have said something nasty, remind yourself that in a few days you will have forgotten all about the agony you are now experiencing. So how important is it? If you let yourself fall into the trap of regarding the present unpleasant feeling as the most important thing in the world, then you will respond to it inefficiently.

Remind yourself that the anxiety you feel right now will have been replaced by another mood tomorrow, and that the new mood will seem just as important as the anxiety appears right now. So if another mood can oust anxiety, how important is the anxiety? It is only a feeling after all, maybe a big feeling, but it is only a feeling and it will pass—so bear it stoically.

* * *

I have mentioned the three ways of developing basic evenmindedness: knowledge that actions have results, knowledge that internal things come and go quickly, and refusing to be thrown by praise or blame. When these three have been developed, you have reached the stage that in traditional Buddhism is called 'controlling the covetousness and dejection that are in the world'.[1]

Now you are ready to develop the second stage of evenmindedness— that of advanced evenmindedness.

What is advanced evenmindedness? It is the stopping of internal dialogue. 'Internal dialogue' is just what it says. It is when you hold a conversation with yourself or someone else in your mind. Internal

1. Adapted from 'Discourse on the Applications of Mindfulness', Horner, I.B. (1976), *The Middle Length Sayings, Vol.I*, pp.70-82, London: Pali Text Society.

dialogue also covers mental chatter and commenting thoughts. All of these we call thinking. Perception, however, is not internal dialogue. Let me give you an example: you hear a sound, and a label comes up which says, 'Ah, that noise is the sound of an aeroplane.' Although it is a whole sentence long, it is still only perception. It is identifying the noise. But the mind may then chatter on and say, 'I wonder what sort of plane it is, a commercial aircraft or a military one. I haven't heard the sound of a plane for several days now. Usually one or two fly over the house every day. I wonder what's happened to them this past week? Perhaps they've flown overhead, but I didn't hear them because the wind's changed direction. I know that wind direction makes a difference to whether or not one picks up certain sounds.'

All that chatter is pretty innocuous stuff. One is unlikely to get worked up about it and so lose the basic evenmindedness, which, by this time, exists for the major part of every day. But even this innocuous chatter must go—it must be switched off for advanced evenmindedness to come into being.

When the internal dialogue is stopped, then there is only one object present in mind. It is the one you have consciously chosen. If you are doing *vipassanā* meditation, then it will be the feeling of the rise and fall of the abdomen.

That one object, the rise and fall, will fill the whole attention. There will be no other object present. There will be no sound or feeling or thought or smell present, only the rise and fall, and you will be *conscious* that you are aware that it is the rise and fall you are watching, rather than, say, a bird sound or a memory of a sunset you once saw.

In this second stage of evenmindedness, the object you have consciously chosen to be aware of, that is, the rise and fall, will appear once, filling the whole mind, then it will appear again and again and again. The attention will remain on that object, not just once but for many repetitions. If internal dialogue appears, then the mind drops out of this second stage of evenmindedness back into the first stage. If you take seriously the content of the internal dialogue, then the mind falls out of the first stage of evenmindedness and down into the state known as 'unliberated', which is where the hindrances dwell.

When mind is in the 'unliberated' condition, it feels as if it is caught in chains, and the more you try to get rid of the hindrance present, whether that hindrance is ill will or sleepiness or restlessness, the more tightly the chains appear to wind themselves round you. The only way to get free of those chains is to be still, to stop struggling, to accept, to be evenminded about the hindrance—then the chains fall away and the mind is liberated. Once it is liberated of the hindrances, you will find yourself back in the level of basic evenmindedness, and you can begin work again to establish yourself in advanced evenmindedness.

In the advanced stage, apart from the object filling the whole of the mind, there must be certain mental factors present. These factors will be a lightness of mind, a workability of mind, and a relaxation of mind and body which will be interpreted as tranquil and pleasurable. The mind will feel spacious, light, bright, clean, enjoyable, and full of interest for the object.

When this stage is reached, the object may change its form and become a circle of light. If advanced evenmindedness is well developed, then that circle of light will be there on and off for most of the hour. However, with *vipassanā* meditation the meditator should not take the practice this far because the mind is too calm, peaceful, and focused on only one object—the circle of light—for too long a time.

Vipassanā wants changing objects. With *vipassanā* you need to hold the attention at the meeting point between sense contact and your response to that sense contact. For example, up into mind pops a picture. It is of a place where you once spent many happy hours. It is a picture of a river with meadows filled with buttercups that are tumbling gently down to the water's edge. The memory picture is full of sunshine and peacefulness. It is idyllic. When you see that picture in mind, up wells a warm pleasurable feeling. That memory is sense contact. It has appeared at mind's door and, by becoming conscious of it, contact was made. Following closely on the heels of that memory will be a feeling. All of this process of memory and feeling is automatic, and 'you' as such have not appeared in the picture yet. 'You' have yet to respond. If you watch the picture come and go and the feeling come and go, that is one response. If you try to add to the pleasant feeling by fantasising about summer days, that is another type of response. And which response produces suffering and which does not is what you want to learn about with *vipassanā* meditation. It is only this type of learning that brings about the lessening and then the ceasing of suffering.

The level of evenmindedness that you need to develop for *vipassanā* operates in a narrow band that lies between the tail end of basic evenmindedness and the beginning of advanced evenmindedness.

When basic evenmindedness is well developed, then if mind is dull or the body is tense or someone is moaning at you, you will respond to that experience evenly. You will still experience an uncomfortable feeling when someone moans at you, but you will not get worked up about it or try to alter it. If you should go ahead and try to alter it, because the mind has been so even for so long, you are able to see clearly the link between feeling and trying to adjust that feeling and how the adjusting inevitably ends up in *dukkha*.

At the beginning of advanced evenmindedness the mind will be filled with rise and fall for several counts of the breath. Then something will cut across that rise and fall, like a sound, and for the split second that that sound fills the mind, there is nothing else. Then it is back to rise and fall again. Then maybe a feeling cuts across the rise and fall and the attention is filled with that feeling. At the beginning of advanced evenmindedness the mind will be light, bright, clear, and joyful, but it will not be on the rise and fall continuously. Internal dialogue will still rise up occasionally, but there will be no disturbance at the content of that dialogue.

Of course, when this mental chatter starts up in mind, one drops from advanced evenmindedness back into basic evenmindedness, but that does not matter in the slightest, because, as already stated, the wisdom that one is seeking to develop is only accomplished by holding the mind in the area that lies between the end of basic evenmindedness and the beginning of advanced evenmindedness.

In spiritual training, impeccability is the first thing that has to be developed. When that is established, then the next thing to be developed is evenmindedness. First to be developed is the evenmindedness that comes from accepting whatever life has to throw at one, whether pleasant or painful, internal or external. Then comes the development of advanced evenmindedness. This cannot happen until the previous two are firmly established. After the establishment of basic and advanced evenmindedness, comes the development of wisdom. Once impeccability, evenmindedness, and wisdom are fully matured, the training is over. And it can be said: what had to be done with this lifetime, has been done—*dukkha* has been understood and *nibbāna* has been realised.

The End of Growth, The Beginning of Learning

Growth is what we get up to before enlightenment. Learning is what we do after enlightenment.

What is growth? When we are young, under the age of fourteen, growth is passing exams and winning sports trophies. In the late teens to early twenties, growth is social activities like going to parties, being part of a gang, forming romantic relationships. From twenty to forty, growth is moving into your own home, getting married, having your first child, then your second, third, and fourth child. Growth is purchasing a pet when previously you had none. Growth is starting your first job or starting your own business. Growth is getting even more educational qualifications than the ones you already have.

From forty into the mid-fifties, growth is getting into leadership roles, like becoming manager of the company you work for, or becoming a headmaster of a school, or a senior nurse. All of these are leadership roles, and when you accept these roles in society, you feel growth taking place. During these middle years, people also grow by joining community projects, such as local councils, local political parties, local charity organisations, and seeking to hold office in these organisations in order to ensure maximum growth.

From the mid-fifties up into one's seventies, growth takes place by passing on what one has learnt to those who are younger than oneself, so that they may grow and realise their potential. One way of passing on such wisdom is by sharing what one knows with one's grandchildren. Another way of growing during this age is by sharing one's accumulated experience and wealth with cultural, educational, or religious groups.

When we are born, we come into the world naked—with no walking skills, no talking skills, no possessions, no money, no qualifications, no husband, or wife, or children—and from the moment we take our first gasp of the Earth's air, we set about gathering to ourselves all the goods we do not have. This gathering of money, possessions, relationships, and the like is called growth. And the more we grow, the better we feel, the more powerful we feel. Those around us, our family and friends, applaud and encourage this growth. How successful we have been at living life is assessed by the amount we have accumulated. Thus, the more possessions we have gathered, the more we have 'grown', the more people are prepared to take notice and listen to us. We feel we are nothing, a nobody, if we have not partaken of this growth process.

Spiritual teachings, however, tell us that it is highly unlikely that we can partake of growth and gain any spiritual depths. Furthermore, they say that the more goodies we collect, the more puffed up we usually become, that growth corrupts, and that the corruption shows itself in a steadily increasing sense of self-importance, and that this separates us even more from the enlightened state.

For example, have you ever witnessed the pride that exists in parents after their first child has been born? They have a new possession and their sense of self-importance grows accordingly. Or there is the pride that often rises up in the older person when he or she comes into contact with a younger man or woman, and older here does not just apply to sixty- and seventy-year-olds—it can apply to thirty- and forty-year-olds too. How quickly the older person compares themselves with the other, realising that, since they have been alive longer, they have collected more possessions and therefore grown more. Thus they judge themselves as better than the younger person. Self-importance only raises its ugly head when we think we are better than, worse than, or equal to another person or another mental quality to that which we ourselves possess.

All the examples I have given you of having nothing when we are born and then gathering to ourselves educational qualifications, friends, husbands, wives, homes, children, and so on, are what is normally understood as growth. Those who dedicate themselves to becoming enlightened, of whatever religious persuasion they may be, will say that this sort of growth corrupts, and therefore it is not compatible with the religious path. They will say that this growth must go if one wishes to be a truly spiritual person.

Such a statement is half right. Growth must go if one is to become enlightened. But what exactly is growth from the meditative point of view? Growth is not the gathering of goods, nor is it the various experiences we go through from birth to death—growth is our *attitude* to these things. Get the attitude right and accumulation ceases— growth ceases, self-importance ceases, and correct living begins. So I prefer to call the various life cycles that we go through and the material possessions we amass 'external growth' and our approach to those cycles 'internal growth'. And it is the internal growth that corrupts and which the meditator needs to eliminate if he or she wishes to experience enlightenment.

What Buddhism means by 'internal growth' is the desire, the lust, to have something other than what we have in the moment. We do this type of growing when we want some sort of pleasure through the senses, like a hug, but there is nobody around to give us a hug, and so we get distressed. That process is wishing to grow through sensual contact.

Growth is also desiring to become something other than what 'I am' in the moment. We do this sort of growing when we want meditation to be clear when it is cloudy, or when we study for yet another educational qualification with the expectation of becoming something other than what we are now. We might say, 'I feel unhappy now. I think that by getting another qualification my life will smooth out and I will become happier.' That is using the learning of a subject for our own ends so as to become something other than what we are now. But if we can study a subject for its own sake, then we have not corrupted the external good into internal growth. Corrupting learning is taking the study out of the orbit of something that is happening in the now and turning it into something that will make me better in the future.

Internal growth's hallmark is 'I want to become something other than what I am now. I want to grow. I want to change, because I do not find the present moment complete.' The truth is that the present moment *is* complete. It is perfection itself. Only when we experience this all the time are we enlightened.

I make the distinction between external growth and internal growth and say that only internal growth corrupts, because if the gathering to oneself of educational qualifications, houses, goods, husbands, and so on prevents enlightenment, then every child who has not yet acquired any possessions, every poverty stricken, uneducated, single adult, every recluse, and every tramp should be enlightened, and they most certainly are not. This is because they indulge in internal growth just as much as the man with many possessions. It is putting a stop to internal growth that the meditative training is concerned with.

However, because internal growth is so closely intertwined with the gathering of external goods, it is often easier to stop the process of gathering possessions in order to highlight just exactly what one is up to on the mental side.

Thus, some meditators opt to become nuns and monks, where they practise poverty, where they have no marriage, no children, no pets, so as to highlight the internal growth process. If you remove the gathering of houses, money, careers, relationships, then the mind is left with only one process to observe, that of internal growth. This simplifying of life, having only internal growth to concentrate on, rather than internal and external growth, makes the meditative training easier for most people.

* * *

So how do we leap from the bad habit of beavering away at collecting internal goods to the stopping of this process? How do we leap from desiring growth, that state of always wanting something other than what we have got, to being content with the perfection of the now?

The clue to the solving of this riddle lies in the one word, 'self-importance'. When we understand what self-importance is, when we truly understand by intuitive wisdom, then our task is done. We are enlightened. However, we can get a good intellectual grasp of what self-importance is long before that time. If you hear the terms 'ego' or 'self-centredness' or 'self-view' used, be assured that it means the same thing as self-importance.

'Self-view' and 'having to get rid of self-view' are statements one hears frequently in spiritual teachings. Getting rid of this 'self-view' is what every dedicated meditator aspires to. But just what is self-view? It is really quite a hard term to grasp. If you have thoughts along the lines of the following, then you have a well-developed self-view: 'I'm not creative enough. In the future, when I've changed this and that about myself, then perhaps I will become the creative person I aspire to be. Right now I don't think very much of myself. I don't like myself much because I have this and that deficiency, but in the future, when I've changed myself, it will be better. I will be happier.'

For the word 'creative' you can substitute 'intelligent' or 'musical' or 'mother' or 'wife' or 'sportsman'. Then there would be such thoughts as: 'I'm not intelligent enough. When I've got this or that degree, I'll be better,' or 'I'm not a good enough mother. In the future, when I'm more giving, more patient, less intolerant with my children, less bored with their childish babble, I'll be a better mother, and I'll like myself better. In the future, when I've brought about the changes in myself which I envisage, only then will I be happy.'

All such thoughts are self-view. There is a dissatisfaction with what I am now and a constant looking to the future when life will be better. Such thinking means the mind is always rushing between the past and the future. It is constantly desiring to grow into something bigger and better. Never does it look at the present *fully*, because it does not like the present. It regards the present as imperfect.

Another way in which self-view manifests is as follows. Imagine you are about to go for a job interview. Weeks before that interview you are turning over and over in mind what you will say to the interviewer, what sort of questions the interviewer will ask you, and what you will say in response. You live that interview a thousand times before you ever get to it. When you eventually do turn up at the real interview, you have twisted yourself all out of shape to present yourself in the way you imagine the interviewer wants to see you. If you cannot maintain the prepared image of the way you want to present yourself, if you lapse for a moment and say something that you think does not present you in the best light, then you go through the tortures of the damned both during and after the interview.

The worrying about the interview before it happens, the twisting of yourself out of shape during the interview, the tortured going over and over the interview afterwards wishing you had said certain things differently—all this is suffering. It is torture. It is self-view.

The anxiety, the pre-plotting, the trying to be something one be-lieves someone else wants, rather than being oneself, can only come about if there is a non-acceptance of conditionality. What I mean by 'conditionality' is this: if you take one person, let us call him Joe Smith, then line up ten of his friends and ask each one to describe Joe's personality, you will get ten different answers. Joe Smith's personality consists of thousands of different facets, which when combined make Joe a unique human being. There is no other human being like him in the world.

Friend number one in the line-up also consists of thousands of different facets of personality such as generosity, neatness, self-discipline, laziness, good memory, and so on, but they are in different proportions to Joe's facets. Also, friend number one has some facets which are different from those of Joe's. So when all of the facets of friend number one are combined, he turns out to be quite a different personality from Joe. Put the two people together and they draw certain of those facets out of one another and one has an event. One could call it a third person that is born as a result of mixing Joe Smith with friend number one. Friend number one may be very generous, so he draws out the generous streak that Joe also possesses. So when friend number one is asked to describe Joe's personality, he will say, 'Joe is a very generous man.'

Friend number two, however, is always moaning about his friends, his neighbours, his job, and thus friend number two draws out of Joe his critical tongue. So friend number two has the opinion that Joe is a very critical man.

All ten people will have a different view of Joe Smith's personality according to what is created when they combine with Joe.

If you have not noticed that you change according to the person you are with, then you have a strong view that you are independent, that you are separated out from the world, and that you are not influenced by it. Also, you have the view that you can control whatever events come within your range. This is the opposite of conditionality, and it means that you have not noticed conditionality operating in your own life.

The definition of conditionality is: dependent on this being present, that comes to be; when this ceases, that ceases.

The truth of the matter is that when you are with another person, you behave and think in a slightly different way to when you are alone. This is because you are connected to the universe. You are influenced by it. You are moulded by it. You are only half the picture, so to speak—your friend is the other half. And when the two halves meet, they create a separate event. I like to call that event 'another being'. It is unique to the two of you on that particular day, because on another day when you and your friend meet, you will both be different. Your moods will be different, and so the 'being' created from your union will be quite, quite different from the previous day, quite unique to that time, that place, and the moods of the two of you at that moment.

You can plot and scheme all you like about how you will react and what you will say and what will happen when you and your friend get together, but whatever picture you build before the event, you can be quite sure that it is a fantasy, that the real event will be quite different from the way you imagined it. That is because in your fantasy you forget to include how the presence of the other person changes you. You disregard their facets and what sort of mood they will be in on the day you meet and how their mood is likely to press all sorts of buttons in you, making pop up such things as anger or love. And if you have decided in advance what the two of you are going to be like with one another, then when you eventually do get together, you will be considerably thrown when it does not turn out the way you imagined. Better not to fantasise, but just be with and experience the event when it occurs.

What has just been described is the fact that how one acts in any given situation is dependent upon a whole host of things such as the other person's mood at the time, one's own mood, one's state of health, and many more things besides. What has been described is how nothing arises by itself. Everything arises dependent upon other things.

If you can begin to detect conditionality—what you say, how you act under certain conditions with certain people, and how you cannot stop yourself being like that no matter how you try—then you will start getting a clue as to just what conditionality is. An experiential understanding of conditionality cuts down considerably the habit of running over in mind an event before you actually experience it. Seeing conditionality clearly is essential to getting rid of self-view.

But one has to notice much more detail about conditionality in order to bring significant advancement on the meditative path. The sort of detail I am referring to is this: you go out into your driveway and notice a pile of wood lying there, and into mind pops a series of thoughts like, 'Ah, that wood must be for the garden shed I ordered. I didn't hear the delivery men arrive. I wonder when it's going to be erected? No doubt somebody will appear shortly to erect it.'

Now how did that thinking arise? Nothing appears out of the blue, remember? Everything, except *nibbāna*, arises dependent on something else. Everything is linked to something else and therefore influenced by it.

If we analyse the example just given, you will see what I mean by things being dependent on other things. You go out of the house into the yard and see a pile of wood, and thoughts about the wood follow. The thoughts arose dependent upon the perception. What was the perception? It was the label, 'pile of wood lying in the yard'. And how did that perception arise? It arose dependent on 'seeing consciousness'. What is 'seeing consciousness'? 'Seeing consciousness' is what takes place when there is a pair of eyes that are functioning and there is an external object for the eyes to see. When the eyes and the external object are close enough, seeing takes place. In the example given, if the wood was piled up one mile away from you, seeing would not have taken place. So for seeing to happen at all, your eyes must be fully functioning *and* the object has to be within the range of eyesight. The eyes only see colour and shape—they do not see wood. It is the mind that adds the label 'wood' to the colour and shape.

Dependent on your having functioning healthy eyes plus an external object—when these two come together you get what is known as 'seeing'. Dependent upon seeing, the label, 'a pile of wood', pops into mind. Dependent upon the perception, 'a pile of wood', a whole string of thoughts about garden sheds and delivery men run through the mind. Not a single solitary thought about garden sheds could arise unless there was first the contact between your eyes and an object out there.

So if a teacher asks a meditator what did all the thinking about garden sheds arise upon, and the meditator says, 'I don't know,' that is the wrong answer. If the meditator says, 'Thinking arose dependent upon the perception of wood, and that perception arose dependent on seeing, and that seeing arose dependent upon contact between the physical eye and an external object,' then the teacher knows that the meditator is beginning to observe conditionality.

Have you ever heard the statement, 'Everything is linked to everything else—all is one'? It is a very romantic statement which many seekers of spirituality from varying religious backgrounds like to use in their conversations. Most do not have a single solitary clue as to exactly what it means, but it sounds good, and so they frequently use the expression, 'All is One.'

What it really means is conditionality. It means the whole process I have just described about eyes and seeing and piles of wood. Intuitively knowing conditionality as it occurs is what breaks down self-view. It breaks down feelings of separation and leaves one actually experiencing that 'all is one' and that everything is interlinked.

★ ★ ★

Once self-importance is broken down, the jewel of enlightenment is revealed. Enlightenment can be likened to a jewel covered with layers upon layers of dirt. When we take up spiritual training and work hard at developing impeccability, evenmindedness, and the stopping of growth, we are rubbing away the layers of dirt that cover that jewel.

We are the jewel—it is just that we have allowed dust and dirt to settle upon us, obscuring our true splendour. When we come to meditation, we have made the decision to put a stop to the build-up of dirt and to rediscover our true nature.

When the mind dwells in its true nature, then learning begins. What is learning? It is when the mind blocks out nothing, but experiences everything, pleasant and unpleasant alike, with utter fascination. Thus a simple unpleasant experience, like going to the dentist, is viewed with total interest. One notices the waiting room, the magazines on the table, the peeling wallpaper, the fear of the people sitting silently on the chairs. One notices the dentist. One notices that one does not pay much attention to his room, his assistant, or what he is wearing because the mind has suddenly become filled with apprehension. One notices the physical pain when the drill contacts a nerve. One notices mind's response to that pain. A hundred and one little things are noticed about the dentist and the surgery and one's response which were never noticed when one dwelt in a state of growth. Why? Because in a state of growth, when one visits the dentist, at least half the period of that visit is spent absorbed in concerns about the past or future. One is caught up in a world which has nothing to do with the dentist and what is going on right now. We further blind ourselves by superimposing on to the present event a memory of the way we usually respond at the dentist. So we do not notice how we are actually responding now, which will be quite different from the way we responded last time.

Learning can only take place when we are *with* what is going on, as it is going on. We cannot learn if we miss half the picture by being caught up in the future or the past or in some dead image of the way we think we respond in a given situation.

The stages we go through from birth to death: the stages of acquiring the capacity to walk and talk, getting educational qualifications, forming a relationship, acquiring a home, starting a career, having children—all these are natural stages of change that a human goes through in a lifetime. Just as a human being in the womb starts off as a single-celled organism, goes through various changes which we call growth, then nine months later ends up as a recognisable human with arms, legs, head, and so on, there is no craving in operation whilst this process of physical growth is going on. The stages of external growth that occur once we emerge from the womb and continue until we die do not have craving within them. However, we ourselves add craving to them, because we do not know how to handle our mental responses to these experiences correctly. We add craving or hatred, thus turning an exciting and fascinating experience into a sometimes tortuous nightmare.

An example: a daffodil starts life as a bulb. Dependent on the right conditions of sunshine, rain, soil, and fertilisers coming together at the right time, leaves and then flowers are produced. That daffodil does not need to crave in order to grow. Growing takes place naturally when the right conditions of bulb, light, soil, and water come together. If, however, the daffodil spent its short life saying, 'I wish I was a tulip,' then that daffodil would have a problem. It would suffer. Why? Because it desires to be something other than what it is.

This desiring to be something other than what you are is what I am calling 'internal growth'. Take that away and you are left with your true nature. Your true nature is Reality. It is Buddha. It is complete. It is right as it is. It is beautiful because of its completeness. It is life living naturally, going through all its different cycles when the right conditions are there.

The Spiritual Mind

Many, on coming to Buddhism, quarrel with the tenet on which this whole practical philosophy is based. They quarrel with the statement that the Buddha made that there is suffering. The newcomer to Buddhism says, 'I don't perceive the world as suffering.' Their snap interpretation of the word 'suffering' is too naive.

They arrive at this interpretation by looking at their friends and seeing that, although their friends moan about bills and the cost of living and about the government and about their bosses, they still have a roof over their heads and plenty of food in their bellies. They can afford to go on holiday abroad, to treat their daughters to the latest new hairdo, and to buy their sons the latest Yamaha motorbike. So they draw the conclusion that their friends are, on the whole, a happy bunch.

Newcomers to Buddhism know that they are not suffering from malnutrition or rampant disease or any other major disaster that strikes some people some of the time. In fact, they know that they are not too badly off. Sometimes they are sad, sometimes happy, but weighing everything up, they come to the conclusion that life cannot be labelled 'suffering'.

But this first noble truth of 'there is suffering' is pointing to a much more subtle state. Apart from referring to the obvious that birth is suffering, death is suffering, old age is suffering, disease is suffering, being parted from loved ones is suffering—it is also referring to how the mind will not stay with the present.

Reality, God, *nibbāna*—give it whatever label you like—is to be found in the present. That coolness, that stillness, that total settledness of mind only manifests when the mind stays put with whatever is happening in the moment.

But what do we see when we take a close look at this mind of ours? We find it is off in the future or in the past, or it is caught up in some visual or mental fantasy. *Anything* is more stimulating than the moment. But it is in the moment, not off in the future, that reality dwells. So in our ignorance we are constantly rejecting reality. We are constantly rejecting God. And, as you continue to meditate, so you come to see more and more clearly that this is the case. And then you begin to realise, with horror, that the only label you can possibly give to that habit of the mind to escape from the present, that habit which desires something other than the present, is *dukkha*, suffering.

The mind which rejects the moment is a very materialistic mind. The more the mind stays still, accepting whatever is going on in the internal or external world, making no movement to adjust or change it but just letting it be, the more it becomes the spiritual mind.

We are constantly trying to adjust and change the moment. By this we are saying that the present is inadequate—it is not good enough. Suffering is not accepting things as they are. Suffering is wanting things to be different. 'I' want to be different. 'I' want to be a better person— more loving, more caring, wiser, more artistic, more spiritual. With these goals driving us, we are dissatisfied with ourselves as we are *now*. But we dream that sometime off in the future, when we have done sufficient meditative work, we will become that ideal we strive for, the wiser, more loving, more spiritual person. So right now we are not good enough, and what is that other than a state of suffering? What is that other than *dukkha*? What is that other than the first noble truth?

★ ★ ★

The teachers here use the terms 'pain' and 'suffering' to mean two clear-ly distinct and different things. Suffering is craving and hatred accom-panied by ignorance. It is an inefficient mental action. We choose to crave. We choose to hate.

Pain is a resultant. From a *kammic* point of view it is neutral. We can do nothing about it. It just rises up dependent upon the past and present supporting conditions. What pain actually is, is unpleasant feeling, either of mind or body.

Pain, as such, is all right. What we do with that pain determines whether we suffer or are at peace. If we make a mental movement to get away from pain or if we try to hang on to it, we suffer. If we let that pain be and totally accept it, we are at peace.

We think we do not like to suffer. Superficially, we are always trying to avoid and get away from turmoil. But it is as if there are two levels to the mind: this superficial level and a deeper level. It is the deeper level which desperately clings onto the painful situation. *It loves to suffer.* The deeper level of the mind does not want to give up its suffering. When it suffers it feels it is really human. It feels it can identify with the human race. It feels it is a worthy part of the universe. Because of this sneaky, submerged wrong view that 'I am only a worthwhile human being if I suffer,' there is an almighty clinging to mental conflict.

However, should that suffering reach an unbearable pitch, then the emotions, which are a mixture of thinking and feeling, say, 'Enough, to hell with this *dukkha*!' and the suffering is given up quite easily, without a second thought and without effort.

The struggle to give up mental torture only exists when we *do not actually want* to abandon it. So there are split loyalties. The superficial part of the mind sees craving and hatred as unpleasant, things to be avoided, and it reasons they *ought* to be given up, because then 'I will become a better meditator' because 'Look! I don't cling so much.' But the second part of the mind—the deeper and stronger part—has no intention of giving up this suffering. Why should it? It is thoroughly enjoying it. It is really relishing getting in there and mentally telling so and so how stupid they are or how petty and mean they are or 'how much everyone's misunderstanding me'.

True, the mind and body get somewhat ragged round the edges from all this internal mental fighting with the world. They feel drained of energy because all the energy has been channelled into the 'fight'. But you do not care. You feel the fighting and the turmoil are worth it for the feeling of pleasure and ego-identity the fight gives. What the mind is doing is settling for a lesser, mediocre pleasure instead of aiming for the highest, for the 'ultimate bliss'. However, anyone who undertakes a spiritual training such as this instinctively realises this and has turned his or her sights towards that bliss.

Vipassanā meditation heightens your awareness of that second level of mind, that part that clings and sees intense pleasure in a pathetically painful experience. *Vipassanā* heightens the awareness of that part of the mind that is attached to the wrong view of seeing pleasure in *dukkha*. Because the mind is normally dull to what it is actually up to, it needs a training in awareness to rid the mind of that dullness so that it can see what is really going on. And the more the clarity develops, from constant systematic practice of meditation, *the more the awareness of suffering increases.* Terrible thought isn't it? But before you mentally switch off or rush out in disgust, let me show you the beauty in increasing your awareness of suffering.

As the mind gets sharper, and sees what is actually going on, it starts to see 'truth'. No longer is it clouding the truth by thinking that suffering is pleasurable. It does not see pleasure in craving and hatred any more. It sees only things as they really are: that suffering is painful. The moment it sees that, the mind automatically, without any effort, stops clinging to pain or to jealousy or to resentment or to fear—in short, it stops clinging to any state that is suffering. It naturally abandons them. It is similar to picking up a hot, burning piece of coal from a fire. There is no trying to decide, 'Should I put it down slowly or should I put it down quickly?' There is an automatic, instant dropping of that piece of coal. It is only when the mind has reached a screaming pitch with suffering that it throws up its hands and says, 'Enough is enough!' and drops the whole burden. But as long as the mind is divided, where part of it views unpleasantness as something to be avoided, and the other part views unpleasantness as something pleasurable, worth possessing and hanging on to, then the suffering never reaches sufficient intensity.

We are then left with the delightful paradox: the more you meditate, the more you increase your *dukkha*, but on the other hand, the more you meditate, the more you increase the pleasantness of life and therefore decrease your *dukkha*. How can we have this contradiction? Well, it is like this. The more you meditate and see how things really are— that is, that suffering is indeed painful and not pleasurable—then there is a spontaneous abandonment of that suffering. And as suffering is craving or hatred, depending on which side of the coin you happen to be focusing on, then an abandoning of suffering is a lessening of inefficient states in the mind. With a lessening of inefficiency, you will feel happier, more balanced, more at peace with yourself and the universe.

★ ★ ★

There are well-defined and documented stages that practising *vipassanā* meditators progress through. They are repeated four times at ever more subtle levels as the meditator travels the four paths to enlightenment, each path culminating in a glimpse of *nibbāna*. These stages show the mind becoming more and more aware of suffering and then spontaneously abandoning that suffering. So when you, the meditator, get to that stage known as 'knowledge of misery and disgust', *dukkha* is at its most excruciating heights. Everything you look at lacks lustre and vitality. It seems not worth the bother. This is true even if you dream up a fantasy that usually gives you a rush of pleasure, like going to Barbados for a holiday—those long deserted white beaches fringed with coconut palms and gently lapped by warm seas—and in your fantasy you picture yourself lying in the sun soaking up its warm rays. If sun bathing does not turn you on, then perhaps seeing yourself galloping along a deserted beach at dawn on a handsome white horse—perhaps this will bring that rush of pleasure. If that does not excite you, then perhaps thoughts of exploring the island and examining carefully its vast array of tropical flora and fauna will fill you with that feeling of warmth.

But at the stage of 'misery and disgust' even these fantasies do not turn you on. Any event that usually gives you joy and happiness is seen as flat and lifeless. With all this misery and disgust with yourself and life generally, there begins to grow in the mind a yearning. At first, it is like a very pale weak flame, but then it grows in intensity into a bright, very large, and constantly burning flame. This flame of yearning is a yearning for escape from suffering into freedom from suffering. The mind sees clearly that all conditioned things are *dukkha*, and it yearns for the unconditioned. The unconditioned is *nibbāna*. It longs for *nibbāna*. And the mind realises that the only way it is likely to experience *nibbāna* is by meditating even more. So it decides that it is going to start at the beginning of the meditation practice again. It is going to go back to step one and really do the meditation properly this time.

The reason the mind does not just drop the misery and disgust there and then and drop into *nibbāna*, especially as this area is particularly stressful, is that it has not actually seen fully and clearly how painful it is. So the suffering has to get more intense yet, and this is experienced in the stage known as 'knowledge of re-observation'.

Now, when the suffering gets intense (and at this stage of re-observation pain will be experienced both bodily and mentally), the mind suddenly says, 'Enough is enough,' and it thoroughly accepts the suffering. That is, it sees clearly that suffering is indeed painful. Then it drops into a stage known as 'equanimity about formations'. This is a delightful stage—calm, peaceful, sharp, mindful, buoyant—nothing disturbs it. Whether the object of observation is painful or pleasant, the mind still stays calm, happy, peaceful.

However, the mind has just one little stage further to go. Remember, the *vipassanā* practice has as its objective the experiencing of *nibbāna*. And the price to be paid for such an experience is the giving up of certain cravings and hatreds, like attachment to rule and ritual or attachment to self-view and doubt or attachment to fine-material existence or conceit. It all depends on which of the four paths you are on as to which aspect of craving the mind zeros in on. In order to totally abandon these cravings and hatreds and thus experience *nibbāna*, intuitive wisdom—which is penetration—has to reach a certain pitch.

This pitch is reached when the meditator sees clearly one of the three marks of *anicca* or *dukkha* or *anattā*. If we take, for example, the mark of *dukkha*, which is suffering, then seeing more clearly into suffering, penetrating into its very depths, is only done by having the mind calm, clear, buoyant, equanimous. In this equanimous state, the mind is totally unbiased. It is therefore in a fit condition to thoroughly penetrate. At the stages of 'misery and disgust' and 're-observation' the mind is not unbiased. It wishes only to get away from the suffering, and this very rejection of it is a prejudice which stains the mind and prevents the mind from seeing clearly the true nature of *dukkha*. Suffering reaches screaming pitch in re-observation, but it only does so because we resist. At this point the mind suddenly lets go, stops resisting, and relaxes into the suffering. Now it is in equanimity, and the mind is unbiased towards the suffering and so is clear enough to take a good look and see how *dukkha* comes into existence and then ceases. When this is fully understood, the meditator gets his or her first glimpse of *nibbāna*.

However, this *nibbāna* is self-created. *You* brought it about by your consistent dedication to the meditation practice and by your persistent striving in trying to understand the real nature of the three marks. It is therefore not that total cleansing, that true *nibbāna* which you seek. Unfortunately, you cannot bring that true *nibbāna* into existence.

No amount of meditation or study, no amount of religious observance or dedication to a system of truth will expose it. That which was never lost, that which is before you and has always been before you and will always be before you, will reveal itself only when you are in a fit state to receive it. And you get yourself into that fit state by walking along the path towards the self-created *nibbāna*. When you have walked that same path four times, you can then consider yourself to be in a fit state to receive true *nibbāna*. You have now reached the 'gateway to enlightenment', and the best you can do at this juncture is sit patiently, mindfully and wait until *nibbāna* visits you. Any movement of your mind to hasten its visit is a movement of self, which only delays its appearance.

★ ★ ★

Zen masters have said that the quickest way to awakening is to struggle with a 'doubt-mass'.[1] A 'doubt-mass' is a gnawing problem that the mind chews over and over and allows you no rest. It allows no rest because there is no intellectual answer to the question, only an experiential one, but the mind goes on and on worrying at the question like a dog worrying at a bone. When the appropriate intuitional experience takes place, only then does the mind quieten down, and at this point it is left filled with a sense of spaciousness, a quietness, a knowingness that the answer that has exploded into the mind, which is so simple, is exactly the right one. Sometimes accompanying this experience are feelings of indescribable bliss and happiness.

Occasionally a person will have this sort of experience, this struggle with a doubt-mass, even before they start on any formal spiritual training. And the experience is so devastating it shakes them to their very core, so much so, that they invariably end up undertaking a formal

---

1. Discussion of the 'doubt-mass' and subsequent anecdotes draw on Kapleau, Philip (1979), *Zen: Dawn in the West*, pp.49–52, New York: Anchor Press/Doubleday.

spiritual training.

Roshi Philip Kapleau in his book, *Zen: Dawn in the West*, tells the story of a gentleman who struggled with a doubt-mass after he had been part of World War II, and the outcome of that struggle was such that it changed his whole view of life. He eventually ended up under Kapleau's guidance, practising a formal meditation system.

This man was a plumber from Brooklyn, New York. He had no formal education beyond elementary school and no spiritual bent or religious affiliation. During World War II he spent four years in the Pacific and witnessed a lot of fighting. By the end of the war he was utterly exhausted and spent. He returned to New York and, as he put it, he could not 'work, play or make love'. Everything seemed pointless. But one question kept turning over and over in his mind, 'What is reality?' He puzzled as to where the question had come from considering he had no philosophical or religious bent, but the question just would not leave him alone. He would be walking along the street and the only thing that filled his mind was, 'What is reality?' Sometimes he would bump into people or buildings, so dazed was he by the question. Even at night the question did not go. Sometimes he would wake up at two or three in the morning, unable to sleep, and the first thing that would pop into mind was, 'What is reality?'

This went on for six months. Then one day an explosion took place inside the man and filled him with a joy he had never experienced before in his life. The question just evaporated into thin air. He found he could work again and do the things people normally do. The feeling of elation lasted for about four months, and all that spoilt it was a new nagging question, 'What has happened to you? All this joy and ease aren't normal to you.' He began to feel bad about feeling so good.

His family and friends told him he ought to see a psychiatrist. They told him that he had been through some pretty brutal war experiences and that his joyous feelings were, perhaps, the first symptoms of something worse underneath. The psychiatrists at the veterans hospital were very interested in his case. They put him through routine tests, gave him a few drugs, and began questioning him every day, asking him about his war experiences and the time after he returned to civilian life.

He had a private room and, unlike the other patients, was allowed free run of the hospital. At first, for about a month, he enjoyed this special treatment, but then he got bored with the whole regime and asked his psychiatrist how much longer he had to stay there and, any-how, what was wrong with him. The psychiatrist told him that the next day there was going to be a special meeting amongst the staff about his case, and so he would know the answer soon. A few days later he got the word: 'You've had a conversion experience.' So delighted was he to have an answer at last and to be able to leave the hospital that he did not stop to question the diagnosis and to ask what he had been converted from or to.

It was ten years later, after a friend had lent him Roshi Philip Kapleau's book, *The Three Pillars of Zen*, that the gentleman finally real-ised that what had happened to him was what the Zen practitioners call a *satori* experience.

How quickly each of you come up with an answer to a doubt-mass depends on how deeply the question grips you and how much it disturbs you that the rational, thinking side of the mind cannot come up with an answer. If you are really disturbed, you will work obsessively to find the answer. A Zen Master once said that to come to full awakening, you must act like a man who has fallen into a hundred-foot-deep pit. His thousand, his ten thousand thoughts are reduced to the single thought, 'How can I get out of the pit?' He keeps it up from morning to night and from night to the following morning with no other thought.

* * *

Towards the end of a spiritual journey, just at the gateway to enlight-enment and before real and final enlightenment occurs, a meditator invariably comes up with one such question.

It is a question that seems unsolvable, like 'What is the difference between total, final enlightenment and the self-produced enlighten-ment which is experienced at the end of each path?' The meditator works at this like the man who has fallen down the pit, focusing all his thoughts and energy on that one question. The mind worries and worries away at it until the question explodes and evaporates into thin air, leaving the mind bare, clean, cleansed of every last vestige of self and in a fit state to receive true *nibbāna*.

The question that drives you, the meditator, right from the begin-ning of your search for understanding, whether you are conscious of it or not, is 'How can I be free of suffering?' How strongly you work at solving that riddle depends on how sensitive you are to suffering and how desperately you desire to be free of it. The meditation increases your sensitivity and so speeds your journey towards enlightenment. If your awareness of suffering is not deep enough, then either you will always settle for an intellectual answer to your intellectual riddle, and your life will never be utterly transformed only quietened temporarily, or you will settle for the lesser satisfaction of boosting the ego by enjoying suffering.

Although 'How can I be free of suffering?' is the overall riddle to be solved during your journey along the road towards the gateway to enlightenment, each meditator will come up with other riddles to be solved, or their teacher will goad him or her towards solving an apparently unsolvable question, often with the pupil not even realising that a question has been asked. The questions may range from 'What is devotion?' to 'What is self?' to 'What is comparison?', but each of these questions is really 'How can I be free of suffering?' in another disguise. So all through your meditative path and right to the end, you are focusing your thoughts on a riddle and driving yourself to solve that with the meditation practice.

Surrendering

I once asked a group of meditators if they had heard the phrase, 'Many are called but few are chosen.' Most of them had not. I asked them to have a go at interpreting the phrase. All came up with roughly the same answer, which was that many may listen to a lecture or sermon or may read a book about a spiritual teaching, and that teaching may be based in Christianity or Islam or Hinduism or Buddhism, but very few will actually get down to putting into practice what they have heard or read.

The interpretation that the meditators came up with was reasonable enough, but it did not really penetrate into the true meaning of the phrase. To be fair, I had not given them the complete saying, which is 'Many are called but few are chosen to enter into the Kingdom of God.' But even with the extra bit added to the phrase, everybody still came up with the same interpretation. It is a Christian phrase, and what it means is that many follow the teachings of Christ, but very few are chosen to have a direct experience of God.

If we put that into Buddhist terms, it means that many meditate and put the teachings of the Buddha into practice in their daily lives, but very few become enlightened. There is many a lay person and many a monk and many a nun who apply the teachings of the Buddha to themselves with great dedication and sincerity, and year after year goes by, they get older and older, death looms on the horizon, and yet still enlightenment eludes them. They are not free of distress and limit-ation despite their hours of meditation and their years of practising the spiritual life.

Why? Why can they not come to the fruits of their labours when they spend so many hours practising? The short answer is—they are not practising in the right manner: they are not surrendering. One can spend many an hour at home doing seated practice, or decide to devote one's whole life to *Dhamma* by taking up the spiritual training full-time and going to live in a meditation centre or in a monastery. Yet if one has the wrong attitude, if one does not know how to surrender, one will not come to the end of the spiritual path no matter how many centuries may be devoted to one's own spiritual development.

Before we take a closer look at the word 'surrender' and what it means and what it is that we are supposed to be surrendering to, it is important to mention that although most people who meditate will not become enlightened, in many senses that does not matter. This is because virtually everybody who does take up meditation and treats the spiritual discipline seriously, as more than just a hobby, finds that the quality of their life improves. They find that many of the ideas expressed in Buddhism make such sense to them that they are thrilled by the new concepts they are being exposed to. They also notice that when they spend time thinking about the various aspects of the teaching like suffering, change, how actions have results, rebirth, and so on, they find that all the little anomalies in life—like why some people are poorer than others—start to make sense, and they find that discovery calming.

If a person gets nothing more out of their practice of *Dhamma* than an overall calming effect, an added richness to the quality of life, and a certain understanding where previously there was puzzlement, they have still gained a great deal. This is worth the many hours that are spent meditating and listening to the teaching.

*   *   *

The word 'surrender' does not sit easily on the ear of the average Westerner, because in the West we hear much of the word 'individuality'. The immediate impression is that the words 'surrender' and 'individuality' appear to be at war with one another. It seems an impossibility to become an individual if one surrenders to another person or to another person's ideas. Along with the word 'individual' seem to go all sorts of other words like 'creative' and 'a powerful personality'. All that is good in life is promised to us if we develop our individuality. We are told that we will become more creative, that we will stand out from the crowd, and that if we stand out from the crowd, we will be more likely to get selected for any job that we apply for, despite there being three hundred applicants for the same job. We are told there will be a greater likelihood of promotion if we are an individual, because there will be more chance of getting noticed by the managers. And we are told that people will be more inclined to want to be associated with us if we are an individual, because individuals are not your Mr and Mrs Average, and Mr and Mrs Average can be so dull.

Some therapies teach that you can only be a free and contented person if you develop your individuality, and some spiritual ways also equate individuality with 'union with the highest'. We are conditioned to believe that the list of good qualities and good things that will come our way if we develop our individuality is endless. The benefits of being an individual, therefore, are highly praised in our Western society. Anybody who surrenders to another or to a group ideal is viewed with suspicion. Sentences such as 'she's been brainwashed' or 'he's been hypnotised' are bandied about to try to explain why the person has done this terrible thing of letting go of his or her individuality and surrendering to another. It is regarded as a temporary personality aberration and that the victim will eventually come to his senses and re-establish his separateness, and thus his individuality, once again.

So when a Western spiritual seeker comes across a teaching that says that he or she must surrender to the teacher and surrender to whatever happens in their life, the seeker immediately stiffens. All the inner alarm bells start ringing because *that* word has been used, that dirty word—*surrender*. But if the word is changed and another word is used in its place, like 'acceptance', the seeker immediately relaxes. That word does not have bad associations. But acceptance means the same thing as surrender. Letting go and detachment mean the same thing as surrender. Devotion means the same thing as surrender.

A meditator once commented that the word 'devotion' had always carried an emotional overtone to him. He had always seen it as being an emotional commitment to a teacher, but he was beginning to gather that devotion is something which can be produced by the intellect—

that if one is intellectually convinced that devotion to a teacher is the quickest way through to the cessation of suffering, then one can, as it were, force oneself to go through the motions of being devoted. One would do this by doing everything the teacher tells one to do and by accepting all the praise and blame the teacher directs towards one, and gradually genuine devotion will start to grow. It is not the case that you are either the devotional type or you are not. Devotion is something that each meditator can consciously develop.

The conclusions that this meditator had come to were correct. Only a few pupils are naturally devoted—the rest have to work at devotion. And devotion, like the ability to speak many languages or dance, is a skill which is developed through repeated volitions. The following story will illustrate the point.

There was a man who decided that he would like to take up the spiritual life seriously and felt that the best way to do this was to go and live in a community that was dedicated to this purpose. He read many books on meditation and spiritual training and through his reading came to admire a particular teacher who was a monk and who ran a monastery. The man made an appointment to see this teacher and during the interview asked the monk if he would accept him as a disciple.

One month later he moved into the monastery. He was given a room that was small, cramped, dark, and noisy, because it looked directly onto a main road. He was rather upset about this. He wondered how on earth he was going to meditate with all that traffic noise filling the room. He hated the room. He hated the darkness, the dirtiness, the noise. He thought it was most unfair that he had been given such a terrible room, and furthermore nobody had even bothered to clean it. He felt most unwelcome. It looked as if nobody cared about him— perhaps they did not even want him there. He knew there were better rooms in the monastery which were unoccupied, because he had seen them only the week before when he had been shown around the monastery.

He was having serious doubts about his decision to follow the spiritual life in this particular monastery. He wondered if he had made a mistake. Perhaps he should pack his bags and leave immediately, or perhaps he should seek out the teacher and voice his concerns and ask for a better room.

He decided to speak his mind rather than walk out. He was just about to leave his room to go in search of his teacher when something he had read in a book came flooding back into his mind. It was a passage about how to overcome self-importance. It had stressed that this could be done by letting go of one's wants and surrendering to what life had to offer. He realised that the way he was supposed to handle this situation, if he hoped to lessen self-centredness and thereby develop spiritual wisdom, was to graciously accept the room he had been given and to be quite willing to stay there for as long as the teacher thought necessary. He also realised that he should let go of all his grumbles about the dirt and the size and the noise. He did this and immediately the turmoil lifted. He realised that he had consciously surrendered to the situation and that, if he could take this approach towards everything that occurred whilst he lived in the monastery, he would develop a devotional type of personality, which is a necessary prerequisite for the development of wisdom.

★ ★ ★

To return to the phrase, 'Many are called but few are chosen,' many undertake some form of spiritual discipline, but very few reach enlightenment, because most are not willing to open up *totally* to life and surrender to everything that comes their way, whether it is pleasant or unpleasant. But surrender is all that is needed for it to become possible for enlightenment to visit you.

Once, when a meditator was asked to give an example of an occasion when he had surrendered, he spoke of his involvement with music, which was a great attachment for him. He loved music, and for years he had been very caught up with it, spending all of his spare time playing in a group and composing songs for the group to play. He had many expensive electronic musical instruments and numerous records, which he would listen to for hour upon hour. During a meditation interview he asked about his music and about taking it up as a career. It was pointed out to him that his music was really leading him nowhere, and it was only hindering his progress on the spiritual path because he spent so much physical and mental time obsessed with it. It would be far more fruitful to him if he were obsessed with spiritual values instead of musical ones. After that interview, although the attachment was still there, the meditator became more aware of the limitations of what music had to offer and eventually felt able to give it up completely.

Now that is an example of surrender. It was a terrible shock to him to hear that he was not sufficiently good at music to take it up full time and a bigger shock to hear that he should give it up entirely. He surrendered to the mental shock of what he heard, and he surrendered to the teacher's suggestion as to what was the best direction for him to turn his energies towards. The benefit that this meditator gained from that surrendering was faster progress along the spiritual path because he was devoting so much time to *Dhamma*, instead of splitting his energies between *Dhamma* and music. Now he is beginning to become obsessed with spiritual development. It has been said that a person must want enlightenment like a drowning man wants air, otherwise enlightenment is not possible.

In order to learn the skill of how to surrender to whatever life throws at one, it is easiest to learn to surrender to the path laid down by a spiritual teacher. It is inconceivable that you could willingly surrender to life and yet object to what the teacher says. It is inconceivable that you could surrender to the teacher and yet resist the pleasant and unpleasant events that occur in your life. Most people find it much easier to surrender and be devoted to a person than to immediately advance to surrendering to every little pain and joy that flits across the mind and every difficulty and excitement that occurs in life. One becomes devoted to the teacher, and through doing so one develops the ability to become devoted to life itself. The devoted, surrendering mind is a soft and pliant mind that resists nothing. Only such a mind is worthy of being visited by *nibbāna*.

For lay followers, devotion to the teacher involves being committed to doing one or two hours of meditation a day in the manner instructed by the teacher and carrying out any changes in lifestyle that the teacher may think necessary in order for the spiritual growth of the pupil to be given the best chance of development. For monks, nuns, and full-timers, though, surrender is taken a stage further. It is a question of surrendering for twenty-four hours each and every day—for all that happens in the life of monks, nuns, and full-timers is decided by the teachers. The teachers say what times the disciples will rise and go to bed, what times they will meditate, and what times they will study, what clothes they will wear, what food they will eat, and what tasks they will fulfil each day.

Having to put up with all this sits very uncomfortably with most characters and can resurrect much craving—craving for different foods than the foods one is permitted to eat, craving to eat when one feels like it rather than at set meal times, craving to have more food than is dished up on one's plate, craving to have more sleep, craving to have more or fewer seated meditation periods, craving for more relaxation time, craving to choose one's own daily routine. The list of possible things upon which craving can arise is endless. Hatred too, often arises on many things—hatred of having to live the same routine every day, hatred towards fellow community members, hatred of the type of work one is given to do. Sometimes a disciple is consistently given toilets to clean, and it can seem to him or her as if others in the community get all the creative jobs, such as designing and constructing pathways. This can cause much dissatisfaction.

The daily discipline for monks, nuns, and full-timers is such that it gives constant opportunity to these disciples to practise surrender. And it is surrender that must be practised, not submissiveness, for surrender is a positive act of mind leading towards a lessening of self-centredness, which in turn produces peacefulness, greater clarity, and ultimately en-lightenment itself. Whereas submissiveness is a totally self-centred act, and selfishness only produces more and more unhappiness.

Surrender is a mental act of consciously letting go of wanting one's own way. It is a letting go of physical pain when it occurs. It is a letting go of mental pain when that occurs. It is a conscious letting go of the joy when one is praised and the hurt when one is scolded. Surrender is a refusal to answer back or in any way defend oneself when one is blamed even when the blame is not justified. Surrender is letting go of examining every slight change in one's meditation practice and wondering if it is a sign of progress. Dwelling on such thoughts is self-centred, which is the opposite of surrendering. Surrender is the letting go of examining all of your actions in life, wondering whether they are selfish or unselfish and wanting only to make unselfish actions. The constant wanting to make only unselfish actions is a selfish action. Surrender is a non-selfish act. Surrender is the letting go of cravings and hatreds.

Surrender is being content with life, even if you have hit a problem. Surrender is to trust that everything about life is right as it is, even if

there are troubles at work or in your relationships or in your meditation. Those troubles are right to be there. They are the results of all
the masses of physical and mental actions you have made in the past.
Surrender to the troubles. Let them be. That would be a non-selfish
act. To complain and constantly worry about the troubles is the height
of self-centredness.

Surrender is a mental act consciously chosen by a spiritual seeker as
a way of handling his universe because it produces stillness of mind. It
is consciously chosen, because whenever it is used it instantly breaks
down whatever craving or hatred may be present in the mind at
that moment. Submissiveness, on the other hand, is a selfish act. It is
employed as a way of handling the world for just the opposite reason
to that of surrender. A person submits only when they cannot see any
other way of getting what they want. They submit, not because they
have the development of non-craving and non-selfishness uppermost
in their mind, but as a cunning way of avoiding unpleasantness.

An example would be when a child has done something wrong,
like stealing a pound out of his mother's purse, but the mother will
not correct the child because she knows there will be a big scene
with much shouting and argument and denial coming from the child.
She just cannot face the unpleasant feelings that will rise in *her* when
she confronts the child, and so she lets the whole issue slide by, doing
nothing about it. She has submitted to the child and his temperament
because she wants peace and she wants the child to like her. She is
more concerned about her own mental state remaining undisturbed.
That is selfish. On the other hand, if the mother had surrendered to
the situation, she would have been happy to fulfil her role as a scolding
parent so as to assist another human being to curb his selfishness—no
matter what it cost her in unpleasant feelings—and she would let go of
the event the moment it was finished.

* * *

Monastic discipline can make monks and nuns feel as if they are being
squeezed into a box and all of their individuality and creativity is
being stifled. Not only can monks and nuns feel like this, but many
a meditator feels the same about meditative discipline. But it is not
true that you are being squeezed into a box where the lid is slowly

being lowered and all will go dark and unwelcoming soon. Rather are you being squeezed through a doorway into another, totally new, universe.

You have to let go of the familiar if you are to journey forth into a new area of experience. If you want to hang on to your old ways of eating, sleeping, thinking, your old routines, that is fine, but it means you will stay put in the mental universe you have known for these past years. If you want to journey through that doorway into a new universe, you have to let go of your old habits, which of course will make you feel temporarily insecure because all the old landmarks that made you feel that you are you, have vanished.

You have to trust that your spiritual guide knows the way and that every instruction, every rule, every task that you are given is given for the purpose of leading you towards and through that doorway into that new universe. If there is ever a time that you need to know the art of surrendering, it is when you get to that stage on the path when you feel that you are being squeezed into a box.

For those outside of the monastic discipline, tendencies towards cravings and hatreds can be hidden for long periods of time because you are able to make your own decisions about what things to do and when to do them each day. For example, many people can instantly rearrange their schedule if they do not feel like getting out of bed in the morning because they had a late night or did not sleep so well and they discover they are feeling tired. They rearrange their early morning routine so that they can have a few more extra minutes in bed but still have enough time to scramble into the office by nine. Monks and nuns cannot do this. When the alarm bell goes at six, they have to get out of bed promptly so that they can wash and dress before appearing in the shrine room for the first group meditation of the day.

If your lifestyle is such that you can choose to remain in bed for an extra five or ten minutes, or even an extra half an hour, then you are far less likely to notice the hatred of tiredness. *Because* you can stay in bed a bit longer than a monk or nun can, the edge of the tiredness wears off so that your hatred of tiredness does not immediately become obvious to you. But the moment a person forces themselves out of bed at a set time, either because he is on a residential meditation course or because he is a monk, the craving to linger in bed and get a few more moments of sleep becomes starkly obvious. And if you have to get out of bed at 6am and start functioning intelligently immediately, you notice tiredness very much more quickly. If you are grumpy about being tired, and you pay proper attention to your mental state, you will come to the conclusion that you must have a problem surrounding the whole issue of tiredness versus non-tiredness. And by observing more closely the next time you have to rise at 6am and discover that you feel tired, you will notice that your problem is *attachment* to non-tiredness and *attachment* to the pleasant feelings that accompany non-tiredness.

When you are tired, the body feels heavy and lethargic, which is unpleasant, and the mind is dull, which is also unpleasant. If you are attached to the pleasant feelings that accompany a refreshed body, then when you are forced out of bed at 6am, you will immediately compare the unpleasant feelings of tiredness with the pleasant feelings that you know accompany a refreshed body, and immediately, resentment arises about having had to get out of bed at all. This is when you get grumpy and others avoid you until 11am or thereabouts. The tiredness is no problem. It is just wanting the situation to be different which is the problem. By immediately surrendering to tiredness, which is letting go of your attachment to wanting to feel alive and awake, all the hatred for the tiredness disappears and suddenly there is no problem.

So there are great benefits to having one's life organised by others provided you know how to approach this situation constructively. There has to be a very good reason why all of the world's major spiritual ways use obedience as one of the main disciplines for those of their followers who take up the religious way full time. Some of these religious ways will talk about obedience, others will talk about devotion, others will talk about surrender. All these words mean the same thing and are out to produce the same effect in their followers, which is to reduce self-centredness. But the followers have to be dedicated enough and courageous enough if they are to find the energy within themselves to put the training of obedience and surrender into practice.

* * *

The Western view that everything which is good in life comes to us when we develop our individuality is very true—it is just that the methods suggested for accomplishing this individuality are false. We are conditioned to believe that individuality is achieved by demanding our rights, by establishing our patch, by going out there and getting what we want to make us whole, and by sorting out our problems rather than accepting them. We are told to get angry with those who deprive us of our rights. This is called justified anger. But all that demanding our rights does is develop within us a greater sense of separation and division, making us more unhappy rather than less. If we go about trying to establish individuality using these methods, we become self-oriented, self-important, selfish people. We lose inner freedom rather than developing it.

True and real individuality does bring about freedom, openness, spontaneity, and concern for one's fellow human beings, but this individuality is brought about by completely different methods to those taught to us through our Western upbringing. If you want to receive, you have to give. If you want to receive the right type of individuality, the 'non-selfish' type of individuality, you have to surrender your individuality. You have to give away your individuality. The answer lies in the opposite direction to that which seems obvious. If you are always making efforts to establish your 'rights' in a relationship or your 'rights' within a group, it may appear on the surface that the reason for your unhappiness is that you do not have any rights. But to even think along the lines of 'my rights' is a self-important act, which just guarantees that you are going to become more separated out and therefore more and more unhappy.

Give up your rights. Give up your individuality. Demanding to be appreciated as an individual is only the cry of the ego. Give it up. Learn to surrender 'your rights'. Learn to surrender what you think you *ought* to have in life. Learn to surrender to pleasure and pain, praise and blame, success and failure. Learn to surrender joyfully to all that comes your way, whether you understand the reasons for it being there or not. The fact that it is there, is right. If you can surrender, then the joy and the beauty of a life without craving and hatred will be revealed to you. Only when there is no craving and no hatred in your nature can you be said to be a true individual.

The Purpose of Life

I want to talk to you about why you are here on this planet Earth and whether there is or is not a purpose to life. Do you know for certain, inside of yourself, the reason for your being alive, or have you decided that life is a pointless, meaningless exercise which must be endured and thank goodness when it is all over? Is life, for you, a matter of 'Life is hard and then I die,' and has it no more point to it than that?

Or do you perhaps read meaning into every puff of wind, every golden sunset, every being that crosses your path, and every black cat you set eyes upon? Do you have so much meaning in your life that you have become confused and forgotten the prime reason for your visit to this human realm? Are you shooting off in so many meaningful directions that you are scattering your energies and not leaving energy to focus in on the task that you have set yourself to do in this lifetime?

And what is that task? Many cannot see any purpose to life at all, look and search as they may. To them it seems that we are born, grow up, get relationships, lose relationships, get jobs, lose jobs, acquire a lot of possessions—and for what? For death! In the end we die and cannot take any of these things with us which we have acquired on Earth. We cannot take our relationships with us nor our children nor our possessions. So why work extremely hard for these things? Why fight and get passionate and make enemies of your loved ones over things which are only going to vanish in the end anyway?

Intellectual acquisitions are not much more satisfactory either.

We twist ourselves all out of shape for an exam. We study hard, feeling constantly under pressure, perhaps breaking out in pimples from the strain of it all—and for what? For the knowledge to be there in your memory one day and then gone the next? How much do you remember of that maths exam you studied so hard for when you were fourteen or that literature exam you crammed for at university? If you were to sit those exams today with no preparatory study, you would fail them. All that such musings point out is that intellectual things are ephemeral too, just like relationships, cars, houses, and children. They come. They go. Is the purpose of life really to sweat and strain and put ourselves under pressure just to acquire intellectual knowledge which is lost to us only a few months after we sit an exam?

Perhaps our purpose in life is to have children. But what of children? They are born, grow up, and then they are gone. And in the raising of those children is yours a story of material sacrifices, sleepless nights, arguments, and worries—all the usual things that accompany the raising of children? Is the purpose of life really to labour hard for children? And for some the story of child rearing will have a very unpleasant twist at the end, with their children leaving home, deciding never to have anything more to do with their parents. Is this your story? Did you really go through all of those years of sacrifice just for your children to reject you? Is there any purpose at all to such a pattern in life? Or were those eighteen years of child raising in the prime of your life just wasted, pointless years?

* * *

So, why are you here? What is it you are supposed to get out of your fifty or sixty or seventy years on Earth? What is it you are supposed to get out of careers, possessions, relationships, and family life?

Well, you are not meant to *get* anything out of life at all. The very experiencing of life *is* the purpose of life. If at the end of your fifty or sixty or seventy years you can stand on one side and say 'Look what I've got out of life. I've got a degree, a spouse, a child, a home. I have all these things. Haven't I done well?'—then you have missed the point of life. You have made the incorrect assumption that the purpose of life is to produce something, when the true purpose of life is the experiencing of a particular lifestyle.

Before we are born we select certain events we wish to experience in our forthcoming life and people we wish to have an intimate relationship with. We may choose to experience poverty or illness or riches or unemployment. We may choose to be a banker or a sailor or a disabled child.

If we have spent many lifetimes doing one particular thing, like being a musician, for example, and we feel that we have thoroughly understood this way of life so that we are no longer developing internally, then we will choose a different lifestyle for our next human life. We may choose to be a manual worker, such as a carpenter, just to experience what it is like to work with our hands. And we will cut off entirely all those centuries and lifetimes of musical knowledge, showing little or no talent for music during our life as a carpenter.

The lifestyles we choose, we choose because we haven't yet experienced them or because we haven't yet had our fill of that particular way of living. For example, a person may be a gangster in one lifetime but does not feel that he has experienced enough of being a gangster in just one short life. He has not fully used up the experience. He has not outgrown it, and so he chooses to be a gangster life after life until he has had enough of that particular experience.

* * *

We have great curiosity about experiencing. You can observe how much experiencing means to you and how experience *is* the end product by taking a look at children and their relationship to smoking. Many children have had a puff on at least one cigarette by the time they get into their teens. And yet most parents would prefer their children not to smoke until they are adults and preferably not even then.

But do children take any notice of tales about how bad smoking is for their health? Do they take any notice of threats of punishment should either of their parents catch them smoking? Do children take any notice of their friends' tales about how smoking is not as great as it is said to be—'You just cough and splutter, and the smoke tastes terrible, and you can feel sick after the first inhalation of smoke'? Children take no notice whatsoever of disaster tales. They take no notice of threats from their parents or threats to their health. Children want to know for themselves what it is like to smoke. They want to experience the act of smoking and all that goes with it—the feel of the smoke in their mouths, and the coughing, spluttering, and nausea, should that be the way they react. They even want to experience that their parents might catch them in the act and punish them. Children want all of this. And the fact that they do not know exactly how the experience of smoking is going to turn out for them is part of the joy. Children do not want to read about smoking in a book or listen to others' tales about it—they want to experience smoking for themselves.

And we are all like that—full of curiosity about life in the human realm, and what it is like to experience being poor or uneducated or educated or a builder or a newspaper magnate. Would you believe it?— we are even curious about what it is like to go through the rigours of a spiritual training. It is the experiencing of the training and the sweat and strain of working towards enlightenment which intrigues us and is what we are after. We are not after the end product of enlightenment. After all, we are already at the end as we are already enlightened. But we have chosen to forget that small fact so that we can play the game of experiencing the spiritual journey.

Because of our curiosity about experience, we love to explore different lifestyles, but in each lifetime we choose to explore only a small fragment of the huge range of lifestyles available to us. The nature of curiosity is such that curiosity takes us into all sorts of areas of life. Sometimes these areas are delightful, but sometimes they are painful. We are happy with both delight and pain, for we want to know what it *feels* like to be delighted and what it *feels* like to be in pain. We want to know what it *feels* like to be a gangster or what it *feels* like to be a spiritual traveller. But we have lost this knowledge that we are happy with all types of experience whether good or bad, pleasant or unpleasant. We have lost the knowledge that we are only after the experiencing itself. The more we lose the knowledge that the purpose of life is to experience, the more our inner world goes dark, and life is no longer fun and exciting. It becomes tortuous and painful because we fall into hankering after something other than the life we have chosen.

For example, if you are a mother and only a mother, you may hanker after having a career as well as being a mother so as to make life more interesting. If you are a businessman with many business commitments and family responsibilities, you may hanker after the quiet life of the monk. If you are a meditator who has difficulty concentrating, you may hanker after being able to concentrate. If you have a short fuse temper, you may hanker after being placid. Whenever you hanker after anything that you do not have, whether that 'anything' is a different way of life or a different personality to the one you have, then your world goes dark and you are in pain.

This is when you take up a spiritual way so as to raise your awareness of why you are here and what the point of it all is. And you learn from this spiritual way that you need to train yourself to live in the moment. When you can do this, then you will be content with whatever life-style you have chosen, whether it is that of a student or that of a mother or that of a father or that of a monk. When you are content with the lifestyle that you have chosen, you will be fully engrossed in experiencing all of the events that occur, all the joys and pains, the ups and downs, that occur within the life you have chosen to live.

★ ★ ★

Why do we sometimes choose painful events like the illness of cancer or the pain of divorce? We choose these when we get stuck, when we settle into rigid patterns and there is no more experiencing taking place, like in a relationship that has become too settled, too automatic. It has become rigid. We no longer look at it. We no longer experience the relationship. We no longer feel the relationship. It has gone dead. When this happens we choose to shake it up by having an affair or getting our partner to have an affair, or we break it up totally and head for the divorce courts just so as to change the rigid pattern our life has settled into.

When we or our partner are having an affair or we are going through a divorce, there is a lot of pain and frustration—but we are experiencing once again. We are feeling once again. There is life in our world once more. It is no longer predictable. It is no longer safe, and therefore it is no longer dead. But be quite clear that, in fact, *you* have chosen the stress and the pain of disrupting your everyday familiar pattern so as to shake yourself free of an unproductive phase. You need to change in order to grow again, in order for you to laugh and feel alive and be joyful once more.

If we are in a stifling marriage, but we do not quite have the courage to walk out of it or to have an affair but know deep down inside of ourselves that the situation must change because we are dying inside a bit more each day, then we manipulate our partner to the point where he or she is the one who has an affair or is the one who walks out on us. The result is exactly the same whether it is us or our partner who walks out. The rigid, unproductive lifestyle we have allowed ourselves to get trapped into is shaken up. Once this happens, we start to experience and live again. We start to look at life from a fresh angle.

The whole point is that we choose whatever happens to us, thus making us masters of our own destiny. We choose to break up the relationship ourselves, or we choose to have the dirty deed done to us. We choose to experience the pain of separation and divorce. We are after the experience. We want to know what it feels like. We are curious about the whole experience of separation. We are not wanting to head away from the separation and divorce and hurry on out to a space beyond the divorce. It is the separation, the divorce, and everything that goes with that event that we are after. It is only when we do not know the purpose of life that we think we are after the space and the time beyond the divorce, which we imagine is a happy space.

So if you have an unsatisfactory job, or your business is going wrong, or you have got the sack, or you are expecting a child and are fearful of what the presence of that child in your life will mean to you and your partner, or you are not expecting a child but desperately want one—stop for a moment and look at what is happening in your life. If your job is unsatisfactory or your business is going wrong or you have got the sack or you are pregnant or not pregnant, that is exactly what *you* want.

Let us take the example of a dead-end job. You find it unsatisfactory. That is what you want. At this point in time you want an unsatisfactory job. You want to experience the boredom and frustration of a dead-end job. You want to experience, in every atom of your being, the frustration and boredom of the situation. You want to experience trying to get out of that situation. Only when you are satisfied that you have wrung every ounce of juice out of being bored and frustrated will you choose to find yourself a stimulating and satisfactory job. Up to this point all doors will be closed to you. Every job application that you send out will either not receive a reply or, should you happen to get to the interview stage, the interviewer will decide you are not suitable for the position and so will not offer you the job.

It is you who choose what happens in your life. When you have had enough of a particular experience and feel that you have learnt enough and have grown enough from that event, it ends. Then new situations and people enter your life, and you set off in an entirely different direction to experience something else. This time you may choose to experience great happiness. You may choose to meet someone and have a love relationship. You may choose to become a mother or a father and experience the joys of parenthood. You may choose to take a long sabbatical so as to experience the joy of not having to *do* anything in particular, like not having to get up at six in the morning in order to be in the office by nine.

If you are to be content with your lot and wring every ounce of juice out of whatever situation you find yourself in at any given time, then it is important for you to become conscious that you are after the experience itself and are not after a space beyond the experience. You are not marking time, waiting till you get to a more meaningful area in your life so that you can begin living. You are not wanting to rush through the experience so as to come to the relief of the end of this difficult time—where you imagine life will suddenly become more peaceful, more satisfactory, more meaningful, more aware.

Life becomes instantly more meaningful, more peaceful, more satisfactory, and more filled with awareness when you wake up to the knowledge that the unsatisfactory job or the unsatisfactory relationship or the childlessness or the being rushed off your feet and not having enough hours in a day has been chosen by you and it is exactly what you want to experience at this point in time.

★ ★ ★

Incidentally, unless we are aware that we choose the life we have now, that we choose the events, the situations, and the people that come into our life and influence us, there will be times when we lose control of our life and mistakenly come to the conclusion that we are victims of life's whims. We see ourselves as innocent, pure as the driven snow, minding our own business, and then others come along and upset the apple cart, or events come along, such as bankruptcy, which mess up our whole life. That is when you hear the cry, 'What have I done to deserve this?'

If we do not become aware that we create the universe we live in, then we will come to the conclusion that we can no longer shape the direction in which our life goes. When this happens, we feel very sorry for ourselves and get locked into a negative state of mind, feeling bitter and twisted about life and how we cannot control it. This negative state is a hell state of desperation and confusion which we may dwell in for months or years.

As it so happens, we have even chosen to experience this hell state which is filled with fears and resentments, phobias, and uncertainties, but by this time we have become so unaware of the purpose of life and what our task in life is that we do not know that we have chosen this hell state or the lifestyle we have. Not knowing these things, we feel that we are so often being tossed from pillar to post, victims of life's ebbs and flows.

★ ★ ★

Our life's purpose is to experience the lifestyle we are now living, which we chose before we were born. Every time we attempt to rush through an experience so as to get to another experience which we believe will be more worthwhile, we cause ourselves a lot of unnecessary pain. Only when we have fully used up one experience, will we move on to another. This happens naturally. When change happens naturally, it means we are still focused only on experiencing. But when we force change, we are no longer focusing on experiencing. Rather, we are focused on getting to an end point and producing something. That something may be a different mental state or it may be a different career. When we stop focusing on just experiencing, our world goes dark.

So our true task in life is to raise our awareness to the point where we come to see that the purpose of life is to sink into and experience all events that come our way. We have to see that we have chosen these events just so as to feel what they are like. Our task in life is to become aware that there is no end point that we are supposed to be getting to—that experiencing what is happening in our lives right now *is* the purpose of life. All spiritual ways drive their followers towards exactly this understanding. Living contentedly with what one finds in the moment is *nibbāna.*

Once we stop looking for something other in life than what we have now, then we start to be content with the way things are. We become content with just experiencing, even if that experience is a divorce. When this happens, we are living in the moment, and there is a lightness and a thrill to life which we have not previously experienced, and we find that we love this game called life, and we play the game with great relish. We do not try to get rid of any of it or preserve any of it. We just let it flow and experience whatever is presenting itself in the moment, being fully aware that the purpose of life is to experience, and therefore it does not matter to us whether that experience is a business succeeding or failing. We have the certain knowledge that we want that, and only that, particular experience at this moment.

* * *

We are all enlightened already. We all have the knowledge that we choose our path through life, and that we take birth in this human realm in order to experience what this realm has to offer. But in order to be born at all, we have had to choose to ignore this knowledge. And because we ignore this knowledge, we end up focusing in on the wrong things like expecting everlasting satisfaction and great pleasantness from the lifestyle we have selected. The life we choose does give us certain pleasantnesses and satisfactions, but it does not give us the everlasting satisfaction we expect.

We choose this lifestyle, then that one, then another, each lifestyle gradually leading us towards a life where our main preoccupation is with spiritual awakening. The spiritual training then leads us right back to the forgotten knowledge that experience is an end in itself, and that to aim for only pleasantness and satisfaction is to focus on the wrong things. The training also leads us back to the knowledge that we choose all the events and people who enter our lives.

When this knowledge is lost to us, we view life as a burden, or alternatively we enjoy life but do not enjoy it to the full because we are so often plagued by thoughts that we have not extended ourselves fully, that we do not know ourselves thoroughly and therefore have not actualised our true potential. When we have the knowledge that experience is an end in itself, we are no longer trapped and sorrowful.

We find life thrilling. We open ourselves up to life, not avoiding any of it and fully understanding our role in the scheme of things.

Meditation and Work

Humanity's lot is to work. Everybody from the seven-year-old to the seventy-year-old has to work. Nobody can live in the human realm and escape the task of work. Every one of us, no matter what our age, sex, or social class, we all have to spend anything from three to sixteen hours a day working.

Seven-year-olds work. They work at their school lessons. When at home they work at their homework and at whatever small household tasks their parents ask them to do.

Eighteen-year-old teenagers work. If still at school, they work at their school work. If at university, they work at their degrees. If they have left school and are not going on to university, they will be searching for employment. It will involve them in many hours of pouring over newspaper adverts, going to a job centre or employment agency, writing for jobs, filling out application forms, going for interviews—all of this is work. When they have finally got a job, they work again, but this time their work is of a different nature to the work they were engaged in when seeking employment.

Newlyweds work. They spend many hours searching for a place to live in together. When they eventually find it, they then have to decorate it and furnish it. This takes work. Often many long, tiring, dirty hours are devoted to decorating. No doubt they both have jobs to go to during the day, which is more work. When they get home, not only do they have to work at the painting and decorating, but they also have to work at feeding themselves, washing their clothes, and keeping their home clean and tidy.

Mothers and fathers work. They go out daily, for eight hours, to some form of employment so as to earn money to support their families. But their work does not end here. They have many hours of cleaning, washing, shopping, and cooking to do, as well as having to nurse their spouses and their children when they are ill. They have to look after and feed children and children's friends. They often help with their children's homework. And they give parties for their children on their birthdays. They may have houses, gardens, and cars. Maintaining these items in a clean and functioning state requires work. Household accounts have to be looked after, and this involves either the husband or the wife in several hours of work per month. All of this involves work.

Retired people work. They have to eat and keep their bodies and homes clean, tidy, and functioning. This takes work and several hours of it per day.

The unemployed and the lady or gentleman of leisure also have to work. Like retired people, they have to feed and wash themselves, keep their homes tidy, pay the bills, and deal with officialdom. It all takes time. It all involves physical or mental work. One might be tempted to think that the lady or gentleman of leisure are the ones who have the least amount of work to do out of anyone, because they usually employ staff to do their cooking, cleaning, and gardening. But staff have to be managed. This takes work. And most people with a lot of money have to invest it wisely or use their money in some sort of business venture, or they very quickly end up with no money at all. Witness football pools' winners who are not used to handling vast sums of money. Research done on them shows that several years after winning, the majority of pools' winners are penniless. Why? Because they do not know how to handle the vast amounts of money of which they are suddenly the owners. They do not invest their money, or if they do, they do not invest it wisely. They do not realise that they have to do something constructive with their winnings in order for them to last their lifetimes. After X number of years of freely spending, there is no money left in the kitty for the majority of pools' winners. Managing a personal fortune involves the owner of that fortune in work.

Recluses, too, have to work. They have to obtain food, which is usually done by begging and may involve the recluse in a couple of hours of walking in order to reach a village where the villagers are happy to feed him. Recluses have to keep themselves and their few meagre possessions clean. All this is work. They also have to work at their meditation and whatever other spiritual disciplines they are involved in, such as studying the holy books.

So you see, nobody, but nobody, no matter what their age or what their station in life, escapes work. It is one of those conditions that goes along with living in the human realm.

Meditators who realise that a vast proportion of every day is taken up with work may well get rather depressed. They wonder how on earth they are going to get anywhere with the meditative life if they have to spend so much of every day working.

To make matters worse, such people invariably have noticed that when they sit down to meditate, their minds are jammed with thoughts about the work they have just done or the work they are about to do when they finish meditating. University students spend much of their hour's meditation thinking about their studies. School teachers think about the classes they have taught that day and how well they did or did not turn out, and they design new ways of approaching the subjects they teach. Parents spend their meditation hours thinking about their day's work, or they are planning menus and shopping expeditions and thinking about the tasks which still need doing before they can call it a day and retire to bed. And unemployed people spend their time fretting about the work they have not done that day. Of course, nobody spends the *whole* hour thinking about work—meditators do sometimes apply themselves to the meditation object, that of watching the rise and fall of the abdomen associated with breathing and all other sensory objects.

You see, the quantity of time that you spend each day absorbed in a certain object conditions the sort of thoughts you will find constantly running through your mind. That is the way the mind works. If you are an accountant and you spend eight hours a day pouring over office accounts, then a great deal of your thoughts and feelings are going to be caught up with figures and balance sheets, profit and loss, and the people who assist you or thwart you in your attempts to carry out your accounting work. So, whatever your line of work is, that is what will occupy your thoughts—that work plus the people involved with you in that work.

This is why people go on retreats. If they spend eight hours a day meditating, listening to lectures on meditation, and reading books on the subject, then thoughts about their worldly work start to fade, and thoughts and feelings about spiritual work and how to become a better meditator start to take over.

A really important question arises. If one's thoughts and interests are conditioned by what one does during the day, is it at all possible to spend the major portion of every day involved in work which is not connected with the meditative life and yet turn it into a meditation? The answer is that it most certainly is. In fact, I would go so far as to say that if you cannot find out how to turn your daily work into a meditation, then your meditative progress is going to move at a snail's pace, because everybody, from the layman to the monk, spends more time each day involved in work than in seated meditation.

So how do you turn work into meditation? There are two approaches to be combined. One is the way of control. The other is the way of understanding. Control is pulling the mind back into the present moment and paying exquisite attention to whatever you are doing in that moment. If you are preparing a meal, pay attention to that activity. Be aware that you are chopping or stirring or frying or selecting ingredients to go into the meal, rather than letting your mind wander off into dreaming about the past or the future, which has nothing whatsoever to do with the meal you are preparing right now.

This constant bringing of the attention back into the present, to be aware of what you are doing in the moment, is meditation. Constant repetition of this process heightens your awareness of what is going on in your body and mind. This is the way of control because your mind is forever wandering away from the object you have placed it on, and you are constantly saying, 'No no, don't wander off there. Come back here and stay put on *this* object.' So you are controlling the mind—you are placing it where *you* want it to be. Conscious control is what is used in concentration meditation. The constant pulling of the mind back into the present moment and being conscious of the work that you are involved in, in that moment, is a form of concentration meditation.

Combining this with attention to the three marks will turn your work into *vipassanā* meditation. This means combining awareness of the moment with the way in which the moment is transient, unsatisfactory, and non-self. It is this approach that develops wisdom, and the development of wisdom is the main aim of *vipassanā* meditation.

★ ★ ★

Let me give you some practical examples of how to turn work into *vipassanā* meditation. I will use the example of mowing the lawn. Forgive me for so frequently using cooking or cleaning or gardening examples. I use these because the majority of you, whether you are male or female, spend a proportion of every week involved in this form of work. Also, it is extremely relevant for our full-time meditators, monks, and nuns, as this is the type of work which they are occupied with each day. So I keep picking examples of activities that I know all of you have done at one time or another.

Let us say it is a sunny, summer day, and you decide to get out the lawnmower and cut the grass. You spend several hours not only mowing the grass, but also trimming the edges with shears where the lawn joins the flower bed. When you have finished, you stand back and admire the work that you have just done. You may even say to yourself or to someone who is standing within earshot, 'That's a job well done. The garden looks so much better now that the lawn has been cut.'

But, by the next morning, what has happened? The lawn does not look quite so good any more. The wind blew during the night, depositing a shower of rose petals across the grass, making the lawn look quite untidy. Also, the grass has grown a few millimetres since yesterday, and so no longer does it have that flat, rolled, immaculate look it had just after you had cut it. And the dogs got out early this morning, chasing one another across your newly cut grass, scuffing it as they dashed about.

The lawn does not look anything like as neat and attractive as it did yesterday. Isn't this somewhat unsatisfactory, this change—the fact that your neat lawn no longer looks so neat, and that the grass has gone and grown, meaning that in four or five days time you are going to have to mow it all over again? Wouldn't it be wonderful if you could mow your grass once and that would be it for life? It would stay in that short, neat style forever, never involving you in any more work again.

Observing the three marks in everything is your task as a *vipassanā* meditator, so let us take a look to see if the three marks of change, unsatisfactoriness, and non-self can be found in the act of cutting the grass.

A lawn, from the moment you cut it and tidy it up, is starting to change—it is growing, things are falling on it. So from the moment you have mowed it, you can start to observe *anicca*, the mark of change, happening to that lawn.

Then look for the second mark, which is that all things are unsatis-factory. Why are they unsatisfactory? They are unsatisfactory because they are not permanent, because they *do* change. Trying to keep your grass neat and tidy is an unsatisfactory task because you cannot do it once and for all and that is it for life. It is a drag that you are going to have to mow that lawn and tidy it up yet again. Being conscious of this aspect of grass cutting means you are observing the mark of *dukkha*, unsatisfactoriness.

Next, look for the third mark, the mark that things are *anattā,* non-self. What this means is that things are conditioned and therefore outside your control. Grass grows due to conditions. It has to be planted in soil if it is to grow. If you laid grass seed down on a concrete path and watered it, nothing would happen—it would soon shrivel up and die. So one of the conditions necessary for grass to grow is soil. Apart from soil, grass also needs the right nutriments in the soil, and it needs water and a particular intensity of sunlight. Remove any of these conditions and the grass will not grow. Remove the sunlight, let it be an overcast, dull January day, and what happens? The grass just does not grow. If the growth of grass was not conditioned, then it would come under the control of your will. You would be able to say, 'Grass, do not grow. Remain the way I have just cut you for the remainder of your days as this makes life easier for me and involves me in less work.' Unfortunately, the growth of grass *is* conditioned, so the lawn is outside your control and will not behave in the manner you would like it to. Point this factor out to yourself. In so doing you are consciously and deliberately noting that things are conditioned. You are noting the mark of non-self with respect to grass cutting.

Can you see that in a simple job of work, like mowing a lawn, your wisdom can grow, *provided* you observe the right things about the mowing of that lawn? For you must consciously observe the three marks during the cutting of and after you have cut the grass. If you are only aware of the present activity of pushing the lawn mower but do not view the task through the filters of the three marks, you are not doing *vipassanā* meditation.

* * *

All the things I have just pointed out about the lawn getting untidy the moment you have finished mowing it and how unsatisfactory this is and that it grows due to conditions are obvious, are they not? Which means you have already observed all the points I have mentioned for yourself, but how conscious was that observation? Isn't all this under-standing lurking below the surface, and hence it is obvious when it is pointed out, but you do not go round *consciously* observing these things for yourself. And to consciously note to yourself these three marks of change, unsatisfactoriness, and non-self with respect to all the jobs you do is the task that you should set yourself if you wish to develop wisdom.

Once you get the hang of viewing work in this way, you will find it is quite easy to do. For example, do you do any painting and decorating? Around your home, perhaps? When did you last paint the outside of your house? Or the outside of your windows? Well, from the moment you finish painting, that paint job is beginning to crumble and decay. A bird flies overhead and does an unmentionable on your freshly painted window sill—instant *dukkha* at this bit of change from freshly painted to not so freshly painted. You can get a cloth and wipe the mess off the window sill, but you cannot stop the rain and the wind and the sunshine falling on your new paint, all of which are the conditions that bring about a change in the paintwork and make it crumble and decay, meaning you will have to repaint the window in a few years time. This is unsatisfactory as it creates more work in your already crowded life.

So next time you paint those window frames, note how their colour and condition changes from the moment you finish the job. This would be observing the mark of change. Note that because the paintwork does not remain the same for year after year, it is unsatisfactory. This, then, would be observing the mark of unsatisfactoriness. And note also that the paintwork crumbles and decays because of conditions like wind, rain, sunshine, birds, and the lack of cleaning, and that you cannot do a thing about it—it is outside your control. This would be noting the mark of non-self.

If you decide that because it is all going to crumble and decay anyway, why bother to do the painting in the first place, note that such an attitude is an act of hatred. By that statement you would effectively be saying, 'Because I cannot control the paint and get it to remain in a permanently good state, I am not going to bother to paint the window frames in the first place.' Sulk . . . sulk.

Remember, the walker along the spiritual path is learning how to throw himself or herself into life and live it to the full with all its ups and downs and yet not hate the downs nor crave for the ups. Everything you do, from cleaning your teeth to making a meal to mowing a lawn to getting married to having children to producing an artistic masterpiece to acquiring fame to acquiring psychic powers, is going to crumble and vanish. You can have the attitude that 'As it is all going to crumble and vanish, why bother to work at anything. I might as well cut my throat now and be done with it.' This is the hate response. Or you can ignore the fact that whatever you work for is subject to change and decay and death and thereby madly, passionately acquire and hang on to this and that. This is the craving response. Both responses will cause their owners a great deal of grief. People who have the hate response suffer because they see life as futile, a waste of time and energy, because everything crumbles and dies in the end. This realisation makes them depressed. People who have the craving response are fine until they cannot get what they want or are parted from one of their possessions, like their relationships ending or their holidays coming to an end, and then they too grieve.

When we have developed wisdom we know that whatever work we do will need doing again. For example, if we clean the house, by tomorrow it will need cleaning again. We know that a clean house is a very temporary thing, that it is *dukkha* to have to keep cleaning it, and that what happens to a cleaned house once we have finished the job is outside of our control. The person who has developed understanding knows all of these things in the depth of his or her being but is not depressed or elated by this discovery. The one who understands lives life *as if* these marks do not exist whilst knowing full well that they *do* exist. He or she lives life intensely, as if every job matters, whilst knowing that nothing matters because everything crumbles and vanishes. The one with wisdom is not disturbed by this knowledge.

If you could keep your attention in the present moment and

remember to frequently stand back from your work and see the marks of change, unsatisfactoriness, and non-self in those tasks, then you could become enlightened through the medium of work. However, most people find that they have so many hindrances running around in mind for so much of the day that they fall into their thoughts and forget all about the work they are engaged in. When this happens, they do their job in a dull, automatic way whilst lost in thoughts of recriminations about the past or dreams about the future.

Then there are those who enjoy their work so much that they have no difficulty in concentrating on what they are doing. However, such people usually get so absorbed in their work that they completely forget to look at it from a meditative point of view. So they do not see it as changing or unsatisfactory or conditioned.

* * *

In order to get the mind to stay in the moment and see your work in terms of the three marks, you have to sit down in a chair each day and meditate. You have to read books and attend lectures so as to remind yourself what it is you should he doing if you wish to develop spiritual wisdom. The reason you get lost and forget all about staying in the moment and viewing things in terms of the three marks is that there is a lack of repetition.

Let us say you were to collect a few stones and place them on a sideboard in your home. Then, four times a day, every day, you dust the stones down, light a few incense sticks, and place these, plus a small dish of fresh flower petals, in front of the stones. If you were to keep this practice up for three months, you will find that at the end of that period you will be much more interested in stones and will know far more about them than you did three months previously. When you go walking, you will find that you notice the stones on the ground beneath your feet. You will realise that before you collected the stones and placed them on your sideboard, you had not really been aware of the existence of stones when you went out for walks. But now you notice their size and shape and colour. If somebody gives you a Christmas present of a book about stones, you will be delighted with the present, whereas three months previously, you would have been horrified by such a present.

This interest and knowledge about stones has come about only because you constantly turned your attention several times a day, every day, towards those stones on your sideboard. This is the way the mind works. Turn your attention frequently towards something, and you will develop an interest and a knowledge about that thing, whether that thing is a career, a relationship, stones, or meditation.

Little wonder then, if you spend eight hours a day in the office, that your thoughts during most of your waking hours are concerned with the office. You do not have to particularly like going to the office or like the type of work you do once you get there—you only have to frequently turn your attention towards the job to discover that you start to spend more and more time thinking about it, and that your knowledge and expertise at your job increases. Apply this same principle of constant attention towards the meditation by sitting down and meditating every day, reading books, and listening to lectures on the subject, and you will find that meditation and how to do it more effectively starts to occupy more and more of your thoughts. You will notice that you are becoming far more interested in the whole subject of the spiritual life.

From this constant turning of your attention frequently towards meditation, one day you will wake up to the fact that you are often living in the present moment compared to the way you used to be, that is, unconscious of what you were up to in mind and body for much of the day. You will realise, too, that your understanding of how craving and hatred come about and how to stop indulging them is also growing because of your constant attention to the three marks of all conditioned things whilst doing the seated practice and whilst working, and that with this growing wisdom your mind is settling. It is becoming less and less occupied with suffering.

Seeking for Happiness Brings Unhappiness

If we come across a new therapy or a new consciousness-raising group or a new religion and it promises us happiness, we are immediately interested. If it promises us a better life, a better future, that we will become better people—more tolerant, more tranquil, wiser—we want this new approach to living. We immediately want to join this new group.

Always we are seeking to become different, which is tantamount to saying that right now we do not like what we are. We consider ourselves not up to scratch. We consider ourselves inadequate in the area of relationships or intellect or career or meditation—it could be anything whatever. This inadequacy disturbs us. We feel sure that some time off in the future we will be more satisfied with ourselves, but only once we have mastered a psychic power or two or have a less hectic lifestyle or when we have more money or have learnt how to overcome the mental hindrances. Once we have corrected what we see as our inadequacies, then we will be more satisfied with our performance as human beings. And we will *really* be content and start living life to the full when we have learnt how to get on to the spiritual path and are heading towards enlightenment. Always happiness and fulfilment lie off in the future when we are different from the way we are right now.

We try to change ourselves and what we are experiencing in the moment because we believe that it is the only way to become happy. Always we seek happiness, and the very seeking makes us feel constricted and unhappy.

★ ★ ★

How many of you sit down to meditate, shut your eyes, and immediately feel heavy, dull, bored, and have various aches and pains in the body? Why? Because you seek. When you meditate you seek to become something other. You find it impossible to sit and be content with the moment—which is true meditation.

You are constantly seeking to change yourself. You seek to become different. You seek to fill your universe with light and joy and happiness. But that very seeking prevents you from getting happiness. That very seeking makes you miserable. That seeking is craving. If you seek happiness, all you get is unhappiness. If you seek calm, all you get is turmoil. If you seek harmonious relationships, all you get is disharmony. If you seek wisdom, all you get is stupidity. You need to learn how to abandon seeking. You need to learn how to abandon your search for happiness, for calm, for freedom. And when you can stop seeking, then and only then will happiness visit you.

The fact that happiness does visit when seeking is abandoned was strikingly illustrated for a meditator whilst he was listening to one of our lectures on enlightenment. When he heard the words, '*Nibbāna* is closer to you than breathing. You do not have to seek for it—just be still and *know* it,' he so fully believed what he heard that he temporarily abandoned his habitual seeking for something other. Abandoning seeking, his mind became full of joy and spaciousness and lightness and the meditation that followed the lecture was a pleasure for him to do. Unfortunately, this state of affairs did not last. As soon as he forgot the words of the teacher, he reverted to his old habitual tendency to seek for something other than what he was experiencing in the moment, and so back came the mental restriction, the body pains, and the dissatisfaction with the moment.

★ ★ ★

Why did you seek to meditate in the first place? Most people start meditation because inside they feel a sense of unease, a lack of true happiness. Even if they have managed to rid themselves of that dissatisfaction from time to time, through a good conversation with a close friend or through buying a brand new outfit of clothes or through clinching a lucrative business deal, the dissatisfaction is only smothered for a while.

It is that sense of inner disturbance that drove you to seek and find a spiritual way. And even now there is no sense of rest within you. You do not feel that you can relax into the moment, that your seeking and your work are at last over. You know that quite soon anxiety or hatred or frustration will return and that the inner disturbance will be back again, triggering you off once more to seek for something that will put an end to the internal disquiet. It is that experience of dissatisfaction that keeps you working at the meditative path.

All men and women are seeking to rid themselves of this inner burden of pain which is so often there deep inside. Some try to free themselves from the pain by taking drugs or drink. Others try to free themselves through careers or travel or relationships. Others seek religion.

All spiritual and religious ways are trying to free their followers from this inner pain. Each has its own methods as to how best to get rid of this suffering. Some recommend that a really moral life is the only way to free a person from guilt, anxiety, and frustration. Others say devotion to God will do the trick. Others recommend meditation. Others say no, the only way to feel good inside is by service to mankind through something like nursing or caring for the mentally disabled. Still others say that you should go and live in a deprived part of the world and help those less fortunate than yourself in order to feel that life has meaning and depth. Many Buddhists believe that only by pledging themselves to the *bodhisattva* ideal, which is to work for the freedom of all beings, will they stand any chance of one day being released from their own inner burden of dissatisfaction.

So people abandon one kind of seeking, that of seeking after material wealth or career or family as the ultimate solution to quieten the inner disturbance. They abandon this kind of seeking for another kind— religion—in the hopes that it will provide the permanent sense of happiness and fulfilment that the other goals failed to provide. Religion, if faithfully followed, will bring its own glimpses of happiness. But how does this help? For getting married or starting a new business or going to a good concert also each bring their own glimpses of happiness. The trouble is that all of these things also bring with them dissatisfaction and pain. None of these things get rid of the inner tension. The only thing that can get rid of unhappiness is the very examination of the seeking itself. That seeking is done within, in your own mind. It is something *you* do. You move the mind. You push it towards seeking after this or that.

Looking at and letting go of this continual seeking is not to be found out there in religion or in psychotherapy or in the act of sitting on a chair with your eyes closed doing something called meditation. It is not to be found in meditation teachers or in their words. Stopping seeking is not available in a religion or in meditation or in spiritual teachers. It is only when you turn your attention back in on *yourself* and examine the mechanics of the seeking itself that you begin to get a glimmer as to why your mind is so often disturbed. When you look directly at the mechanics of seeking, no longer do you search for peace and calm and enlightenment. No longer do you seek spiritual truths. No longer are you interested in travelling along a spiritual path. For you understand and see clearly that it is the very seeking for these things which is the problem, and it is that seeking which brings about the inner constriction and unhappiness.

* * *

Does abandoning seeking therefore mean that one should do nothing? Let us explore a few examples. Many have looked within and have seen this inner disturbance. A woman sells her home and moves to another town. The whole experience is disturbing. Dealing with the solicitor, organising the removal men, ensuring they do not damage family heirlooms, settling into a new town where she has no friends, getting used to new rooms and the unfamiliar positioning of cupboards and stairs—all this is disturbing. Inside there is pain, an inner constriction, feelings of insecurity, loneliness, masses of wonderings as to whether she has done the right thing. So disturbed is she that she vows never to move again.

A man organises his day in such detail that he knows exactly what he will be doing at 11.05 today, tomorrow, next week, and next month. He knows what time he will rise, what time he will shave, what time he will have his breakfast, what time he will read the newspaper, and what time he will set off for work. He knows what day he will visit his mother and how long he will stay. He knows which day he will go on vacation and which filling station he will stop at to buy petrol. He spends his week's holiday in the same beach cottage on the same stretch of Dorset coast that he has rented every year during the first week in June for the past fifteen years. In advance he knows what he will do every minute of every day for the next ten years. With this military regime that he has worked out for himself he feels safe, which eliminates a great deal of the inner disturbance.

On the way to his beach cottage, his car breaks down. He did not plan for this. This event is not scheduled in his daily timetable. It is 9pm—his timetable says he should be at the cottage by now, unloading his luggage. His car has broken down on a deserted country lane. There is no house in sight. It is getting dark and it has begun to rain. And he never did join an organisation that offered a car breakdown recovery service. He chews over in mind how being towed away at night will cost a fortune, which will throw out of balance his carefully calculated finances. As he walks along the dark, wet, deserted country lane he feels wretched. He is disturbed inside. He vows never to drive again.

A man meets a woman. He is attracted. He wants to ask her out on a date. 'Will she reject me if I ask her out? She's taller than me. Perhaps she doesn't like men smaller than her?' He feels disturbed. He feels unconfident. He does not like this feeling. He wants it to be different. He wants to feel good inside. His solution to his inner disturbance? He decides not to ask her out. Furthermore, he resolves never again to ask any woman out. After all, any woman will eventually leave him and that will hurt, and so what is the point of dating a woman in the first place? He has looked inside himself and he has seen disturbance.

The woman moving house, the man going on holiday, the gentleman who wanted a date, they all looked inside and what did they see? They all observed suffering within. Each one chose a way of handling that suffering, and all three of them chose exactly the same approach. Having observed the tension that is always present when a person moves from the familiar to the unfamiliar, they responded by immediately seeking happiness.

The woman who moved house observed the tension within her that arose at having to deal with solicitors, removal men, and a new house—all new things. She had never dealt with solicitors or removal men before. She had never changed residence before. All of these things were new. Change was in operation. She was leaving the familiar and the known and stepping into the unknown. Unpleasant tensions arose with all this change. All of this is very normal and natural. Tension is part and parcel of new events and is no problem. It only becomes a problem when those that experience the tension that is inherent in change think that it is unnatural and should not be there. They think that somehow or other they are lesser, inadequate beings for experiencing this tension. They do not want it and seek instantly to rid themselves of it. They seek to become something other than tense in the moment. When this seeking occurs, then they are disturbed, dissatisfied. Inwardly they are constricted and in pain.

All three people in these examples chose to get rid of the tension by deciding never to do that activity again. The woman vowed never to move house again. The man vowed never to drive a car again. And the gentleman who found starting relationships with women painful vowed never to go out with a woman again. But were those three decisions, decisions that would lead to the lessening of inner dissatisfaction? Those making them thought so. But the only way to lessen inner pain is to abandon seeking.

These three people were, most definitely, seeking. They sought to have feelings inside of themselves different from the feelings they actually experienced. They sought to be free from the inner pain, and to accomplish this, they chose not to move house, not to drive a car, and not to date. With time, they will discover that the action they chose to rid themselves of inner pain with, does not work, but rather it will increase their inner disturbance. For they have chosen the method of avoidance rather than the method of facing up to the pain. When one faces pain, one steps right into the middle of it, and when one does this, one chooses the path of non-seeking.

* * *

Hardly a week goes by without you being presented with a problem— the washing machine breaks down and floods the kitchen or your child breaks an arm or there are storms and the greenhouse gets blown over or the telephone bill arrives and it is larger than you had budgeted for, and so arguments rage as to who is overusing the phone.

Life is painful. It is full of problems. It is a continuous series of problems, some minor, some major. Problems—whether they are how to stop wrong concentrating when meditating or how to live with terminal cancer or how to mend a plug if you are non-mechanical—usually arouse in us feelings of frustration or anger or depression or anxiety. All are unpleasant. All are uncomfortable. All are painful. All cause inner turmoil. Immediately when a person becomes conscious of this inner turmoil, he or she makes a decision, makes a movement to get away from it. Every decision you make, whether it is to shift your position whilst sitting meditating or to change job or house or relationship, is made because you want to get away from the painfulness of the moment. And whatever decision you come up with has only one consideration in it—it should take you towards a state which is happier and more comfortable than the state you are experiencing right now. But many of the decisions we make are very unwise, for although the action we take relieves the turmoil in the moment, it usually brings twice as much pain tumbling down upon us some time later.

The man who steals a video because he does not have sufficient cash to buy one certainly solves the problem of the pain of the moment. He no longer feels angry and resentful at not having what others have. But when his stealing habits put him behind bars, the inner frustration and pain that he will then experience will be greater than the dissatisfaction that drove him to steal the video in the first place. So the movement he makes to get away from inner dissatisfaction does not work because in the long run it brings an increase in inner conflict.

Those who come to realise that unethical behaviour brings about a tremendous amount of inner conflict tend to give it up, not because their parents tell them to or because their religion or their counsellor or their neighbour tells them to, but because they wish to lessen their inner suffering, and they have come to realise that ethical behaviour makes for more peace within.

But even for the ethical there are still problems. Moving house, developing new relationships, getting ill, reaching the age of forty, the age when you most commonly hear the phrase, 'it's not fat, it's muscle'—all these events stir within us a myriad of feelings, many of which are unpleasant. Because of this inner unpleasantness, we regard moving house as a problem, getting to know new people as a problem, getting ill and getting old as a problem.

Because life is full of problems, we moan. We moan about moving house and look forward to the day when it is over. We moan about being ill and look forward to the time when we are free of it. We moan about getting old and pretend it is not happening. Or we moan about how life has settled into a rut, how we have been living the same existence for the past ten or fifteen years. Often this is when the husband or wife goes off with a new partner, which solves one problem—they are no longer in a rut—but brings lots of other problems in its wake that have to be adjusted to, like angry ex-partners, angry children, divorce, less money, a new partner and home. Such a person is back on the treadmill of inner conflict. They have made a major life decision in order to get away from inner conflict only to find that their decision has changed many events and relationships in their life, and whenever there is change there is tension, there is *dukkha*, so they discover that they still have inner suffering. Nothing has been solved.

★ ★ ★

It is only when we develop a totally new and revolutionary approach to problems that they cease to be problems. And what is that revolutionary approach? It is seeing clearly that change and tension go together. You cannot have one without the other. If you go on holiday there is a change in your daily routine, and along with that change will come tension. All that accompanies the festival of Christmas—meeting up with relatives you hardly ever see, buying lots of presents, eating lots of food at unusual times of the day—all is a change from your normal routine, and therefore it will be accompanied by tension, by *dukkha*.

Everyone realises that the death of someone close is a sad event and is likely to give rise to much inner turmoil. But few observe that even pleasant events like going on holiday and Christmas also bring inner turmoil. Where there is change there is suffering. That is the Law. Change and suffering are as inseparable as your nose is from your face. If you turn your face to the left, your nose turns to the left. It is unthinkable that your nose should stay pointing forward whilst your face turns.

This is why some who have come to observe that there is inner suffering whenever they instigate a change in their life make the decision never to introduce change. These are the people who stay in the same job in the same house with the same relationships for life. It was because of this very observation that the woman who experienced suffering when she moved house decided never to move again. It was because of the realisation that suffering accompanies change that the man who made sure he did the same activities at the same time every day, year in year out, organised his life in this manner. He was so terrified of inner suffering, which he knew came about because of change, that the only way he could think of to lessen that suffering was to introduce massive control over what he did each day in order to make the pattern of events so predictable that there would be no change and therefore no suffering. And observing that change brings suffering, the gentleman who was attempting to form relationships with women decided to abandon his attempts.

All three people could not tolerate the inner suffering that accompanies change, and the solution they came up with to solve their problem was to try to control life by introducing non-change. This is to stifle life, to rob it of its richness, for it is the very problems themselves which give life meaning. It is the tussle with and the solving of problems which brings about inner maturity. The challenges they present give us the opportunities to develop all sorts of talents and mental qualities that we otherwise would not develop. It is the anxiety or guilt or fear or hatred that various life events stir within us that drives us to examine what we are doing and challenges us to come up with a healthier mental attitude to the problem. It is the very challenge that makes us feel alive. To attempt to put a stop to that change and that challenge is to slowly die within, and when this cut off, isolated feeling is present, the inner suffering is excruciating. It is far worse than the suffering accompanying change.

There is a much wiser way to handle inner suffering than to try to crush it out through control. Finding that solution is the challenge of life—it dares us to come up with the answer. When you take up *vipassanā* meditation you take up that challenge. You set yourself the task of discovering the right way to handle inner suffering.

Some may say, 'But I don't experience life as continually filled with pain and problems. In fact, I quite often get a great deal of pleasure from life. I get pleasure from deep conversations, from watching dramatic sunsets, from listening to classical music, from laughter.' However, if you look closely at pleasure, if you investigate its real nature deeply enough, you will discover that it does not last, it falls away, it changes into something other. And the fact that it does not last is disturbing. You cannot feel safe with it. You cannot relax into it. You cannot think, 'Ah, at last I have arrived at permanent happiness. Now I can relax, let go, and everything will be just fine and pleasant and wonderful from here on in.' Pleasant feelings die away. They change and, wherever there is change, there is suffering. So the true, but hidden, nature of pleasure is that it is painful.

Once you realise that life is filled with suffering—that no matter how much you may adjust it externally by avoiding challenges, by being ethical, by following this or that therapy, or by joining this or that religious group, life is still painful—once you come to accept the fact that change is a part of life and therefore suffering too must be a part of life, that both are unavoidable, then you stop fighting, you stop avoiding. Instead, you head straight into the suffering. You open your arms to it. You cease to seek for happiness.

When you seek for happiness, what are you seeking for? When you look at it closely, you see that to seek for happiness is nothing less than to seek to experience something different from what is being experienced in the moment. When you turn 180 degrees inwards and look intently at the mechanism of seeking, you will be startled to discover that seeking is a refusal to acknowledge the obvious—that life is full of change and that change is painful. Because you refuse to accept the obvious, you are always seeking to change it. You are constantly wanting the moment to be different than it is. So you are constantly dissatisfied with yourself, feeling that you are not good enough at meditation or not good enough as a marriage partner or not good enough as a boss or not good enough as an employee. What is this other than self-hatred? When you have got that low opinion of yourself in operation, inside there is constriction, a continuous dull ache—it is called inner dissatisfaction, inner suffering.

When you do accept the obvious, that life is filled with change and that change equals suffering, no longer do you seek for the moment to be something other than its inherent nature. Not seeking freedom from the painful, you find that the mind flips right over and suddenly, unexpectedly, it is free of suffering, and it is free of inner constriction—*it is free!* And for the first time in your life, there is continuous enjoyment.

The Only Way to Practise

How many of you have, at some stage or other in your life, gone on a diet? Most of you, I am sure. Have you noticed how conscious of food you become when you are on a diet? Have you noticed how you are always thinking about food—if it is not about the calorific content of the food, then it is about how hungry you feel. And if you let that diet slip for an instant, then you go on an eating binge, the likes of which you never indulged in when you were not concerned about your food intake.

When you are on a diet, those cream buns displayed in the cake shop window seem to leap out at you and beg to be bought. Normally, you would walk past that cake shop and not even notice those buns. But when you are on a diet, your relationship to food changes. Thoughts about food seem to lie waiting to spring into mind at every opportunity. In short, you become obsessed with food.

There was a young man once who applied to come on one of our introductory courses. He had a characteristic of constantly talking when he was nervous. He was, naturally enough, nervous during the interview for the course. He did not listen much. He tended to talk over us, and what he talked about was food, diets, health. He was obsessed with health. Diet was part of his physical health regime, so he talked about his diet. What he learnt about meditation in that interview I will never know, but we certainly learnt a lot about the calorific content of food. We learnt how many calories are contained in a slice of chocolate cake two inches wide by four inches long. (He had a great weakness for chocolate cake.) We learnt how many calories are contained in a slice of pizza, a cup of tea, a salad, a lamb chop, and many more items. We learnt how, if he caved in and allowed himself to be tempted by a slice of chocolate cake, then he would have to drastically reduce his food intake for the rest of the day.

It disturbed him terribly that he could decide at the beginning of the day exactly what he was going to eat that day and in what quantities and yet, in spite of his firm resolutions, he would find himself only too frequently breaking that resolve because he was tempted by a favourite food that was banned from his daily diet sheet, and it was banned because it had an unthinkable amount of calories in it. When he broke his diet, he got so depressed that he swung to the opposite extreme—he became a glutton for the day. Afterwards, he was left riddled with guilt and grief at what a spineless, weak character he was, seeing that he could not stick to a simple diet.

This young man came to only a few classes and then dropped out. However, we did get to see him for a meditation interview after one of those classes, and for most of it he talked about food, his diet, and calories. There was a young man obsessed with food.

If we concentrate on reducing our food intake, on fasting, or on dieting, then we become obsessed with its opposite, which is food. If we concentrate on celibacy, and a person can do this whether single or married, then we become obsessed with its opposite, which is sex. Our thoughts are constantly turning towards how to get it or how to avoid getting it. If we become dedicated to peace, then we become obsessed with war, with violence and destruction. If we focus in on becoming good, then all we become aware of is its opposite, evil.

When we want to become good, we want to eradicate our faults. Those journeying along a spiritual path, this is what they want to do—they want to eradicate their faults and be left with only positive qualities. Even if these spiritual travellers say, 'All I want out of the meditation is to become calmer and more able to cope with the demands of modern living,'—that very statement implies that these people see themselves as being deficient in calmness. They therefore have a fault. They feel they get worked up too easily, too readily. They want to calm down their fault of overwoundness. They want to eradicate that fault. They want to put in its place the opposite quality of calmness. They see calmness as good and non-calmness as bad. So they become obsessed with their non-calmness. They are terribly aware every time they get tense, and that they are therefore not reaching their heart's desire of a calm, cool, laid-back approach to life.

* * *

The prime aim of the Buddhist teaching is to eradicate craving, hatred, and delusion, and to come to that state of *nibbāna*, which is utter freedom from those three negative factors of mind. From what I have just said, however, if you focus in on getting rid of those three negatives and substituting them with the opposite 'good' qualities of non-craving, non-hatred, and non-delusion, then all that is going to happen is that you are going to become obsessed with how much craving you have got, how much hating there is in you, and how much you ignore in your mental universe.

Trainee *vipassanā* meditators do not bother with their good and bad points. They focus their attention between the opposites. They focus their attention on a neutral object, an object that is neither good nor bad, and that object is the feeling of the rise and fall of the abdominal region as they breathe naturally, in and out. Spiritual travellers work with that object. When they have built up sufficient concentration on that particular neutral object, then they move on to focusing their attention on another neutral object, the second neutral object being the rise and fall of *all* objects. They do not ever place their attention on their good and bad qualities. If they did they would become obsessed with good and bad, and whichever way they turned they would see themelves as the most despicable beings alive, as they would always be failing at the self-improvement tasks they set themselves.

If people want to overcome good and evil, this can only be done by rising above and beyond these opposites, and to do that spiritual travellers must focus on objects that have nothing whatsoever to do with good and evil, but which they can view as neutral and then observe them with careful, thorough, detailed attention. This way good and evil solve themselves.

When meditators suffer, so often it is because they fall into self-assessment. They will mumble away to themselves about, 'I'm not good enough. I'm very bad. I'm always falling short of what I want to be. If only I hadn't made that biting retort to the boss. If only I hadn't lost my temper with the kids. If only I could concentrate better, I'd be a better meditator.' Intense agony always follows such assessments of one's own worth.

So meditators are not concerned about their worth or lack of it or what they should or should not become. They focus their efforts on 'neutral territory' so to speak. That way what they 'should do and become' grows naturally and rightly, without their generating self-hatred and confusion. Self-hatred and confusion arise when they start playing the game of self-assessment, and the very mental states they are trying to avoid by self-assessing rise up and take over the mind.

However, meditators do take upon themselves to follow the five precepts, the Buddhist rules of training concerned with cultivating harmlessness in physical and verbal action. Those five rules of conduct are there to give them some guidelines, some framework of morality, whilst they are trying to come to spontaneous true morality. And those guidelines are there only to stop the mind from constantly diving into this area of self-assessment and becoming tortured and twisted and caught up with how bad one is. With a few basic guidelines of what one should and should not do, if those are adhered to as best one can, then the whole question of trying to become a 'good' person is put aside, and the meditator focuses his or her attention, energy, and drive on the neutral object of the rise and fall of phenomena. That way, with time, the mind settles down more and more, day by day. It becomes cleaner, and—surprise, surprise—it contains less craving and hatred. It becomes 'good' without you ever focusing directly on 'goodness'.

* * *

Meditators who come to us receive the instruction right from day one that is designed to develop the qualities of concentration and mindfulness within them. However, in the early days, slightly more stress is put on concentration than on mindfulness. This is because it is essential to get a certain amount of calm and one-pointedness in the mind. With this calm and one-pointedness, it is very much easier to look mindfully at an object and not grab hold of it and hang on to it. Without concentration the mind does not remain still when viewing an object. It grabs hold of the object, and when this happens, the mind readily craves or hates that object.

When there is sufficient strength of concentration, backed by the mindfulness, then the mind does not fall into the object but is happy to remain still and just watching. It is not disturbed if the object is pleasant. It is not disturbed if the object is unpleasant. It remains still and equanimous towards whatever it is viewing.

Some people, when they come here, come with many years of meditation practice behind them. Some have been meditating for as long as fifteen years before they came to us. The system they had been practising for those many years is invariably a form of concentration meditation. When this is the case, then the meditator has concentration developed to a sufficient pitch for the *vipassanā* practice, and the aspect of the meditation the teacher will emphasise now as needing development will be mindfulness, specifically mindfulness of the rise and fall of all phenomena. The stress is taken off concentration and placed on mindfulness.

Concentration is developed to a sufficient pitch for the *vipassanā* practice when the five hindrances of ill will, sensual desire, worry and restlessness, sloth and torpor, and doubt are absent most of the time, and when objects such as thoughts, sounds, tangibles, smells, and sights are still floating through the mind. If the mind becomes too concentrated, then these objects get blotted out, and one is left with the first object, the one the meditator started with, in other words the rise and fall of the abdomen. If there are no sounds or thoughts or smells or visual objects or feelings, bodily or mental, cutting across the rise and fall, then you have become too concentrated *for the vipassanā practice.*

It is not necessary to first develop *jhāna* before you can develop *vipassanā*. '*Jhāna*' is the Pali term for a very deep state of concentration. Sometimes this Pali term is translated as trance, sometimes as absorption. If a meditator develops these states of absorption, it is like going on a giant detour. It is an unnecessary side-track *off* the path to *nibbāna*. The path leading to these concentrated states is quite different from the path that develops *vipassanā*. And it is the *vipassanā* path that leads towards *nibbāna*. And that is the only path that leads towards *nibbāna*.

You do want concentration developed to a certain depth but no further, because if it goes too deep, you are left with more concentration at your disposal than you need. And if the concentration is overdeveloped for the *vipassanā* practice, it will produce states of deep calm, bliss, and joy, and it will throw up lights and visions, and the student will have awful difficulty tearing himself or herself away from the glamour of these objects.

He or she will become attached to these objects. It will be like the person who goes digging for gold, and a few feet under the earth he finds a number of items of jewellery covered in gold plate, and he is so attracted to these trinkets that he abandons his original quest to find gold and settles for the cheap imitation of gold-plated trinkets. The meditator is after the genuine gold of liberation. He does not want to get trapped and side-tracked by beautiful objects that only give temporary liberation and which are a pale imitation of the genuine article, and this is more likely to happen if the concentration is overdeveloped.

Another reason why a state of deep concentration is such a drawback to the development of *vipassanā* is that the meditator finds the pleasure, the calm, and the peacefulness of the very concentrated states so desirable that there is a longing for these, and when the meditator eventually gets into one of these states, he or she tries to stay in it. And when the calm is too deep, there is no interest whatsoever in developing wisdom because to turn the mind towards *anicca*, *dukkha,* or *anattā* is to destroy that calm. This is when a meditator has become addicted to calm and peacefulness. When there is addiction, then defilements of the mind increase. The defilement of craving for the calmness increases, and the defilement of hatred for the non-calm state also increases.

So a meditator must guard against getting too concentrated because of this danger of addiction and the increase of defilements. However, on the other hand, if the mind is not calm and concentrated enough, then wisdom will not develop either, because the mind gets caught up with the object it is viewing. It cannot see clearly, and then it readily hates or craves the object.

So whichever extreme the mind goes to, the extreme of too much concentration or the extreme of too little concentration, it loses out. The only time the mind is workable for *vipassanā* is when it is on the middle path between these extremes.

When the mind is on that middle path, it is still. This is good. With this stillness it is easy to watch the movements of mind and body, how they arise and how they pass away. By watching this impermanence, one comes to experience true stillness, true peacefulness. Only when the mind is still, do meditators come to see that all is impermanent, even the peacefulness that is being watched will die and pass away. If meditators become attached to peacefulness, they suffer, but by watching the impermanence of peacefulness time and time again, they give up that attachment to peacefulness. They allow peacefulness to be born and to die. They do not hang on to it and stop its natural flow. Then, and only then, will they know true peacefulness.

When the mind has fallen off the middle path and fallen into the extreme of too little concentration, then it becomes overcrowded with objects. It is so crowded with sounds and feelings and thoughts running hither and yon that it is impossible to distinguish one object from another. They all crowd into one another, clamouring for attention.

In this state of crowdedness the mind is unclean like a stirred up muddy pond. Someone peering into that muddy pond would not be able to make out any objects. They would not be able to see the rocks and fish and water snails clearly. It is just the same with the unclean, stirred-up mind as with the unclean, stirred-up pond. It is very difficult to make out any objects clearly. When a meditator cannot distinguish different objects because there are so many, he or she is always falling into those objects, becoming trapped by them. Only with concentration does this myriad of objects settle down, like stirred-up mud in a pond settling to the bottom. When this happens, then one object rises slowly out of the mass and is clearly seen. Then another object rises slowly, and it in turn is clearly seen because it is not surrounded by masses of other objects. This way it becomes easy to see the beginning, the middle, and end of these objects.

When the mind has become sufficiently concentrated to practise *vipassanā,* it is easier to see the beginning, the middle, and end of objects because the mind contains fewer objects. Also, there is a calmness in the mind that does not overreact to whatever it is looking at. You may, for example, be looking at the object of sleepiness. If the mind that is viewing that object is not calm, then it gets involved and caught up with the object. It cannot see the beginning of sleepiness, and it cannot see the end of sleepiness. It falls into sleepiness, and it falls into its likes and dislikes of sleepiness. And then, before very long, the meditator is dejected because the practice is not going the way he or she thinks it ought to.

To not like sleepiness is to practice *vipassanā* meditation incorrectly. The correct way to practise is first to be aware of the presence of sleepiness, then second to avoid getting involved in likes or dislikes for that state so as to keep your response to sleepiness still, and then third to watch the way sleepiness has arisen and how it ends. To regard the state of sleepiness as 'me' who is experiencing sleepiness is again the wrong way to practise meditation because this reinforces the erroneous view of a personality which is separate from the object it is looking at, a personality which judges, assesses, manipulates, and which can control and order out sleepiness. The correct way to practise is to view sleepiness not as 'my sleepiness' but as a mental state called 'sleepiness' which has come into being dependent upon certain conditions joining together, and to watch that mental state fade away when those conditions cease. All you can do is accept the presence of sleepiness and just watch. The sleepiness will come and go as it pleases. It will last for as long as the supporting conditions last and so cease in its own time. It takes no notice whatsoever of the meditator demanding that it should not be present. No matter what the meditator may think, he or she actually has no control over the objects that appear in the mind.

It is not the purpose of insight meditation to get rid of a state of sleepiness. It is the purpose of insight meditation to watch that sleepiness without any interference—without wanting it to go away or wanting it to continue. It is the purpose of insight meditation to watch that object in an unbiased way so that you can learn, by direct seeing, how that object of sleepiness has come into existence and how it ceases.

If you can manage by sheer effort to get rid of that sleepiness, then you will be very pleased with yourself because you will think that you are doing the meditation correctly since you have got rid of this unpleasant object, which you think, erroneously, is preventing you from meditating properly. But if you do this, then you do *vipassanā* meditation incorrectly, for you do not give yourself the opportunity to learn about the object because you have forced it out. Also, by forcing it out, you build up a craving for wakefulness and a hatred of sleepiness. So you are bending the mind towards prejudice and bias when what you want is a mind that is free of prejudice and bias.

* * *

To spend a greater part of your meditation hour thinking about your job, your neighbour, your holiday, the wall that needs building, the parties that need arranging—that is not meditation. That is indulging in thinking. Meditation is not wiping out thinking completely, for you have thought since the day you were born and will think till the day you die, but meditation is allowing thinking to settle so that objects other than thinking can be seen clearly. When the mind has the right amounts of concentration and mindfulness present and is therefore still, when thinking does arise, it is no more than one sentence long and can be seen clearly. If you try to banish thinking, that implies hatred in the mind, and all that that will produce is the stirring up of thinking and more thoughts than ever flying around.

So you still and clean the mind in the same way that you would still and clean a pond that had become cloudy. If you were to agitate the mud that lies at the bottom of a pond with a stick, the water in the pond would instantly become cloudy and muddy. If you leave the mud alone, it settles to the bottom, leaving the water clear. Note, it has not got rid of the mud. If you leave thinking alone, not agitating it with the stick of indulging thoughts one moment and hating yourself for indulging the next, if you do not use this stick, then the thoughts settle down and the mind is left clear and can see the other objects in mind easily. Note that you have not got rid of thinking forever. You have just let it settle so that it is no longer filling and obsessing the mind. To stop yourself from constantly picking up that stick and having a quick stir, you turn the attention to another object, an object dissociated from thinking, and that object is the feeling of the rise and fall of the abdominal region. And once you have turned the mind to that object, you resolutely refuse to pay any attention to thinking but just keep turning the mind time and time again towards the object of rise and fall.

Once concentration is strong enough, the meditation teacher will place more stress on watching the rise and fall of phenomena, returning the mind only occasionally to the rise and fall of the abdomen.

* * *

When an object is present, and the object may be feeling or hearing or smelling or seeing or touching or thinking, be aware of that object. Be with it right in the present moment, in the now. Do not reach out for that object or chase after it once it has gone. Know the object just as it is. Know it as being feeling when it is feeling.

When it is feeling, it is not thinking or seeing or hearing—it is feeling. Know the object clearly. Do not add to the object more than what is present. Do not add and obscure the object by thinking, 'This is an unpleasant feeling in my back.' The object is feeling. Be clearly aware of that. If there is added afterwards, 'Oh dear, what an unpleasant feeling in my back,' then be clearly aware that feeling has ceased and thinking has arisen. This way you will be aware of each object as it arises, and you will be with that object in the moment. If feeling and thoughts run together and you are not aware of the two separate and distinct events, then you will not be aware that feeling has arisen and ceased, and that thinking has arisen. You will not be experiencing the raw data as it occurs. Instead, all the objects run together and form a solid mass, and there is confusion as to what is actually taking place.

Do not let the mind ramble off into 'What is it that I am experiencing? Is it *anicca* or *dukkha* or *anattā* or is it a hindrance?' This is indulging in speculation. It is concerned with *my* practice and what is happening in *my* meditation. It is not insight practice. It promotes the hindrance of doubt, doubt in your capacity to do the meditation correctly. Keep the practice simple. Keep driving the mind in towards the raw data of feeling, hearing, touching, tasting, smelling, seeing.

When a true knowing experience of one of the three marks or one of the hindrances takes place, it will present itself to you. You will not have to go looking for it. You will *know* it directly. If you have to ask yourself, 'Is it *anicca*?' you are not having a direct experience of *anicca*, but instead, you are caught up in a concept of *anicca*.

If you say to yourself, 'Now I will watch the mark of transience,' you are, again, not having a direct meditative experience but are playing conceptual games, which is not the insight practice. For example, when you are irritated and in a bad mood, you do not have to say to yourself in words, 'Now I am in a bad mood.' You *know directly* that you are in a bad mood. It is the same with the meditation. When the mind stays in the present moment, watching alertly, consciously, the arising and passing away of objects, then it is a direct experience of transience. It *knows* transience in exactly the same way that you *know* when you are in a bad mood.

The word '*vipassanā*' means insight. And that means seeing clearly, as it occurs, that mind and matter are different and separate and that they do not last. They are forever changing. 'Insight' also means seeing directly that mind and matter are unsatisfactory because they are forever changing and they are impersonal. What 'impersonal' means is that what we take to be 'self' or 'ego' is a view. It is a wrong view that has arisen from not being able to observe, in an unbiased way, what is actually occurring in mind and body from moment to moment. When we can observe in an unbiased, clean way, then we discover the truth—the truth that the imagined, permanent 'self' is but a very rapid series of births and deaths of mind and matter that continues ad infinitum. This is insight, and the more insight grows, the more craving and hatred decrease, and the wiser we become. Insight develops wisdom. And that is the sole purpose of insight meditation—to develop wisdom, so as to destroy craving and hatred and ignorance permanently. Whereas the purpose of concentration is to develop calmness and tranquillity and to destroy craving and hatred temporarily.

* * *

These three characteristics of transitoriness, suffering, and non-self exist naturally. They are not created by doing the meditation. They exist in life for anyone to observe, no matter what a person's sex, nationality, or religion may be. No matter whether anyone knows about the existence of these three characteristics or not, they still exist. These three characteristics are therefore called facts of existence or facts of life. And what we are wishing to accomplish when meditating is to eventually arrive at a point where we can see *for ourselves* these facts of life. Then there is no necessity to blindly agree, or blindly disagree, with what somebody else says are the facts of existence. When we see for ourselves, we know. When we *know,* we are wise.

The reason why we do not see these facts of existence naturally and why we have to bother to meditate at all is that we do not observe in an unbiased way. Our minds are coloured, stained with defilements and views. You have heard the expression, 'viewing the world through rose-tinted glasses'—that expression means not seeing clearly the object one is looking at, but seeing it with a bias in the mind. Because we look at mind and matter, the world, through coloured glasses, we look at them with a bias, in other words, through defilements. This distorts what we see, and therefore we cannot see these three characteristics of all phenomena. What we end up seeing is the opposite of the three marks. We see permanence, happiness, and a self.

So we have to cultivate a way of looking at the universe that will allow us to see these three characteristics. Mindfulness meditation is such a way. It is the only way.

Mind and matter change so rapidly and with such an amazing speed that unless we have developed a capacity of calm, concentration, and mindfulness, we are unable to notice this speeding birth and decay, and therefore we experience mind and matter as solid, running together, and permanent. When we begin to calm the mind down, we develop some experiential appreciation that mind and matter do change, but then we fall into the trap of believing that, although the objects observed are changing rapidly, that which observes does not change. So we *still* end up with a universe that is distorted because a bit of it appears to be permanent.

The aim, therefore, of *vipassanā* is to calm the mind down, get it concentrated and mindful, and then turn it time and time again to observing objects in the moment until one of the three marks of existence becomes clear. This is the *only way* to practise. This is the *only way* to come to freedom from craving, hatred, and ignorance. This is the *only way* to enlightenment.

The Path

One hears from time to time the word 'path' used in connection with Buddhism. I myself have likened meditators to travellers and have mentioned that you are all 'spiritual travellers journeying along a path'. But what is 'the path' that is being referred to here?

One hears about the eightfold path in Buddhism—is it that? Or is it perhaps the path of streamwinner or the path of once-returner or the path of non-returner or the path of *arahant*? 'Path', here, means the way that leads directly to *nibbāna* and includes the paths of streamwinner, once-returner, non-returner, and *arahant*.

It can help if one imagines the spiritual path as a physical path which winds its way up a mountain side. The mountain is very large and very high and has many different types of terrain that you, the traveller, have to journey through. Sometimes the ground is steep and rough and difficult to traverse, where the hardships of the journey are so great that you are tempted to abandon the whole idea of climbing to the summit. At other times the path winds through delightful meadows where cool crystal-clear pools are shaded by tall slender trees, tempting travellers to put down roots, settle and enjoy the beauty of the surroundings and forget all about completing the journey.

'Traveller', here, refers to you. Travellers who climb actual physical mountains have to have certain qualities such as stamina, drive, determination, courage, and sheer guts if they are to reach their destination—the top of the mountain. Likewise you, the traveller along the spiritual path, need the selfsame qualities as the mountain climber if you are to reach *nibbāna*, the top of your spiritual mountain. And it is no easy task, because just as physical exhaustion can prevent a mountain climber from continuing his journey, what stops a spiritual traveller dead in his or her tracks is doubt. Doubt saps the energy and prevents further travelling as surely as physical exhaustion cripples the mountain climber.

One of the rather sneaky aspects of doubt is that it has a subtle side to it which one does not expect to be there, and so one does not notice its presence. In its grosser form, doubt is easily detectable. The spiritual traveller is aware of it, and, being aware of it, he or she can then choose to find the antidote and get rid of it. But in its subtler form, it goes quite unnoticed and so wreaks havoc because the meditator, being unaware of its presence, does not put a stop to it.

* * *

Before I explain what the subtler forms of doubt are and give you examples of them, let us just talk a little more on the subject of the path. This path, which I have likened to an actual path up a mountain side that has certain difficult patches and certain pleasant areas, both of which have to be travelled through but not succumbed to, relates in Buddhism to the paths of streamwinner, once-returner, non-returner and *arahant*.

Although traditionally these paths are described as four separate paths, they are not in fact different paths. Rather are they four separate sections on the same path. So the path of streamwinner can be likened to the first section of the path up the mountain side, once-returner to the second section of that path, non-returner to the third section, and *arahant* to the fourth and final section which leads directly to the summit, in other words to *nibbāna*.

In addition to picturing yourself journeying up a mountain path with all its attendant difficulties, you have also to imagine starting your journey at the bottom of the mountain with an enormous number of goods strapped to your back. You are carrying such things as a piano, a pair of hedge clippers, a football, a chimney-pot, a plant, a standard lamp, and a sofa—things which are of no possible assistance to your journey. In fact, they are a definite hindrance, wearing you down, exhausting you, and making it impossible for you to travel through narrow ravines and up the steeper sections of the mountain. These goods have to be abandoned if you are to reach your destination successfully.

The piano, the hedge clippers, the football, and everything else you have strapped to your back are a simile for the ten fetters which you carry around with you on your spiritual journey and which are useless items. They are items which do not help your quest in any way at all. They only hinder it. These fetters have first to be detected and then let go of if you wish to be successful at journeying up that path to the summit. These useless items called 'fetters' are doubt, attachment to rule and ritual, belief in a self, sensuous craving, hatred, craving for fine-material existence, craving for immaterial existence, conceit, restlessness, and ignorance.

★ ★ ★

A favourite question of meditators is 'Am I on the path yet?' To answer the question, those who are journeying along the first section are technically termed meditators who are on the streamwinner's path. To get on to the path and to complete the first section is *the* most difficult part of the whole journey. The problems which bother the meditator on the streamwinner's path are exactly the same problems that bother those who are not yet on the path—in other words doubt, attachment to rule and ritual, and belief in a self. These are the problems that the majority of you will be faced with time and time again until you have learnt how to recognise them and how to handle them without any movement of the mind for or against these problems.

A person who has doubt also has attachment to rule and ritual and attachment to the view of self. The three problems are linked—you cannot have one without the other. This may come as something of a surprise to some of you, for you may well recognise that you have plenty of doubt in your mental makeup but would regard yourself as far too sophisticated to be attached to rule and ritual. You may think that that is for primitive tribal people, surely? After all, isn't it attachment to rule and ritual when a person is convinced that, by bowing down before a stone carving of a Buddha a hundred times a day, every day, that this act alone will result in his or her becoming enlightened?—and you would certainly not believe that. Yes that is attachment to ritual—but ritual has a much deeper side to it than that, which I hope to reveal to you shortly.

If the question is not 'Am I on the path yet?', then it is 'Where am I on the path?' Usually, the meditator receives a non-committal response from the teacher, which is interpreted either to mean they are just about to become enlightened, or, if the meditator is feeling a bit negative, it is interpreted as 'I'm a million lifetimes away from even getting on the path.' The truth, as usual, lies somewhere between these two extremes.

The question that often follows on the heels of 'Am I on the path?' is 'How long does it take to travel to the end of the path?' How long it takes you to get on to the path and then to complete the first, second, third, and fourth sections of that path is governed to a very large extent by your past actions. If, in the past, you have spent much time and effort devoted to the religious quest, then your spiritual journey will be quick and smooth. And by the 'past' I mean not only the immediate past few years but your past lives as well.

Let us say that it takes fifty lifetimes of devotion to the religious quest in order to become enlightened. Do not take that figure seriously—I have made it up. I do not know whether it takes seven or fifty-seven lifetimes to become enlightened. All I know is that it definitely takes more than one lifetime. So fifty is just a convenient round number. Let us say it takes fifty lifetimes from the time you decide you want to overcome suffering and become enlightened to the time that your goal is achieved. In each of those fifty lifetimes you spend considerable quantities of time meditating, studying religious texts, and listening to wise discourses. Maybe you have even had a try at ascetic practices like eating only a few grains of rice a day or standing on one leg staring into the sun. Perhaps you have spent hours spinning prayer wheels on some snow capped mountain in the Himalayas believing that this activity was exactly the right one to loosen you from the bondage of suffering.

One thing is for sure, however, and that is that all of the different practices would have been undertaken because you sincerely believed that they were the ones that led directly to that highest of the high, enlightenment itself. You go through one lifetime after another dis-covering that this or that particular practice does not get you where you want to go. Then you discover a practice which looks as if it will get you to the summit of the mountain, provided you follow its tenets in the correct manner. Let us say it is meditation that you decide holds all the answers—specifically *vipassanā* meditation. Once you have discovered meditation, you spend several more lifetimes practising it, and some of those lives are spent as a monk or a nun. Eventually it dawns on you that certain qualities of mind such as faith and investigation are not sufficiently developed within you for you to make the necessary headway with the meditation, and that this lack is temporarily blocking your journey up the mountain side. Having made this discovery, you now spend a few more lifetimes developing the qualities that you are currently deficient in, whilst still continuing to meditate.

It is impossible to predict the length of time it is going to take you to complete your spiritual journey. So much depends on the work you have done in previous lifetimes. Some meditators are only on their tenth life, and so, for them, the whole of the spiritual endeavour is a bit of an uphill struggle. But for those who are in their forty-seventh life of dedication to the religious ideal, understanding the teaching comes easily, as does spending much time practising meditation and associated disciplines. For such people there is a great love of the spiritual way and everything to do with it.

There is no short cut for anyone. Everyone has to do the same amount of work. Everyone has to go through each of the fifty lifetimes and learn what they are supposed to learn in each one. If it looks as if a fellow meditator is advancing faster than you are, it only means that, at some earlier time, he or she did the work that you are now doing. And you cannot opt out and say, 'Because it looks as though it's going to take me lifetimes of work, I think I'll sit this life out, thank you very much.' You cannot opt out because you have to do the work at some stage or other, as the whole purpose of existence is to come to understand, through direct seeing, that you create your own universe and therefore you create your own suffering. This understanding can only come about through the spiritual training. If you put off the spiritual training to a later date, then, when you eventually do get down to it, it is even more of an uphill struggle. Provided you work steadily and evenly at the training, it gets easier and easier as the years go by. If you work in jerks, stopping and starting, the training becomes a continuous battle.

Should you ever feel like getting the sulks and giving up because you cannot become enlightened right *now,* and it all looks like too much work, well, do pause and consider for a moment how fortunate your conditions are—you are attending this meditation centre and so you have found a way, you have found a couple of guides, and you have sufficient wealth to allow you leisure time, which you can use for meditation and study. You have your health, and so you can travel to lectures and hear the *Dhamma*, and you can come on residential meditation courses. If you were sick and confined to bed, attending lectures and residential courses would be out of the question. Reflect on the fact that in a future lifetime, conditions may not be so fortunate, and so it is best to make full use of them whilst you have them.

There are two popular and opposing beliefs in Buddhist circles. One is that it takes many, many lifetimes before one can become enlightened. The other is that the task can be done in this very lifetime now. Those who think it takes many lifetimes say that it is not possible to become enlightened in just one lifetime. Those who believe it can be done in this very life say that this view is nonsense. They say that if we are already enlightened, then all we have to do is open our inner eyes and merge with what is right under our noses to realise *nibbāna*.

As it so happens, both these views are correct. One view does not contradict the other, provided one looks at them both from a slightly different standpoint. It *does* take many lifetimes of working at the religious-mystical way in order to become enlightened, but if this is life number fifty, then it is one's last lifetime, and so enlightenment is going to happen in this very lifetime.

* * *

How do you get on to the path? If already on it, how do you get through that first section? You get on to the path and you get through that first section by letting go of attachment to doubt, rule and ritual, and the view that you are a separate and discrete self. Let us look at each one of these fetters and define their obvious and not so obvious meanings.

Doubt means to doubt the spiritual discipline you have chosen to follow. You doubt that it is effective. You doubt that it leads to what it says it leads to. You doubt that *Buddha-dhamma*, the teaching of the Buddha, leads to enlightenment. This fetter also means that you doubt the ability of the guides you have chosen to lead you. You doubt that they know the way to the top of the mountain from their own experience. If you are confident that they do know the way to the cessation of suffering, you doubt that they understand *you* sufficiently to help you get there. Or if you are confident that your guides are fully experienced, you doubt your own ability to become enlightened. You doubt too that there is any value to be gained in spending lots of time practising meditation or going on retreats or spending a longer period still at the practice by becoming a monk or a nun.

How often have you done an hour's seated practice after which you have sighed and said, 'Well that was a waste of time, wasn't it? A whole hour of torture, for what? This meditation is too difficult.' To you, the period was a complete waste of time. You might just as well have spent the hour enjoying yourself, with your feet up, watching the television. If you have ever made a statement like that, you have experienced the fetter of doubt.

To put those doubts in perspective, consider the following: how many of you drive a car? Were you, the very first time you got behind the steering wheel, an instant 'Stirling Moss'? No, you only became a skilled driver because you got into that car and practised, practised, practised your driving skills. If you had dwelt at all on the doubts and frustrations that beset you whilst you were learning, you would not be driving around the streets today—you would have abandoned your attempts long ago.

The same goes for the spiritual training. If you take any notice at all of your doubts and frustrations, at best you will prevent yourself from getting anywhere with the training, and at worst you will abandon the practice entirely. If you give up in the middle of a seated practice because the meditation is not going the way you want it to, at that instant you abandon meditation, you abandon *Dhamma*, you abandon your climb up the mountain side, all because you have fallen prey to the fetter of doubt. You fall prey because you could not let go of those doubtful thoughts—you just *had* to act on them. And until you have mastered the capacity to note but not take any notice of doubtful thoughts, you stop yourself from journeying along the path. It is only a temporary stoppage because you invariably pick yourself up the next day and start again, but, each time you handle doubtful thoughts incorrectly, you sap your energy, you damage your joy in living, and you make the whole of the spiritual training that much more of a battle for yourself.

When a meditator consistently applies too much effort to the practice, he or she is instructed to spend the following hour of meditation doing nothing but just sitting and watching and to abandon returning the attention to the rise and fall of the abdomen and the counting. He is told he must spend the hour doing nothing. For a while he is happy. He is enjoying doing nothing. It seems a bit like a holiday. But then the mind starts to wander and daydream and fall asleep. From the meditator's perspective he does not seem to be achieving anything by following the instruction to 'sit and do nothing'. It all seems a waste of time. At least when turning the attention to the rise and fall he was *doing* something—he was going places in his spiritual training, even if it was accompanied by a headache, which he believes is a small price to pay as long as he is getting somewhere. So what does he do? After about fifteen minutes of following the teacher's instruction to 'do nothing', he abandons that and returns the attention to rise and fall.

That meditator, by his actions, shows doubt. He doubts the teacher. As far as he is concerned, the instruction the teacher gave him was useless. He cannot see that following the instruction leads anywhere worthwhile at all, and so he abandons it and returns to concentrating on the rise and fall. He believes there is something intrinsically more worthwhile about rise and fall than sitting doing nothing. Bear in mind that at this stage he does not know anything about the path, because he has not been along it yet. He does not really know what will be gained by paying attention to the rise and fall. He just *believes* it leads somewhere profitable because he was told in the far and distant past that it was a worthwhile thing to do. He has lost sight of the fact that it was the teacher who told him that in the first place.

This meditator, by applying too much effort in the meditation, was actually going down the wrong eightfold path. To stop him from continuing down that wrong path, the teacher changed the instruction and would have kept him on the new instruction until he had gained sufficient experience of what was too much energy and what was too little. Once the meditator had gained this experience, the teacher would then change the instruction again and perhaps get the meditator to return to concentrating on the rise and fall, knowing that now that the meditator had more understanding of energy, he would not travel down the wrong path quite so frequently. But the meditator could only have gained the experience of the difference between too much and too little energy by carefully following the teacher's change in instructions.

The example given shows clearly the fetter of doubt. But how does attachment to rule and ritual and self-view relate to that same example? The meditator insisted on practising a former instruction, the one of continually returning the attention to the rise and fall, and by that action he or she showed both attachment to rule and ritual and self-view. Let me explain: a meditation technique is only effective if it is right for that person at that moment in time, with the supporting conditions that exist at that time. If a teacher changes the instruction, it is because the meditator and the conditions have changed. If the meditator insists on continuing with a past technique, he is effectively saying that he has not changed—and declaring that he stays the same is self-view.

Insisting on staying glued to the rise and fall at all costs, even when told not to, shows an attachment to a previous rule. There is a belief that there is something intrinsically magical and worthwhile in the rule of 'Pay attention to the rise and fall of the abdomen.' If the meditator did not have that attachment to the rule he received when he first came to meditation, then he would be quite happy to follow the teacher's new instruction, wouldn't he?

★ ★ ★

How do you overcome attachment to doubt, rule and ritual, and self-view? You overcome them by letting go of them, but also you overcome them by developing their opposites. The opposite of doubt is faith. The opposite of rule and ritual is adaptability. The opposite of self-view is conditionality.

There are a hundred and one ways in which a meditator can show doubt. Perhaps you read a book on *Dhamma,* and, finding a technique described in that book which you have not heard about before but which looks good, you decide to give it a try. Perhaps the technique described is to open your eyes slowly after a period of meditation, and so you do just that. Your teacher has not told you to practise in that fashion, and so why do you do it? Why must you follow past instructions, instructions from previous teachers, instructions you read in books, instructions you make up yourself, to help you cope with a painful practice? Why can't you just take the instruction that is given and practise that and only that? You cannot do it because doubt is still a part of your makeup.

A meditator has been meditating for years and at the end of every course he says, 'What should I do with my meditation over the next few months until I next see you?' His question shows that he is both doubtful and attached to rules and rituals. Why does he not just continue with the last instruction? Why does he doubt that the teacher is giving him the latest up-to-date information on his meditation? Why does he have to keep checking up to make sure that his teacher is on the ball *vis-à-vis* his personal meditation instructions? Why does he need to be given further fresh instruction, in other words a rule, in order to feel safe?

Another meditator is told not to join the three hours of group meditation that morning but to go and work instead. She explains to the teacher how she could fit in the work and the meditation. By her actions she shows that she doubts that the teacher has her spiritual welfare at heart, because surely the more meditation she does the more she increases her chances of becoming enlightened—so how can the teacher be so uncaring as to ask her to give up her seated practice for that day? The meditator also shows attachment to a ritual—the ritual of the seated meditation. She secretly believes that the summit of the mountain can be reached only through seated meditation. She ignores all the teachings she has heard which say that she must learn how to meditate whilst sitting, standing, walking, lying down, and attending to the calls of nature.

Attachment to rule and ritual breeds a rigidity of mind. The person wants to stay doing the same thing even when conditions change. When a teacher detects this rigidity, he or she will give instructions that involve the student in changing direction, thus forcing her to let go of her cherished routines and become more adaptable. Adaptability is the opposite of attachment to rules and rituals, and thus will weaken the fetter.

In order to carry out the teacher's instructions at all, the student requires faith and devotion. Until a meditator has got through the first section of the path, he or she is going to be constantly plagued with doubts and attachments to old routines. Although superficially it will look as if the meditator is carrying out the instruction, he will be subverting it and hanging on to his own idea of the way he should be treading the spiritual path. The meditator sincerely believes that he is doing exactly what his teacher has told him but is in fact fooling himself.

So how do you overcome this catch-22 situation where it seems you are constantly deluding yourself until you have got through the first path? You overcome it by developing devotion. If you have sufficient faith, then even though you do not want to spend an hour just sitting doing nothing, and everything in you screams to abandon the instruction and return to concentrating on rise and fall, you will not be able to. You have so much faith that the teacher knows what he or she is talking about and that there is something to be discovered by following the instruction, that the pull to go in the direction the teacher has indicated is greater than the pull of doubts and attachment to past routines and the pull of your own view of the way it ought to be done.

Recently, a Bulgarian couple were motoring through Germany when their car broke down. The husband said he would go for help and he told his wife to stay in the car. Three days later he returned. His wife was still sitting in the car in the lay-by. And the husband's explanation for taking so long to return? He had forgotten where the car had broken down! This is reported to be a true story, and the radio commentator who told it was most fascinated by the wife's devotion to her husband's instructions.

My teacher, Kapilavaddho Bhikkhu, said that if his meditation teacher had asked him to climb to the top of a very high building, open a window, and jump out, he would have done just that. The most difficult thing his teacher did ask him to do was to sit and meditate until he returned. His teacher went off, leaving him to sit there cross-legged on the floor. Twenty-four hours later he returned. Kapilavaddho had not moved a muscle in the whole time. Several monks had to carry him away and massage his limbs, because his legs had developed cramps and had set solid in the one position. That is the depth of devotion you need if you wish to be successful at walking the path and reaching the summit of the spiritual mountain.

How to Become a Spiritual Adult

As long as we hang on to our worries of yesterday, our arguments of yesterday, our wants of tomorrow, our imagined problems of tomorrow, there is no release. Life becomes a long, grey, dull tunnel. That which we call living becomes a mixture of worries, of wants, of arguments, of problems, of battles, stretching on and on and on. We allow the mind to become a mechanical machine that just churns on and on, going over and over the same old material, with no rest, no silence. We become weary. We become dull. We keep walking down those long, grey, endless mental tunnels. We know every crack in their walls, every hole, every slight change in colour, every bend, every gradient. It is all the same every day. Long, endless, continuous, dull tunnels constructed from the same old worries, the same old fears, the same old dreams. We know it all. It is endless. It is exhausting. There is no freshness in those tunnels. No sudden burst of light. Nothing new. Only dull familiarity. Dull because it is familiar.

As soon as we become conscious of this dullness and wish to change it, we begin a journey, a journey which takes us from spiritual child to spiritual adult.

If we are to experience a freshness, a brightness, a silence, a joy, we must die to that tunnel. We must be reborn. To be reborn, we must stop this continuous, endless walking down long, dull tunnels. Our hanging on to and going over and over worries, problems, arguments, past mistakes, future hopes, what I want, what I do not want—all of this mental churning is the building blocks for those tunnels. And although part of us desperately wants to escape the dullness, part of us is terrified of anything new and unfamiliar. We cling to security no matter how dull and stifling it is. And the churning, robot-like mind is familiar. The familiarity makes us feel secure. But that security slowly chokes us and stifles us and kills us.

How to get free? How to experience a newness, a freshness, another dimension?

Those long endless tunnels have been created from inner conflict. Hatred is conflict. Wanting things to be other than they are is conflict. Value judgement is conflict. Resistance to what is going on in the moment is conflict. Comparison is conflict. *All* conflict, *all* resistance makes the mind dull. It goes dull because the mind in conflict will only see certain things. It refuses to see anything that is different from what it expects and wants. So the material presented to the mind is always the same. If it is always the same, the mind grows bored and dull. To overcome dullness, one needs to see clearly.

To see clearly there must be freedom from wanting—freedom from wanting things to be different, freedom from wanting happiness, freedom from wanting success, wanting a relationship, wanting fulfil-ment, wanting spontaneity, wanting enlightenment. The mind needs to free itself from this incessant wanting—because wanting distorts the mind and a distorted mind becomes dull. The dull mind cannot see clearly.

In order for the mind to be capable of clarity and direct penetration, it must be quiet. A wanting mind is never quiet. It is a continual babble, like a Saturday morning street market. And its babble is concerned mainly with what 'I' want: 'I want a better job,' 'I want a more fulfilling marriage,' 'I want fewer financial concerns,' 'I want to live a simple, uncluttered life,' 'I want to be religious,' 'I want my meditation to be going places,' 'I want this moment, right now, to be more stimulating than it is.' This continuous 'I want' fills the whole mind, the whole be-ing. It crowds it. It makes it cluttered, makes it noisy. And this noisy mind looks out through a thick fog of wants onto the world. It is too busy, absorbed in its wants, to notice subtle changes. And yet it is the very noticing of these subtle changes and the non-resistance to them that introduces us to a newness, a freshness, a spaciousness.

If we are to learn the art of clear seeing, if we are to learn how to live fully in the moment, then we have to learn how to let go of this total absorption in ourselves, this total absorption in what 'I want'. All this wanting makes us see partially—we never see anything fully. How can we see fully and clearly if we are looking at everything through a thick fog of wanting and conflict? If we see only partially, then we are only half living. Part of us is dead. We are not living to the full capacity of which we are capable. When we are part dead, then the world gradually becomes dull and lifeless. And this dullness and heaviness slowly creeps further and further into all the corners of the mind—even into those areas we used to enjoy and derive pleasure from.

★ ★ ★

How do we escape from the creeping paralysis of dullness? Only by direct seeing. By becoming aware of how we never experience things directly but are always experiencing our image of the thing. Have you ever had the following experience? The front doorbell rings, and at the sound of the bell there forms in mind an image, a concept of who is at the front door. Let us say you picture your mother standing on your front doorstep. You open the door and for some seconds it is as if you are blind. You cannot see the person standing on that step in front of you. You see only who you expect to see—your mother. Then gradually the blindness fades, and you see it is not your mother—it is your next door neighbour, with cup in hand, requesting the loan of some sugar.

If you analyse that episode, you will be able to pull out what exactly went wrong. When the front doorbell went, it was 11am, and you had been expecting your mother for coffee. At the sound of the bell, you formed a mental image of your mother, and you went to the front door with that image. Whoever is standing on that doorstep the eyes do not see. The mind lays over that person the image of the mother it is expecting for coffee. The mind and the eyes see only the mental image. As the image begins to fade, you stare at this thing on the doorstep which you do not recognise, and it takes some little while before the mind gets into gear and compares the features of the person in front of you with similar features in memory, and then eventually the mind throws out the label 'Mrs Jones, our next door neighbour'.

The main point here is the image the mind created, which it then projected over the person standing at the front door. The mind in this example is not seeing clearly, not seeing directly. It is seeing only its image of what it expects to find. And this is what we do with everything. We falsify the world by never seeing it directly but seeing only our image, our idea of it. So we are always out of contact with the Real.

The 'I want' is an image: 'I want success,' 'I want a better job,' 'I want a job,' 'I want money,' 'I want quietness,' 'I want *jhānas*,' 'I want enlightenment.' When we create an 'I want', what exactly are we doing? What we are doing is building a picture in mind of ourselves *in the future*, with lots of money or a happy relationship or a quiet lifestyle. Then we yearn for that picture. We strive to materialise that picture in the outside world. We hold the picture in mind for hours, days, months, sometimes years. We hold that picture before the mind, for however long it takes to build that event in our everyday world. Sometimes we do not manage to achieve what we want, but it does not stop us from keeping that image frequently before the mind's eye. If we do manage to build the event, that is, when we have a lot of money or the quiet lifestyle, we then move in to possess it, thus satisfying our want. But wants are insatiable. Once we have devoured one want, we create another.

What is dangerous about these images we form in the mind? What is dangerous is that whilst we hold in mind an image of ourselves in the future becoming, say, a highly successful, well-adjusted being, we cannot see anything else. The mind can only be aware of one object at a time, and so if it is churning through masses of images of different wants most of the time, all you will ever see are those mental images. Those images you will keep laying on top of whatever is present in the now. You will never see what is actually present and living and breathing in the moment. All you will see is an image. And an image is a ghost. What is actually present is the Real. You are wanting, you are obsessed by a ghost whilst the Real, the alive, the dynamic lives with you all the time, but you cannot see it because you are so absorbed in the image.

The other danger with images is that they keep us within the realm of the familiar, and the Real lies in the unfamiliar. Even though, when we begin our journey towards becoming a spiritual adult, we want to throw off the familiar and the dull, yet we are frightened of the unfamiliar. But we do not know what the unfamiliar is. We have not consciously experienced it, but nevertheless we are frightened of it.

Those words and mental pictures that are familiar to us, those words which we go over and over in our minds—we use them to put together a picture of the unknown. *Nibbāna* is the unknown. *Nibbāna* is the unfamiliar. In our picture we may imagine this state of *nibbāna* as being filled with endless joy from morning till night, the type of joy we experience when we get a pleasant surprise or pass our exams or enjoy a concert. And we picture our days being filled with that and we like the taste of it. With that picture, we have created another tunnel, made from some of the bricks of the old familiar tunnels. We have created a new tunnel, but it is made from the old—so it is not new at all. It is the same dull, endless, familiar tunnel. If we are to build the new, we must die to the old.

Perhaps our picture of the unknown takes a slightly different form—perhaps we imagine it being empty, lifeless, dark, with endless hours of nothing to do. If that is the picture we build of the unknown, of *nibbāna*, it will frighten us, for we do not want to be alone and in the dark. So we cling even more mightily to those endlessly long, grey tunnels, those tunnels made up of conflict and worries and momentary joys and 'I wants'. After all, they are familiar and we feel secure with the familiar.

But the picture of endless days of joy and the picture of endless days of emptiness are only mental pictures made from words or visual images. We put them together in mind, and then we believe that they are the Real and react to them accordingly. We must grow beyond this weird belief that our mental images are reality if we are to experience the freshness, the newness, the fullness, the Real. *It* lies beyond our mental words and pictures and worries and fantasies and wants. *It* lies beyond the familiar. *It* lies beyond the known.

We think that if we have an image of ourselves becoming more successful in the future or more tranquil or more mindful, that this is good. We think that it is good to create goals of self-improvement to strive towards—that life as we know it would be unbearable, rootless, even aimless if we were to drop all goals. We think we will become spineless, going nowhere, lumps of jelly. We feel we need goals and images to strive towards in order to be happy. But do we? Or are we perhaps making a mistake? When we have become established in the art of direct seeing, it is borne in upon us, very strongly, that we have indeed made a mistake.

We notice with direct seeing that when we produce an image in the mind, conflict arises—conflict between what is actually present (me, being unmindful, for example) and the image of what I *want* to be present (me, being totally mindful all the time). The difference between what is present and what we want to be present is painful.

All you have to do to contact the Real is to see clearly. There is nothing else you have to do. You do not have to change anything—or improve anything. You do not have to do away with thinking or love or laughter or tears. All you have to do is see clearly.

When you see directly, you will see that you have an image of something and that it is not the same as the actuality. When you see this clearly, you no longer believe in your image. You no longer take it seriously. You see it as the mind playing games, which is what the mind loves to do. You see the image for what it truly is—a phantom ghost. When you no longer take seriously the images that the mind creates, then you see through them to what is actually lying beneath the images. You see through to the real event.

When you are no longer taking your images seriously, when you are no longer regarding them as real, then no comparison can arise. Comparison cannot arise because previously, when there was no clear seeing, you were always comparing between the image, which you regarded as real, and the actual experience, which you also regarded as real. But now, with direct seeing, you have the real, living experience in the moment and a ghost. The mind does not bother to compare between Reality and a ghost. It focuses straight in on the Real. And with no comparison, there is no conflict.

* * *

But how *do* you see clearly? Well, we think we have to learn to see clearly. But having to learn to see clearly means we do not think we see clearly right now. So before we even start we have comparison. And if we have comparison, we have conflict. We compare between what is now 'me who cannot see clearly', and what we wish to become, 'a super-duper clear-seeing being'.

I say you do not have to 'learn' to see clearly. All you have to do is accept whatever is in the moment, each moment, and that is seeing clearly *right now*.

When you have an image of yourself becoming the perfect meditator somewhere off in the future, and you compare it with the way you see yourself right now (this unmindful, unconcentrated, unwise meditator), then you have duality. You have 'me as I am now' and 'me as I wish to become in the future'. So there are two of you. That is duality. Abandon, give up, let go of that image of what you will become in the future, and then there is no longer two. There is no longer duality. There is no longer comparison. Without comparison there is no longer conflict. No conflict *is* enlightenment.

But you do not believe this. Not one of you believes that you can give up your conflicts, your comparisons, your images just like that. You believe that enlightenment lies at the end of a long, hard slog of training and beating and moulding the mind into happier and happier states. You believe it lies at the end of a step-by-step training of mind control, where you have forced out all ill will, bad moods, irritability, lust, gossip, and where nothing is left but the positive states of loving-kindness, joy, happiness, serenity, lofty thoughts. And when all of this positivity has reached a climax, a peak, then there is this mighty explosion in the mind and *there it is—Enlightenment*—a marvellously blissed-out state that you have been waiting for, craving for, training for, for years, even lifetimes.

Well, that is not enlightenment, nor is it the way to enlightenment. Enlightenment does not lie off in the future after a long, rigorous training and after you have been good boys and girls for a sufficient number of years. It lies right here, now. Open your eyes and see it.

But you do not believe that. Even if you do intellectually, you do not emotionally. So to get over the emotional block, you have to meditate. Nothing else will do. You have to become an expert meditator—an expert at awareness meditation, not concentration meditation. You have to train and work and study and devote much time and love to becoming this expert meditator.

Once you have achieved all the accolades possible—have gone through the four paths of *vipassanā*, know backwards by meditative experience all the hindrances, know what wrong concentration is, what overconcentration is, how and why comparison, images, goals are destructive, know exactly, from experience, what is meant by hatred, craving, ignorance and why they produce suffering—when you know all of this from intuitive experience, then you can be said to be an expert meditator. You can also be said to be a spiritual child well on its way to becoming a spiritual adult.

* * *

I do not wish to denigrate awareness meditation to the point where it seems like a useless activity engaged in only for the purpose of removing an emotional block. It does more than this. It most certainly loosens the attachment to wanting and the attachment to images, but it does not do the whole job because to meditate at all is to create an image. It is done because you yearn for a state that is better than the one you have right now. You do not see the present as perfect, and so there is a movement of the mind away from the *now*. You *want* something out of meditation and that very wanting is craving. Craving is selfish, it is self-oriented, and it is an act of the ego. And acts of ego and enlightenment do not go together. There is no ego in enlightenment.

So even meditation must be given up. But it can only be given up once you are an expert at it. There is no point in giving it up before then because nothing will happen. You will just have the same conflicts, the same joys and sorrows, the same addiction to images you have always had. You certainly will not find yourself living in a fresh, totally new mental universe.

When you have become this expert meditator, only then will you emotionally *know* that meditation does not end in enlightenment. For you realise that although you have become this expert meditator, you are still not totally released from conflict. If you are not released from conflict, you are not enlightened, and only when you get to this point of being an expert meditator, and at no other time, will your whole being—mind, body, and emotions—accept that there is nothing you can do to become enlightened. It is only now that there is a very real possibility that you will give up your attachment to all images. It is only at this point that the opportunity opens up for total abandonment of all self-oriented movements of the mind.

When this total abandonment of wanting takes place, then the Real, which has always been there, is revealed. It is not found. You cannot find something that was never lost. Hence, you can never learn to become enlightened, because learning implies acquiring, and you cannot acquire something that you already have.

That which is revealed has been called by many different names. It has been called the state of bliss, the state of permanence, final destiny, total release from conflict, Unchanging Truth, The Absolute, the state free from decay, the state that has no end, the deathless state, the state of coolness, liberation, God, *nibbāna*. When that state of bliss, that state free from decay is a constant companion then, and only then, can you be called a spiritual adult.

Glossary

A Note on Pronunciation:
The pronunciation of Pali words should present no serious difficulty.
There are only a few points to remember:

> c – 'ch' as in 'church'
> h – always as in 'boathook', never as in 'this'
> ā – as in 'far'
> ī – as in 'meet'
> ū – as in 'blue'

anattā—Non-self. See *three marks*.

Anguttara-Nikāya—One of the books of collected discourses of the Buddha. See *Pali Canon*.

anicca—Impermanence. See *three marks*.

arahant—See *fetters, paths*.

attā—Self-view; the belief that the self exists as a separate entity. It is the antithesis of the *anattā* view. See *three marks*.

becoming, canker of—The wish to become something other. This involves rejecting what occurs in the moment in the attempt to experience a preferred state. See *cankers*.

cankers—Four unwholesome biases or stains that pollute the mind and thereby distort perception. The four are sensual desire, desire for becoming, views, and ignorance.

conditionality—All things arise and pass away dependent upon conditions and do not have any independent existence. This understanding undermines self-view.

craving—The desire to acquire or perpetuate some thing or state. It is the chief cause of suffering and the perpetual round of rebirths. See *fetters, four noble truths, ignorance*.

deva—The Buddha described a number of worlds or realms in which beings are born, live and die. Some of the realms that are more pleasant than the human are called *deva* realms. Beings are born there as a result of their wholesome actions.

Dhamma—Law, teaching; the teaching of the Buddha which is summed up in the four noble truths.

doubt—Doubt in the Buddha, Dhamma, and Sangha, or wavering and indecision. See *fetters, hindrance*.

dukkha—Suffering, pain, or unsatisfactoriness. See *three marks, four noble truths*.

eightfold path—The path leading to the end of suffering (*dukkha*). It is the last of the four noble truths and can be divided into the three sections of (1) wisdom: right view and thought; (2) ethics: right speech, action, and livelihood; and (3) mental development: right effort, mindfulness, and concentration.

enlightenment—See *nibbāna*.

feelings—In the Buddha's teaching three types of feelings are identified: pleasant, painful, and neutral. Not understanding that feelings have the characteristics of the three marks, we respond to them with craving or hatred and thereby cause ourselves to suffer.

fetters—The ten fetters tie beings to the perpetual round of rebirths. They are (1) personality belief or self-view, (2) sceptical doubt, (3) attachment to rule and ritual, (4) sensuous craving, (5) hatred, (6) craving for fine-material existence, (7) craving for immaterial existence, (8) conceit, (9) restlessness, and (10) ignorance. The first three ties are broken at the fruition of streamwinning. The fourth and fifth are attenuated at the fruition of once-returner and broken at the fruition of non-returner. The remaining five are broken at the final fruition of *arahant* when the training is complete. See *paths*.

fine-material existence, craving for—See *fetters*.

flurry and worry—A state of agitation caused by dwelling on past and future concerns. See *hindrance*.

four noble truths—The Buddha summarised his teaching in four noble truths: (1) all forms of existence are unsatisfactory and subject to suffering (*dukkha*); (2) there is a cause of suffering, namely, craving (or hatred), which arises from ignorance of reality; (3) there is a final end of suffering and rebirth, namely, *nibbāna*, when craving is completely eliminated; and (4) there is a way (the eightfold path) by which the end of suffering may be realised.

hatred—Ill will, aversion; desire to get rid of some thing or state. See *fetters, four noble truths, hindrance*.

hindrance—A hindrance is a conditioned mental action or habit that obstructs the development of concentration and mindfulness and prevents the perception of what is present. There are five main kinds: sensual desire, ill will, sloth and torpor, worry and flurry, and doubt.

ignorance—Delusion, confusion, unawareness, blindness; also, perceiving a mental or physical object or quality and immediately refusing to acknowledge it, often while unaware of the process. Of particular importance as a condition upon which craving, and hence suffering, arises is ignorance of the transient, unsatisfactory, and non-self nature of all physical and mental experience.

ignore-ance—See *ignorance*.

ill will—Hatred, aversion; desire to get rid of some thing or state. See *hindrance*.

immaterial existence, craving for—See *fetters*.

jhāna—Absorption; alert and lucid states of mind divorced from five-fold sense consciousness and achieved through the exercise of concentration. During these there is a complete, though temporary, suspension of fivefold sense activity and of the five hindrances.

kalyāna mitta—Noble friend; one who is both teacher and friend; one who personally guides a student in his or her search for wisdom.

loving-kindness—Friendliness, goodwill; the desire for beings to be happy and well. 'Loving-kindness' also refers to a specific meditation used to cultivate this attitude.

marks—See *three marks*.

mindfulness—Awareness and clear comprehension; the knowledge of what is taking place in the present moment.

nibbāna—Freedom from desire. *Nibbāna*, enlightenment, is the complete absence and elimination of all craving, hatred, and ignorance. It is the end of all suffering and the goal of the eightfold path.

noble eightfold path—See *eightfold path*.

noble truths—See *four noble truths*.

non-returner—See *fetters, paths*.

non-self—*Anattā*. See *three marks*.

once-returner—See *fetters, paths*.

overconcentration—Focusing attention on a single object more than necessary for *vipassanā* practice. If done skilfully, with mindful attention to mental states and objects, then a state of *jhāna* may result. If done unskilfully, the meditator drifts into daydream or sleep. In either case, insight cannot be developed at that time.

Pali—The language in which the original teachings of the Buddha were first spoken and recorded. It has close associations with Sanskrit.

Pali Canon—The texts of the Theravada school of Buddhism. They are divided into three parts: (1) the books of the rules of discipline (*Vinaya*), (2) the books of discourses (one of which is the *Anguttara-Nikāya*), and (3) the books of the higher teaching (*Abhidhamma*).

path—See *eightfold path*.

paths, the four—The four supermundane paths to freedom. Each path is a moment of coming to realise *nibbāna*, the realisation itself being the fruition. The fruitions of the four paths are called streamwinning, once-returning, non-returning, and *arahant*. Each path arises due to generating sufficient insight (*vipassanā*) and utterly transforms one's understanding of life. Each of the four paths reduces or eliminates specific impurities of mind. See *fetters*.

perception—The label, based on memory, that identifies an object that comes into consciousness.

precepts, the five—The five precepts or rules of training form the basic ethical standard for lay people. There are more for those under rigorous training and many more for monks and nuns. The five rules are to train oneself to refrain from (1) killing or harming any living being, (2) taking that which is not expressly given, (3) unlawful sexual intercourse, (4) lying, slander, and all harsh speech, and (5) intoxication by drink or drugs.

restlessness and worry—A state of agitation caused by dwelling on past and future concerns. See *hindrance*.

rule and ritual, attachment to—See *fetters*.

Sangha—Literally, the orders of Buddhist monks and nuns. In terms of the three refuges, it specifically refers to the *ariya-sangha*, the noble ones—those who have attained one or more fruitions of *nibbāna* regardless of whether they are in the ordained orders or not. See *fetters, paths*.

self-view—*Attā*; the view that the self exists as a separate entity. It is the antithesis of the *anattā* view. See *three marks*.

sensual desire—Desire for experience through the five physical senses, namely, the eyes, ears, nose, tongue, or body. See *cankers, fetters, hindrance*.

sloth and torpor—Sleepiness or rigidity of mind due to a lazy approach to the practice. See *hindrance*.

streamwinner—See *fetters, paths*.

suffering—Dukkha. See *three marks, four noble truths*.

three marks—All relative, mundane things, material or mental, have these marks or characteristics. All mundane (conditioned) things are in a state of flux, changing from instant to instant (*anicca*); hence they are unsatisfying and painful (*dukkha*); and there is nowhere to be found, either in the mundane world or in *nibbāna*, any unchanging or independent self, soul, ego, person, or being (*anattā*).

Vinaya—Those parts of the Pali Canon that set out the rules of discipline for monks and nuns. See *Pali Canon.*

vipassanā—Insight; the direct perception of one or other of the three marks. Insight is the only factor which destroys ignorance and hence craving, though it can only be developed along with training in ethics and mental development (see eightfold path). Insight is not intellectual understanding, but arises based on careful and systematic meditative observation of all material and mental objects and processes.

worry, flurry, and restlessness—see *flurry and worry*, *hindrance.*

wrong-concentration—A torpid, unwieldy state of mind caused by excessive effort in directing attention onto an object of meditation.

Under the spiritual guidance of **Alan James**, the Aukana Trust provides a wide range of facilities from introductory evening classes in meditation and Buddhist philosophy right through to full-time monastic training. All the activities are held at the House of Inner Tranquillity in Bradford on Avon.

If you would like further information, please contact:

Aukana Trust
9 Masons Lane
Bradford on Avon
Wiltshire
BA15 1QN
England

e-mail: info@aukana.org.uk
wwww.aukana.org.uk
Telephone: (01225) 866821
International: +44 1225 866821

A MEDITATION RETREAT

Alan & Jacqui James

The Buddha said that there is just one way to overcome the suffering seemingly inherent in the human condition. The practice of mindfulness generates insight into the way our minds work, revealing why it is that we feel dissatisfied and distressed, and exactly how suffering can be overcome.

With a clarity and directness of approach that can only come from understanding, Alan and Jacqui James elucidate the practice of mindfulness, covering such topics as how to meditate, hindrances to the practice and how to surmount them, the relationship between teacher and student—and enlightenment itself, the final goal of the spiritual journey.

While many of these talks were especially designed for the new meditator embarking on his/her first retreat, they will all provide inspiration and a wealth of wisdom for novice and experienced meditator alike.

*Based on profound experience and very clearly written ... there is much throughout the book which will prove of benefit to many - **The Middle Way***

*A very informative book about the nature of the practice ... of benefit to both beginners and more experienced meditators - **Visuddhacara Bhikkhu**, author of* Curbing Anger, Spreading Love

ISBN 10: 0-9511769-0-0

ISBN 13: 978-0-9511769-0-0

216 x 138mm   224 pages

MODERN BUDDHISM

Alan & Jacqui James

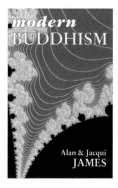

'The Buddha's teaching is as relevant today as it ever has been. It describes the facts of human life which are observable by anyone who cares to take the trouble to investigate.'

Presenting timeless truths in a current context, *Modern Buddhism* provides answers to questions that have always haunted mankind.

Death and dying: a wasted and terrifying experience—or an opportunity for spiritual growth? A meditation teacher describes the way she helped her mother approach the doors of death.

Family relationships: why do some families live in harmony, whilst others are constantly at war? What is the purpose of the family unit?

Sexuality: what sexual habits are most conducive to progress along the path?

Alan and Jacqui James belong to the tradition of teachers who present the essence of Buddhism in a way which is totally in tune with the needs of their own time and culture.

In a confused and dark world, the book is like a ray of light showing the path to sanity and peace - **Buddhism Today, Brisbane**

ISBN 10: 0-9511769-1-9
ISBN 13: 978-0-9511769-1-7

215 x 135mm   176 pages

THE UNFOLDING OF WISDOM
The Buddha's Path to Enlightenment

Alan James

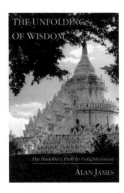

' ... it is like having lived all your life in a dark cave, never being sure where the walls, the ceiling or the exits were, never being sure of the real shape of the space around you. When at last you bring in some light to the darkness, immediately your old idea of the cave disappears. The illumination of true vision eliminates what had been total darkness, including all your speculations about the reality of the cave.

'When this occurs, there is never any need to refer to your earlier idea of how things were; it simply becomes irrelevant. Now you know things as they are. What interest can speculative fantasies have for you now?'

The Unfolding of Wisdom is uncompromising. It presents the facts about spiritual progress. It is not for those who would speculate about symbolism or metaphor but for those who would dare to approach truth directly.

Hardback: ISBN 10: 0-9511769-4-3   *240 x 165mm   224 pages*
                ISBN 13: 978-0-9511769-4-8

Softback: ISBN 10: 0-9511769-5-1   *230 x 155mm   224 pages*
                ISBN 13: 978-0-9511769-5-5

INNER TRANQUILLITY
The Buddha's Path to Freedom

Alan James

'The successful spiritual traveller completely understands suffering. He knows through experience its conditioned nature, its origins and its cessation. Having won to the deathless, he knows with a knowing that goes beyond words that he is free—that the universe is love—that the journey is ended— there is no more to do. He is finally at peace.'

Inner tranquillity is a universal goal.

Inner tranquillity, it could be argued, is *the* universal goal, the goal of all existence, however various our attempts to reach it.

The Buddha uncovered a systematic, comprehensive and—most importantly—effective pathway to the attaining of that which all of us seek.

In this collection of lectures, Alan James draws on over thirty years of teaching experience to illuminate this path to the ultimate peace.

There is much that is wise and helpful here ... a detailed and useful guide to meditation - **Buddhism Now**

Written with a down-to-earth tone ... James gives lots of practical advice ... from the perspective of someone who has travelled the path - **Living Traditions, Australia**

One of the best books on the teaching of the Buddha, written by a person of great learning ... in lucid simple language and in a clear style - **Buddhist Publication Society Newsletter**

ISBN 10: 0-9511769-8-6
ISBN 13: 978-0-9511769-8-6

234 x 156mm   224 pages

BUDDHISM: THE PLAIN FACTS

Robert Mann & RoseYoud

A clear, systematic guide to *vipassanā* meditation, the practice of insight at the heart of Buddhism, this book focuses on the original teachings of the Buddha and shows how they can be applied today.

This is Buddhism without history, politics or jargon—the plain facts about the Buddha's path to enlightenment.

ISBN 10: 0-9511769-7-8
ISBN 13: 978-0-9511769-7-9

216 x 138mm   176 pages

BUDDHIST CHARACTER ANALYSIS

Robert Mann & Rose Youd

Food, sleep, relationships, sex: do you go for quality, quantity or moderation? Or would you prefer to live without them?

Buddhist Character Analysis is a practical guide to the infinite complexities of human behaviour.

You are offered your own TV show. Do you think, 'What took them so long?' Or would you rather die?

Based exclusively on observable facts, **Buddhist Character Analysis** identifies our fundamental motives and assumptions.

Does your heart sink at the prospect of a quiet weekend? Or do you believe that the world could be a wonderful place if it wasn't for all those people?

Skilful use of **Buddhist Character Analysis** leads to a greater understanding of human nature and increasing happiness in daily life.

How do you see the enlightened person? An aloof Himalayan hermit, master of self-control? Or a charismatic leader using his powers to create a better world?

Combined with a spiritual training**, Buddhist Character Analysis** deepens insight into the true nature of reality.

A thoroughly readable introduction to the subject - **Holistic London Guide**

ISBN 10: 0-9511769-3-5
ISBN 13: 978-0-9511769-3-1

197 x 125mm   144 pages

BUDDHISM IN A FOREIGN LAND

Robert Mann

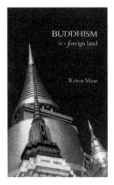

As Buddhism is taking root in the West, evolving new forms to suit new conditions, much of its traditional oriental context is being called into question.

In this intriguing and provocative collection of talks, Robert Mann addresses many of the issues which confront Buddhism as it adapts to modern western culture.

Rebirth and traditional cosmology, the role of ethics in a global consumer society, the dangers inherent in confusing therapy with spirituality—these are just some of the topics included in this controversial book.

*Covers in an admirably clear manner the fundamentals of the Buddhadharma ... a book to be recommended - **Journal of Buddhist Ethics***

*A pleasure to read—lucid, unambiguous and expressive - **Buddhism Now***

ISBN 10: 0-9511769-6-X
ISBN 13: 978-0-9511769-6-2

215 x 135mm   192 pages

LIFE AS A SIAMESE MONK

Richard Randall

May 1954, Bangkok—10,000 people converge on the outlying temple of Wat Paknam to witness a historic ceremony. Forty-seven-year-old journalist Richard Randall is taking the saffron robe to ordain as a Buddhist monk. Known henceforth as Kapilavaddho Bhikkhu, he is the first Englishman to enter the monkhood in Thailand. After an intensive meditation training and some remarkable experiences in concentration and insight practice, Kapilavaddho later went on to play a key role in the introduction of Buddhist meditation to the West.

An exceptionally fine Dhamma-read - **Buddhism Now**

An inspiring story of Buddhist devotion - **Light of Peace, Bangkok**

ISBN 10: 0-9511769-2-7   *230 x 150mm   224 pages + 8 pages b/w photographs*
ISBN 13: 978-0-9511769-2-4

These books are available by mail-order:

The Purpose of Life	£8.95
A Meditation Retreat	£7.95
Modern Buddhism	£7.95
The Unfolding of Wisdom	
softback	£8.95
hardback	£10.95
Inner Tranquillity	£8.95
Buddhism: The Plain Facts	£6.95
Buddhist Character Analysis	£6.95
Buddhism in a Foreign Land	£8.50
Life as a Siamese Monk	£8.95

Prices include postage and packing

Please send order and payment to:

Aukana Trust
9 Masons Lane
Bradford on Avon
Wiltshire
BA15 1QN
England

e-mail: info@aukana.org.uk
wwww.aukana.org.uk
Telephone: (01225) 866821
International: +44 1225 866821